MW01252837

International Political Economy Series

General Editor: **Timothy M. Shaw**, Professor and Director, Institute of International Relations, The University of the West Indies, Trinidad & Tobago

Titles include:

Hans Abrahamsson
UNDERSTANDING WORLD ORDER AND STRUCTURAL CHANGE
Poverty, Conflict and the Global Arena

Andreas Bieler, Werner Bonefeld, Peter Burnham and Adam David Morton
GLOBAL RESTRUCTURING, STATE, CAPITAL AND LABOUR
Contesting Neo-Gramscian Perspectives

Morten Bøås, Marianne H. Marchand and Timothy M. Shaw (*editors*)
THE POLITICAL ECONOMY OF REGIONS AND REGIONALISMS

Paul Bowles, Henry Veltmeyer, Scarlett Cornelissen, Noela Invernizzi and
Kwon-Leung Tang (*editors*)
NATIONAL PERSPECTIVES ON GLOBALIZATION
A Critical Reader
REGIONAL PERSPECTIVES ON GLOBALIZATION
A Critical Reader

Sandra Braman (*editor*)
THE EMERGENT GLOBAL INFORMATION POLICY REGIME

Edward A. Comor
CONSUMPTION AND THE GLOBALIZATION PROJECT
International Hegemony and the Annihilation of Time

Giorel Curran
21st CENTURY DISSENT
Anarchism, Anti-Globalization and Environmentalism

Martin Doornbos
INSTITUTIONALIZING DEVELOPMENT POLICIES AND RESOURCE STRATEGIES IN EASTERN
AFRICA AND INDIA
Developing Winners and Losers
GLOBAL FORCES AND STATE RESTRUCTURING
Dynamics of State Formation and Collapse

Bill Dunn
GLOBAL RESTRUCTURING AND THE POWER OF LABOUR

Myron J. Frankman
WORLD DEMOCRATIC FEDERALISM
Peace and Justice Indivisible

Marieke de Goede (*editor*)
INTERNATIONAL POLITICAL ECONOMY AND POSTSTRUCTURAL POLITICS

Graham Harrison (*editor*)
GLOBAL ENCOUNTERS
International Political Economy, Development and Globalization

Patrick Hayden and Chamsy el-Ojeili (*editors*)
CONFRONTING GLOBALIZATION
Humanity, Justice and the Renewal of Politics

Axel Hülsemeyer (*editor*)
GLOBALIZATION IN THE TWENTY-FIRST CENTURY
Convergence or Divergence?

Takashi Inoguchi
GLOBAL CHANGE
A Japanese Perspective

Kanishka Jayasuriya
STATECRAFT, WELFARE AND THE POLITICS OF INCLUSION

Dominic Kelly and Wyn Grant (*editors*)
THE POLITICS OF INTERNATIONAL TRADE IN THE 21st CENTURY
Actors, Issues and Regional Dynamics

Mathias Koenig-Archibugi and Michael Zürn (*editors*)
NEW MODES OF GOVERNANCE IN THE GLOBAL SYSTEM
Exploring Publicness, Delegation and Inclusiveness

Craig N. Murphy (*editor*)
EGALITARIAN POLITICS IN THE AGE OF GLOBALIZATION

George Myconos
THE GLOBALIZATION OF ORGANIZED LABOUR
1945–2004

John Nauright and Kimberly S. Schimmel (*editors*)
THE POLITICAL ECONOMY OF SPORT

Morten Ougaard
THE GLOBALIZATION OF POLITICS
Power, Social Forces and Governance

Richard Robison (*editor*)
THE NEO-LIBERAL REVOLUTION
Forging the Market State

Fredrik Söderbaum and Timothy M. Shaw (*editors*)
THEORIES OF NEW REGIONALISM

Susanne Soederberg, Georg Menz and Philip G. Cerny (*editors*)
INTERNALIZING GLOBALIZATION
The Rise of Neoliberalism and the Decline of National Varieties of Capitalism

Ritu Vij (*editor*)
GLOBALIZATION AND WELFARE
A Critical Reader

Matthew Watson
THE POLITICAL ECONOMY OF INTERNATIONAL CAPITAL MOBILITY

International Political Economy Series
Series Standing Order ISBN 0-333-71708-2 hardcover
Series Standing Order ISBN 0-333-71110-6 paperback
(*outside North America only*)

You can receive future titles in this series as they are published by placing a standing order.
Please contact your bookseller or, in case of difficulty, write to us at the address below with
your name and address, the title of the series and one of the ISBNs quoted above.

Customer Services Department, Macmillan Distribution Ltd, Houndmills, Basingstoke,
Hampshire RG21 6XS, England

Consumption and the Globalization Project
International Hegemony and the Annihilation of Time

Edward A. Comor
Associate Professor
and
Rogers Chair in Journalism and New Information Technology
University of Western Ontario
Canada

First published 2008 by
PALGRAVE MACMILLAN
Houndmills, Basingstoke, Hampshire RG21 6XS and
175 Fifth Avenue, New York, N.Y. 10010
Companies and representatives throughout the world

PALGRAVE MACMILLAN is the global academic imprint of the Palgrave Macmillan division of St. Martin's Press, LLC and of Palgrave Macmillan Ltd. Macmillan® is a registered trademark in the United States, United Kingdom and other countries. Palgrave is a registered trademark in the European Union and other countries.

ISBN-13: 978-0-230-52224-4   hardback
ISBN-10: 0-230-52224-6   hardback

This book is printed on paper suitable for recycling and made from fully managed and sustained forest sources. Logging, pulping and manufacturing processes are expected to conform to the environmental regulations of the country of origin.

A catalogue record for this book is available from the British Library.

Library of Congress Cataloging-in-Publication Data

Comor, Edward A., 1962–
    Consumption and the globalization project : neo-imperialism and the
    annihilation of time / Edward A. Comor.
        p. cm. — (International political economy series)
    Includes bibliographical references and index.
    ISBN 0-230-52224-6 (alk. paper)
    1. Consumption (Economics) 2. International economic relations.
        3. International relations. I. Title.

HC79.C6C6354 2008
339.4'7—dc22   2008011810

10   9   8   7   6   5   4   3   2   1
17   16   15   14   13   12   11   10   09   08

Printed and bound in Great Britain by
CPI Antony Rowe, Chippenham and Eastbourne

From my parents, the past
With my wife, the present
To my son, the future

Contents

Illustrations and Table

Illustrations

Table

Preface

Shortly after September 11, 2001, US President George W. Bush urged his compatriots to go shopping. If Americans fail to go about their lives as normal–visiting malls, buying things, racking up debts – the 'evil-doers' will win.

On this rare occasion, George Bush was correct; the edifice of the contemporary political economy is, in fact, built on the grounds of a consumption-dependent framework.[1] In the context of the contemporary globalization project, this framework's construction is secured more through consumerist identities than workplace satisfactions, more as a result of acquisitive aspirations than civic achievements. As Bush's post-terrorist-attack appeals underline, this emerging world (dis)order also at times reveals itself as something of a house of cards, instantaneously interconnected and vulnerable to a range of consumption-related disruptions – from inflation to deflation, from energy shortages to 'liquidity' crises.

Despite the ecological implications of our systemic compulsion to produce and consume evermore, and the geopolitical ramifications of this dynamic (involving a deepening dependency on both oil and cheap labour), consumption itself arguably has become *the* core indice of not just individual 'success' but also national 'development'. Capitalist consumption - as a historically constructed way of thinking, acting and relating - constitutes an essential but contradiction-laden institution. Its core agent - the much-vaunted 'sovereign' consumer - is ideally free to do virtually anything except withdraw from consuming. After all, if that choice were acted upon, the edifice would collapse.

Remarkably, consumption, and, more generally, the commodification of social (and international) relations, remains a relatively neglected subject among political economists and students of international studies. One reason for this could be that consumption often is regarded as a local if not individual activity, thus not the ontological concern of international political economy (IPE). Another explanation, most relevant for neo-Marxists, is the tendency to focus on production (and labour more specifically) as the essential moment in the political economic cycle rather than examining production and consumption (as well as circulation and exchange) as inter-dependent elements of the political economy's production process.[2] Additionally, we might speculate that students of IPE, as with other academics, tend to underassess subjects entailing unfamiliar heuristics. Certainly, consumption - especially its anthropological, sociological and psychological aspects - warrants the application of theories and approaches that generally lie outside the typical IPE specialist's area of expertise.[3] In particular, consumption elicits conceptual tools associated with the study of the complex (and thus often simplified) subject of culture. This book constitutes an interdisciplinary step towards correcting this lacuna.[4]

Outside the purview of IPE, Samuel Huntington's clash of civilizations thesis[5] - dismissed by many as simplistic and empirically unsubstantiated - magnified the profile of culture within international studies. While his work both reifies culture and generalizes its relationship to nation states, Huntington raised the possibility of conflict and resistance during the halcyon days of globalization. Also prescient was Benjamin Barber's 'Jihad vs. McWorld'.[6] To Barber's credit, it similarly anticipated conflict – a conflict rooted in religious, tribal and nationalist responses to a corporate-led, US-facilitated promotion of neoliberalism, consumerism and modernity. Importantly, neither the parochial nor the corporate (the two main 'combatants' in Barber's version of the civilizational clash) furthers democracy. 'An efficient free market,' wrote Barber, '... requires that consumers be free to vote their dollars on competing goods, not that citizens be free to vote their values and beliefs ...'[7]

Barber's general point is suggestive – particularly for those grappling with consumption's role in the twenty-first century. Perhaps consumption, when structured and practised in particular ways, constitutes a nodal point facilitating hegemonic stability or, in other contexts, rebellion. In this book, we look into this very possibility. More specifically, by assessing capitalist consumption as an institutional mediator of power, we consider its constitutive influence in light of three possible developments: First, consumption may be mediating (structurally and sociologically) an international acquiescence to neoliberal norms. Second, consumption practices and priorities may be undermining the contemporary hegemonic bloc's capacity to recognize its own contradictory trajectories. And third, this institution, as a component part of a complex political economic dynamic, also may implicate anti-status quo actors in a pernicious cycle of unreflexive, 'time-annihilating' strategies – strategies that are as reactionary as those being pursued by globalization's primary agents, corporations and the American state.

Herein we also substantiate Justin Rosenberg's argument that an empire of civil society has emerged.[8] Through property rights, contracts and the alluring institution of capitalist consumption, a neo-imperialist (dis)order has been cast that emphasizes quantity, speed and market access. And while some places and collectives now seem well situated to respond critically, creatively and possibly progressively, our study reveals that time is running out. Structurally and conceptually, capitalist consumption widens and deepens our political economy's more general neglect of history and duration in favour of efficiency, fashion and immediate gratification. This overwhelming focus on spatial reach and control to the neglect of time may well constitute globalization's most irrepressible contradiction.

George Bush's concern about the American public's shopping habits after 9/11 revealed a neglected truth: consumption can't be taken for granted. Years later, when asked about how history will judge his decision to invade Iraq, 'History,' the president responded, as he shrugged his shoulders, 'history, we don't know. We'll all be dead.'[9] More than affirming Bush's dearth of historical imagination, the President's words convey a deeper truth – a truth regarding the power of historical structures and their implications on consciousness; the truth about how empires that abhor reflexive thinking sow the seeds both of international violence and, ultimately, their own demise.

* * *

This book is the culmination of research, observations and discussions spanning some ten years. Innumerable people shaped, informed or directly influenced its development. Particular thanks to Robert Babe, Jody Berland, David Blaney, James Compton, Ken Conca, Matthew Davies, Gigi Herbert, Martin Hewson, Timothy Luke, Christopher May, Craig Murphy, Mustapha Pasha, Randolph Persaud, Thomas Princen, James Rosenau, J. P. Singh, Kees Van Der Pijl, Paul Wapner and Frank Webster for their intellectual contributions. Thank you to Stephen Anderson, Robert Crozier, Paul Fox, Karl Gerth, Philippa Grand, Vincent Manzerolle, Paul Mitchell, Phil Mitchell, Timothy Shaw, Mark H. Williams and Hazel Woodbridge for their support and assistance at various stages of the project. Thanks also to research assistants Marta Banat, Samantha Burton and Rob Sibbald.

Components of Chapter 4 appeared in *Global Governance: A Review of Multilateralism and International Organizations*, Vol. 4 No. 2 (© 1998 by Lynne Rienner Publishers, Inc.) and *International Studies Quarterly* Vol. 45 No. 3 (© 2001 by Blackwell Publishing). Also, sections of Chapter 6 originally appeared in *Topia* No. 10 (Fall 2003). Thanks also to Benjamin Barber, John Hodge, DNA Films and *Studies in Political Economy* for their epigraph permissions.

Finally, this book would have been impossible without the love and support of Larissa Webb. To you, Larissa, I promise to work less and play more.

Abbreviations

BBC	British Broadcasting Corporation
BJP	Bharatiya Janata party (India)
GCS	global civil society
GCS	global consumer society
GDP	gross domestic product
ICT	information and communication technology
IMF	International Monetary Fund
IPE	international political economy
MEFTA	Middle East Free Trade Area
NGO	non-governmental organization
NSS	National Security Strategy
OECD	Organisation for Economic Co-operation and Development
OPEC	Organization of Petroleum Exporting Countries
PBS	Public Broadcasting Service
PNAC	Project for the New American Century
PRC	People's Republic of China
UN	United Nations
UNDP	United Nations Development Programme
UNESCO	United Nations Educational, Scientific and Cultural Organization
USSR	Union of Soviet Socialist Republics
WTO	World Trade Organization

Abbreviations

1
Introduction

Consumption is the motor force of capitalism and the
motivation of consumer demand is indispensable to capitalism's continuing development. There are significant cultural variations ... but, on the world scale, aspiration
towards the American and west European model has been
the dynamic behind market liberalization in the Third
World, China and the ex-Soviet empire, and the driving
force of economic globalization.

—Robert W. Cox

In a 1949 memorandum prepared for the advertising firm J. Walter Thompson,
social scientist Vergil Reed likened the task of modernizing India to shov-
elling smoke or putting 'a rubber band around a gaseous mass'. Due to their
cultural 'introspection' and aversion to 'the practical', Indians, reported
Reed, were obsessed with eternity rather than the here-and-now priorities of
modern consumption. Faced with this apparent obstinacy and in response
to corporations seeking new markets, Reed prescribed a kind of cultural
retraining programme. 'The medicine of modernization,' he reported, 'may
taste strange and bitter at first, but it can't help the patient until taken.'[1]
Indeed, it would be decades before an elixir of commodified social relations
and consumerist practices would turn the patient (India) around, supplant-
ing Gandhian austerity with immediate-gratification priorities.

Paradoxically, unlike Reed's assumption that the institutionalization of
capitalist consumption constitutes an essential step *en route* to modernizing
humanity, consumption itself involves the forging of identities, meanings
and relationships that have more to do with smoke-and-mirrors than
modernism's rationalism and light. As disparate populations experience an
ever-more complex division of labour, more than just existential complexities and organizational bureaucracies abound; reifications and magical associations emerge also. The latter not only fill the social-psychological
vacuums that accompany modernization, they also mediate otherwise

1

disparate thoughts and activities. For example, all kinds of things and relationships magically become comparable and valued through their transformation into commodities. Fundamental indices of existence, space and time, become 'emptiable'. Irrevocably inter-dependent human beings become seemingly autonomous. In modernity, as Marx argued, 'individuals are ... ruled by *abstractions*'.[2]

This is not to say that modernity, as expressed through capitalism, urbanization and now globalization, is based primarily on illusions. Material ('real') human relationships and concrete capabilities still constitute the stuff of existence. Instead, abstractions, such as the smoke-and-mirrors of capitalist consumption, emerge to become essential nodal points of interaction and meaning. More than just the means through which commodities are sold, the *camera obscura* world of capitalist consumption, once in place, becomes a central mediator of virtually all human relations.

Through what this book calls 'the globalization project', we venture beyond the fact that this institution and its dynamic (and often problematic) development is being widened and deepened in the post-Cold War world – widened and deepened by mostly corporate/capitalist vested interests, crucially accommodated through the American and other states. Herein, we also argue that capitalist consumption has itself modified the globalization project, particularly in terms of how people have come to conceptualize it. Globalization, more precisely, constitutes the latest chapter in the ongoing story of capitalist development and modernity – a story that features capitalist consumption as a central medium shaping political economic structures and consciousnesses. In sum, capitalist consumption has become a crucial institution in the international political economy's hegemonic order and potential disorder. This book sets out to explain this as well as its implications and contradictions.

* * *

The time is ripe to examine the role played by consumption in the international political economy. 'Consumption,' to repeat what Robert Cox said at the start of this chapter, 'is the motor force of capitalism and the motivation of consumer demand is indispensable to capitalism's continuing development.'[3] Despite this fact, consumption remains undertheorized and strategically underassessed among many critical analysts. Unlike production, distribution or exchange, consumption generally is taken for granted – seen as the subject of extraordinary manipulation[4] or, taken to another extreme, viewed as a potentially subversive activity.[5] Mainstream theorists fare no better, exhorting free market policies based on the supposed sovereignty of rational consumers while paradoxically bearing witness to billions of dollars being funnelled into a much different consumer logic. Indeed, it has long been common practice in the West for advertisers and marketers to promote commodities by associating them with the social-psychological needs of individuals, as opposed to their utilitarian applications. Not only are the balance sheet calculations of *homo economicus* largely absent in the real world of capitalist consumption but, as Goodwin et al. demonstrate, 'On no matter is [mainstream] economics more in contradiction with itself than in its view of consumer behavior and motivation ...'[6]

In this book we conceptualize consumption as a complex institution – a historically constructed, power-laden way of thinking and acting. As with other political, economic and sociological institutions – such as law, religion or family – consumption-related norms are neither natural nor inevitable. Instead, people are directly involved in its ongoing development, and the power of consumption (and other such institutions) directly involves the fact that an almost countless number of people are its primary agents – historical agents who usually treat the institution as a universal, timeless fact of everyday life.

Today, in a period of rapid change, uncertainty and ongoing social-economic injustice, consumption – at least in its contemporary capitalist guise – serves the globalization project by dampening or fragmenting collective and sustained modes of resistance. Speaking more generally about what he calls 'market civilisation', Stephen Gill argues that 'it tends to generate a perspective on the world that is ahistorical, economistic, materialistic, "me-oriented", short-termist, and ecologically myopic'.[7] Beyond this, in these pages we argue that through the (usually problematic) integration of capitalist consumption into daily lives, individualism, immediate gratification time frames and even *change itself,* all become (or prospectively become) 'naturalised' – taken-for-granted elements of everyday 'common sense'.[8] While, to repeat, the saliency of all institutions involves their apparent timelessness and universality, *capitalist consumption is different in that what it prospectively makes timeless and universal is a lifestyle that paradoxically eradicates time.*

* * *

Conceptualizing consumption as an institution connects debates about how our world (dis)order is being structured with the kind of world people actually or prospectively want. It does this by relating macro-historical developments with the everyday. Indeed, consumption compels us to assess relationships involving both the individual and the collectivity, the local and the global, the past and the future through questions concerning how people live, their material and cultural aspirations, and what is (or is not) imaginable.[9] In the context of the globalization project, the capitalist consumer, as a mythically free and rational individual, is 'exemplary of the new world and integral to its making'[10] – a new world characterized by complexity, contradiction and smoke-and-mirror relationships.

The history of capitalism is directly linked to and inter-dependent with consumption and other institutions such as private property, the wage labour contract and, still more abstractly, state sovereignty. The globalization project, through trade agreements, new technologies, the internationalization of property rights and other reforms, now has set the stage both for capital's expansion and resulting tensions and contradictions.

Having recognized this, the form, direction and mode of potential resistance will be shaped (as it always has been) by the organizational and intellectual capacities of variously situated human beings. In what follows, we argue that the thoughts and activities of vested interests supporting the globalization project *and the thoughts and activities of many of its opponents* are being increasingly mediated, with important implications, by the extraordinary institution of capitalist consumption.

Consumption and growth

Capitalism requires consumption. Without the latter, the system, and thus the entire political economic order, falls into crisis. North America and Western Europe, together constituting just over 10 per cent of the world's population, consume about 60 per cent of everything produced.[11] The consumption practices of the American consumer are especially important. In itself, the United States is the world's largest marketplace – just over 5 per cent of the earth's population accounts for almost 32 per cent of total consumption.[12] The American marketplace, in fact, is so important that signs of the US consumer's demise – as indicated by unprecedented consumer debt loads, the outsourcing of jobs overseas, rising energy costs and other looming problems – directly threaten the economic feasibility of global capitalism.

One threat to consumption involves the tepid growth of American wages – wages essential for the economic system to remain buoyant. Unlike the decades following the Second World War, when the median wage earned by workers grew in real terms by 80 per cent, since the 1980s most American wages have been stagnant.[13] This means that the centre of world consumption, the United States, is not able to purchase more because the majority of its workers are making more money. Instead, lower prices, mass access to cheap credit and, of course, a domestic cultural-psychological obsession with consumption are the primary means through which Americans have continued spending.

Fortunately for the beneficiaries of capitalism and proponents of the globalization project, consumption continues to grow. From 1960 to 2000, the total amount spent on goods and services by households worldwide increased from $4.8 trillion to $20 trillion.[14] Both population growth and the growth of overall wealth have been central to this; but, more recently, for the reasons noted above, as well as because of expanding efforts to promote consumption through advertising and marketing, more people are buying more things. One question concerning mainstream and other analysts is this: is this growth sustainable?[15]

The perpetuation of US-based consumption, following a brief downturn after September 11, 2001 (9/11), is crucial, particularly because other world centres of consumption – Western Europe and Japan – have been lagging. From 1995 to 2003, domestic consumption in the United States increased by an average of 3.7 per cent each year, twice the growth rate of the rest of the 'developed' world.[16] For some economists, free trade agreements, new information and communication technologies (ICTs) and other tools of contemporary globalization will keep the engine of worldwide consumption growing, at least at a rate and scale needed to counter-balance a prospective US slowdown. But when measured in terms of income growth (or GDP) per person, from 1980 to 2000 – the years in which 'free trade', ICTs and neoliberal regulatory reforms first were widely applied – the rate of growth in these countries has been less than half of what it was during the preceding 20 years.[17]

Among other things, such empirical facts speak to the importance of promoting more consumption in as many places as possible. Theoretically at least, by creating new demands, workers will want more; their governments will accommodate more business activity and capitalist interests will flourish, leading to, it is assumed, economic growth and, thus, more consumption. And while global economic growth is weaker today than it was before the 1980s (before, to repeat, the contemporary globalization project began), spending inside and outside the United States on advertising has increased steadily. In the United States, from 1980 to 2003, real dollar advertising expenditures rose from about $135 billion to $231 billion.[18] In response to slower growth rates and stagnant wages (and, of course, more commodities competing for consumers), this intensification of advertising and marketing activities has been predictable.

Consumption, consent and American foreign policy

Consent, tolerance or acquiescence for the post-Cold War globalization project has been attained, in part, through the promotion of a vision and, with it, a promise. The vision has been the universalization of the material living standards enjoyed by the already well off. The promise is that such material improvements, leading to the relatively extravagant lifestyles enjoyed by many in the North, can be achieved through the capitalist marketplace. According to the Bush administration, '[m]ore open markets, sustainable budget policies, and strong support for development will unleash the enterprise and creativity for lasting growth and prosperity'.[19] The globalization project constitutes more than a leap of faith. It promises, quite literally, to deliver the goods.

Wanting what globalization has promised has become a core motivation for billions of people to at least temporarily go along with changes associated with the project; namely, the opening up of borders for capital, the repeal of state-based protections and programmes, and the institutionalization of property rights and related reforms. Through this project, goods and services previously out of the reach of many are being widely promoted. Previously unimaginable commodities are being made available, regardless of where a person lives, so long as one has money. Items and services, once thought of as luxuries – computers, dry cleaning, air conditioning, carbonated soft drinks – are becoming lifestyle necessities.

Beyond such material inducements and rising expectations, as Marx observed some time ago, the realm of exchange – the moment in which a commodity is purchased – entails an illusion. Human relations, in this endlessly repeated transaction, appear to be both free and voluntary. Class differences momentarily vanish; marketplace decisions are made by seemingly autonomous individuals.

> A worker who buys a loaf of bread and a millionaire who does the same appear in this act only as simple buyers, just as, in respect to them, the grocer appears only as a seller. All other aspects are here extinguished. The *content* of these purchases, like their *extent*, here appears as completely irrelevant compared with the formal [institutional] aspect.[20]

But, despite the fact that an unprecedented number of purchasable things now are available almost everywhere, huge numbers of people have been excluded from taking part. One-third of the earth's population, as of 2004, accounted for just 3.2 per cent of human consumption. Since 1990, in some parts of the world, poverty has worsened. Even among the 'poster children' of globalization – China and India – domestic income disparities have grown.[21] And while overall poverty has declined over the past few decades, according to the World Bank, almost 1.5 billion people still try to survive on less than $2 a day.[22]

The richest one-fifth of the world's population consume 45 per cent of the meat and fish while the poorest one-fifth consume 5 per cent. The wealthiest fifth own 87 per cent of all the motorized vehicles. The poorest fifth own less than 1 per cent.[23] Equally disturbing is the apparent *decline* in the number of nations that have a substantial middle class – defined by World Bank as countries in which over 40 per cent of residents earn incomes that enable them to consume more than what's needed just to survive. Since 1960, their number has declined, from 41 to 31.[24]

Officials working for the US Department of Defence and various American intelligence agencies are concerned about these disparities. This concern, however, is not based primarily on questions of fairness or social justice. Instead, many US officials implicitly recognize the power of exchange – specifically, the constituent illusion of social equality that Marx identified – as a means of maintaining consent.

After the attacks of 9/11, two inter-related foreign policy principles have come to the fore: the 'disconnectedness defines danger' security paradigm and the Bush administration's 'freedom doctrine'. According to the former, those parts of the world in which capitalism and its constituent social-economic relations (including capitalist consumption) are well established constitute what US foreign policy strategist Thomas Barnett calls the 'functioning core'. Because Western Europe, Japan, Australia, Canada and others are fully participating in the globalization project, they are thought to be relatively secure components of a US-led international order. At the other extreme are countries largely disconnected from globalization's inter-dependencies and development opportunities – countries mostly located in much of Africa, Central and Southwest Asia, and the Middle East. Together, these are called the 'non-integrating gap'. In addition to their poverty, these 'gap' countries have failed to participate in the globalization project. Barnett, a chief proponent of the 'disconnectedness defines danger' paradigm, explains that if

> a country is ... losing out to globalization or rejecting ... its advance, there is a far greater chance that the US will end up sending forces ... Conversely, if a country is largely functioning within globalization, we tend not to have to send our forces there ... to eradicate threats.[25]

Beyond the need for the United States to 'export security' to the gap, Barnett argues that the task of 'making globalization truly global' will 'ultimately depend ... on private investment'.[26]

As for the 'freedom doctrine', it sanctions the use of American security and military forces to remove regimes that oppose 'free markets' and their assumed correspondence with 'free democratic governance'. As President Bush stated during his second inaugural speech, '[t]he survival of liberty in our land increasingly depends on the success of liberty in other lands ... The best hope for peace in our world is the expansion of freedom in all the world'.[27]

The globalization project

The United States has become an extraordinarily important proponent of the globalization project. In the 1990s, this project was pursued through the construction of a largely consensual world order, forged by trade agreements, intellectual property arrangements, ICT applications and infrastructures, the diktats conveyed to governments through international organizations and, of course, the direct interventions of American state and corporate personnel.

The project, involving efforts to shape what is imaginable, acceptable and rational, has been driven forward by powerful agents structuring 'media' (broadly defined) – international and domestic institutions, organizations and technologies. Through these, the globalization project entails explicit and implicit efforts to widen and deepen general conditions found in all capitalist political economies: a systemic obsession with spatial expansion, organization and control within ever-shortening time frames, and the related neglect of historical and social conceptualizations of time.

While the expansionist tendencies of the United States have been well documented by historians,[28] only in recent years has the notion of a grand neo-imperialist project been the subject of open debate in Washington. By the term 'neo-imperialism', we mean a post-colonial empire – one in which direct control through territorial occupation has, with notable exceptions, been replaced by efforts to re-structure the essential mediators of international and domestic relations. Through the institutionalization of domestic media such as private property and the wage labour contract, often enforced through international organizations such as the World Bank and IMF, neo-imperialist policies can be applied with limited resistance. National populations – many of whom are free to vote in or out the governments of their choice – may not recognize that asymmetrical power relations have, in fact, been entrenched. More than this, under this neo-imperialism, civil society itself becomes the site of institutions, organizations and technologies whose mediation of relationships generally legitimize and enculture ways of thinking and acting that deepen inequalities. As we develop in subsequent chapters, the institution of capitalist consumption is among the most significant of these media.

Nevertheless, the globalization project is generating its own contradictions and, from them, a sporadic but potentially dangerous opposition has emerged. In this context, and in response to 9/11, neo-imperialism became an in-vogue part of Washington think tank discourse – a discourse only softened as a result of Bush administration blunders in Iraq.

Echoing the self-assumed benevolence of the British in the nineteenth century and Rome after Augustus, proponents of a neo-imperialist, American-centred world order emphasize the virtues of liberal democracy and the material benefits of the market system. The latter, framed in terms of what George Soros calls 'market fundamentalism' (involving the lowering of taxes, pro-growth regulatory reforms and the opening-up of markets for investment and trade), in effect constitutes a system of international political economic dominance with the American state as its core nodal point of power.

Reflecting this position, the Bush administration released its defining foreign policy document – its first *National Security Strategy* (*NSS*) – in 2002. In it the White House makes innumerable references to the principles of market fundamentalism. Democracy, development and free markets are intimately associated with lower taxes, pro-marketplace regulations and expanding trade regimes. Together, they constitute what is called 'a single sustainable model for national success'.[29] This recipe, says the *NSS*, 'transcends mere economic theory: "free trade" arose as a moral principle even before it became a pillar of economics. If you can make something that others value, you should be able to sell it to them. If others make something that you value, you should be able to buy it. This is real freedom, the freedom for a person – or a nation – to make a living'.[30]

Following the writings of Justin Rosenberg[31] and David Harvey,[32] in this book we argue that such freedoms – instituted through the globalization project – entail both more inter-dependence *and* enhanced territorial differentiation. As capital is granted more mobility to invest, produce and sell its commodities in virtually any country (an ability made possible by media such as trade agreements, ICTs and domestically enforced property rights), the resulting insecurities for local/national workers and governments impel a simultaneous emphasis on 'comparative advantage' efficiencies. While these may lower overall costs (thus, indirectly, reducing prices for consumers), such single-sector or one-commodity export dependencies also magnify vulnerabilities. In such a sped-up, inter-dependent and (especially for countries possessing few if any comparative advantage) crisis-laden political economy, cultural turns to various forms of nationalism, chauvinism and, in some cases, religious fundamentalism are predictable. In this context, a 'freer', more open world (dis)order generally entails greater insecurities and reactionary conflicts.

Capitalist relations are historically unique in that their structures and institutional mediators, including consumption, can be organized and extended without the formal expansion of one sovereign state into another. Indeed, coercive measures usually are frowned upon as costly and sometimes counter-productive (as the US occupation of Iraq reaffirms). According to Rosenberg, 'in capitalism we have an historical form of society in which *uniquely* it becomes possible even for relations of production [including consumption] to extend across political orders ... *without* diminishing the sovereign territoriality of the states involved'.[33]

Globalization and commodification

Before proceeding, we need to link these policies to consumption more directly. 'Capital', it should be underlined, compels the commodification of human relations. This compulsion is rooted in the fact that capitalist production requires workers to sell their labour *as a commodity* – a requirement stemming from the crucial role labour plays in capital's drive to accumulate more capital.

In capitalism, people must be willing or compelled to work for a wage. Typically, this is achieved through various means, one outcome of which is to deny communities their economic self-sufficiency. To do this, the structured power relationship commonly called 'private property' needs to be institutionalized. Once in place, most have to enter into wage-labour contracts. If they don't, they cannot earn the monies required to purchase the goods and services needed or desired – goods and services now privately owned rather than autonomously made or communally accessible.

Today, this process of institutionalizing private property and waged labour has generated both a geographically diverse working class and the globalization of capitalist consumption. To repeat, once private property is imposed, people are compelled to sell their labour power as a commodity. Wages, for many, thus become the primary means of survival. The modern worker *and consumer* emerge hand in hand. Both, after all, 'are born of the same social relation'.[34]

The globalization project, the disconnectedness paradigm and the freedom doctrine, all suggest that the primary challenge now facing capital (and those nation states most influential in mediating its activities) is not the presence of an alternative political economic model, as was the case during the Cold War, nor the sporadic threats to commerce posed by al-Qaeda. Instead, the core challenge facing capital is the challenge it has always faced – the challenge of institutionalizing capitalist relations, primarily by establishing the worker/consumer through a complex of both material and smoke-and-mirror developments. More than just ensuring that at least some consumers have the means to buy what is produced (usually through higher incomes, lower prices and/or the capacity to sell more commodities more quickly), capital also seeks to commodify 'traditional' and 'alternative' relations. In the words of Boal et al., capitalists are compelled to move 'outward, to geographies and polities it can plunder ... [and to] drive *inward*, deep into the fabric of sociality ...'[35]

Examples of this abound. The former constitutes what Marx referred to as *primitive accumulation*. By this he meant the process, involving violence, through which communal or state-controlled things and relationships are criminalized or, to use a contemporary buzzword, 'privatised'. Historically, primitive accumulation played a core role in the industrial revolution by creating masses of people who were stripped of their means of subsistence, compelling them to become waged producers and commodity consumers. This history continues and, today, the globalization project is as much about human displacement and coercion as it is about the 'global village' and high-tech 'freedoms'. The imposition of neoliberal policies on the world's poorest countries and the 'fire and blood'[36] that flows from its explicit application (as in the occupation of Iraq) is primitive accumulation at work.

As marketing executives at Coca-Cola used to boast in the 1990s, rather than viewing other soft drink manufacturers as their main global competitor, coffee, tea or whatever indigenous beverage was favoured by a local population constituted the corporation's primary target for displacement and growth. Since then, Coke has joined others in commodifying the most essential of all drinks – water. To take another food-based example, in the United States the growth of fast food, processed food and instant food has been extraordinary. By the end of the 1920s, when most meals were made 'from scratch', a few hundred foods were available. In the 1960s, nearly 800 new food products were introduced each year. By 1985, this number rose to 5617. In 1995, 16,863 new food items were introduced into the American marketplace.[37]

With commodification, all kinds of relationships, activities and things become exchangeable through the use of money. This is one of the most profound secularizations in history. A skill, someone's time, a bag of potatoes, a poem, a ton of steel and even human sexuality magically become quantifiable, comparable and seemingly 'manageable'. Prices, through commodification, become the culture's core measuring rod of value and, in the process, inherent, historically established or intrinsic values are trivialized or erased. In this emerging world, because virtually everything has a price and almost anyone can become a consumer, everyone theoretically is free to have whatever he/she wants. Through capitalist relations, muscularly endorsed by the United States, the individual worker/consumer is free to choose what he/she needs or wants and, indeed, the consumerist lifestyle of his/her choice. But more than this, as people and their communities become increasingly dependent on selling their labour as the means of acquiring what is needed or desired, workers/consumers are integrated into the complex that is global capitalism.

Materially, structurally and psychologically, commodification generally and consumption specifically constitute linchpins of the globalization project. For all the diversity that persists (including an array of capitalist/non-capitalist political economic 'hybrids' found in many local and 'developing' communities), the commodification of labour and consumption constitutes a pervasive and universalizing process, sometimes involving coercion. '*McDonald's*,' writes Thomas Friedman (without apology), 'cannot flourish without *McDonnell Douglas*.'[38] More profoundly, in the words of Benjamin Barber (borrowing from Marcuse[39]), 'commodification does not so much kill as crowd out other meanings and values', eventually rendering the exchange value of things (rather than their use and intrinsic values) predominant.[40]

Hegemony and consumption

In the face of globalization's promised consumerist freedoms (as billboards, commercials and innumerable other promotions remind people dozens, hundreds or, for some, thousands of times each day), the carrot of consumption remains remarkably seductive despite persistent inequalities. Connecting the world through a web of material possibilities and individual aspirations is all well and good as long as such possibilities and aspirations can be *experienced*. In their effort to explain the rise of al-Qaeda, Boal et al. reference 'the billion new city-dwellers' in globalization's gap countries. These, they argue, are more than just places of 'misery and disorientation': they are also breeding grounds for anti-status quo militants. Never before, they write, 'have the wretched of the earth existed in such a bewildering and enraging hybrid state, with the imagery of consumer contentment piped direct into slum dormitories rented out by night, at cutthroat prices, to hopelessly indebted neo-serfs'.[41]

The power of capitalist consumption to contain even those harbouring little hope of becoming 'free', materially secure consumers (not to mention the already well off), warrants our direct attention.[42] To develop a precise and prospectively comprehensive understanding of the role of consumption vis-à-vis the globalization project (the core goal of this book), the puzzle of its power – or, more accurately, the power implications of its institutionalization in social relations – needs to be assessed with care.

Consumption rather than socialism (or perhaps even democracy) has become globalization's (and capitalism's) most compelling idea. More than just an ideal, capitalist consumption also has become *a shared yet individualistic way of thinking* – one whose norms entail the expectation that things, people and relationships are immediately accessible, interchangeable and disposable.

By addressing consumption as an institutional moment in *and mediator of* the production and reproduction of global capitalism, this book aims to develop consumption as an analytical category. In so doing, we hope to articulate strategic possibilities leading to progressive political economic change. As we develop in what follows, our approach resonates with neo-Gramscian political economy, particularly its concept of hegemony – the process of rule through consent.

According to Gramsci, workers, peasants and citizens provide capitalist liberal democracies with a modicum of potential stability as a result of their capacity to participate in their own governance. Whether these capabilities are used or not, the presence of elections, a 'free' press, laws protecting individual liberties and other such institutionalized norms provide the regime at hand and its ruling class with an air of legitimacy. In these political economies, consumption, through its institutionalization of the individual as an active or prospective consumer, reaffirms this legitimacy. If one 'plays by the rules', one can earn the monies needed to take part.

In developing political economies, where a range of political-legal opportunities to participate have not been historically concretized, capitalist consumption provides people with at least the potential to take part in constructing their fortunes, not through the ballot box but, instead, via the marketplace. Through this relatively limited but tangible mode of participation, we hypothesize that some form of legitimacy is conferred to status quo interests, especially among those whose spending capabilities are improving.[43]

But having said this, changing or modifying consumption, as with all institutions, does not and, indeed, cannot take place automatically or quickly. Institutions, once integrated into a complex of institutional, organizational and technological media (or, more abstractly, into a culture) are difficult to change. After all, institutions – from the law to family norms to consumption – constitute multifaceted, historically established, inter-subjective human relations – relations that are almost always explicitly or implicitly defended by organized and unorganized vested interests.

The institution of capitalist consumption, at the very least, requires sufficient incomes and the availability of purchasable goods and services. In its 2004 report on global consumption, the Worldwatch Institute claims that about 1.7 billion people, half of whom live in North America, Western Europe and Japan, can be classified as the world's 'consumer class' – defined as those whose lifestyles routinely involve the consumption of highly processed food, the active pursuit of bigger homes and more expensive cars, and a devotion to the accumulation of other non-essential goods. If we accept this descriptive definition, it can be argued that, for billions more, capitalist consumption is either an institutional 'work in progress' or something altogether external to their lives. For the latter, their relative poverty, while a source of unfathomable misery, provides little or no traction for consumption to play its prospectively hegemonic role.

Beyond its hegemonic utility, consumption serves capital through its dissemination into and influence on other institutions. This is why it is a mistake to assess consumption in isolation. Advertising, for example, does not (and, indeed, cannot) *itself* trigger consumption. Instead, the messages communicated through advertising only 'make sense' if established norms or complementary institutions are in place. As the institution of capitalist consumption is entrenched, at least within a particular sub-culture (such as middle-class Hindu teenagers living in Mumbai), others, such as patriarchy or the educational system or even religion, are implicated. In extraordinary circumstances, people informed by or acting through such media might organize themselves in ways that promote or resist it. For example, capitalist–worker conflicts over the past century have become increasingly framed in terms of consumption-related wages and cost-of-living disputes. Schools now teach children the tools they will need to get the commodity lifestyles they, as in a prophecy, 'inevitably' will want. Christmas, through a complex of historical forces and processes, has become a consumerist orgy in the West and a marketing vehicle in many non-Christian countries.[44] A crucial component of consumption's power thus stems from its integration into innumerable affecting institutions, organizations and technologies. Through this process, capitalist consumption becomes a taken-for-granted aspect of daily life in an extraordinarily diverse range of political economies and cultures.

Globalization, time and space

In the task of elaborating the process of rule through consent or rule in the absence of explicit coercion, we need to know more than just what people think about. We also need to understand *why people think in the ways in which they think*, not only to clarify why capitalist consumption is so attractive to so many (which will help us specify why capitalist relations have been successfully inculcated and reproduced) but also to assess the possibility of widespread and sustained *changes* in thought and action. As we develop in subsequent chapters, the power of capital to shape how humanity *thinks* constitutes its most formidable tool in shaping what policies are feasible or not feasible, what social trajectories are imaginable or unimaginable.

One outcome of globalization and commodification – at least in the eyes of many post-structuralist and liberal commentators – is the emergence of innumerable hybrid identities and cultures. Rather than a global consumer society emerging as a homogeneous 'McWorld',[45] a multitude of new relationship norms and meanings have been constructed. This perspective, however, tends to assess the globalization of consumption (however defined or measured) in terms of an either/or conceptual framework: *either* Westernization is an all-engulfing tidal wave *or* a plurality of responsive individuals and communities construct their own 'self-determined' realities. In this book, commodification, generally, and capitalist consumption, specifically, instead are conceptualized as established or potentially *constituent* conditions *through which* cultures, identities and ways of thinking are modified or entrenched.

Established structures and institutional media cannot simply be swept away by capital (at least, in most cases, not right away). Nor can individuals just will them into oblivion. Power and history are everywhere; they structure human capacities through the institutions, organizations and technologies that mediate the political economic (dis)order. In this book's analysis, at least, we thus argue that the autonomous actor is pure mythology.

From a status quo perspective, in the long run, a successful globalization project would involve the defence or re-structuring of core technological, organizational and institutional media. These would constitute the means through which consciousnesses and, thus, 'realities' could be structured, thereby securing consent or quiescence. Ways of thinking and acting that both 'excuse' primitive accumulation and normalize commodification subsequently become possible. But clearly this is a tall order, especially as the tensions and contradictions facing the project are profound. For one thing, policy elites, whose consciousnesses also are influenced through consumption, generally conceptualize time in ways that neglect the complexity of historical processes. Moreover, thoughts and activities that shape the globalization project – including the drive to organize space in order to manage (logistically and conceptually) production, distribution, exchange and consumption – tend to involve an accompanying neglect of time. In what follows, this neglect of time is shown to be both the outcome of and itself a precipitator for its metaphorical 'annihilation'. In opening up international commerce through trade agreements, institutionalizing capitalist relations through property rights and accessing consumers through ICTs, almost without regard as to their location or the time of day, the temporal dimensions of life are being reduced to what Marx famously called 'the twinkling of an eye'.

Arguably, neorealist international relations, the quantitatively oriented, state-centric, and epistemologically ahistorical approach favoured by most US foreign policy agents, is incapable of the strategic sophistication needed to manage the globalization project over the *longue durée*. In American-centred efforts to construct a hegemonic twenty-first-century world order – involving both the smoke-and-mirrors *and* experiential realities of commodity consumption – current trajectories, we argue, are laying the groundwork for its prospective collapse.

* * *

The view expressed by Vergil Reed, just 60 years ago, that forging a consumer culture in India was as unlikely as was the prospect of 'shoveling smoke', underlines the power not just of commodification but of capitalist dynamics *writ large*. The fact that even India (or at least a growing 'middle class' within it) – the nation of Gandhian austerity, utilitarianism and, for many, abject poverty – has begun to embrace the individualistic, materialistic and immediate-gratification norms of modern consumption tells us something important about the globalization project and its implications for billions worldwide.

On the other hand, the complexities of India's (far-from-complete) transformation into a Western-style consumer society also conveys some revealing insights as to the limitations, tensions and contradictions at hand. Here, as in China, Russia and other world (dis)order 'hot spots', aspects of the West's history are being roughly replicated, but, significantly, at a much accelerated pace. This, itself, presents agents of the globalization project with a range of problems, not the least of which is the normalization of accelerated modes of decision-making and related ahistorical responses.

Amidst all the unpredictability of what appears to be unfolding, our analysis reveals one thing with confidence: the globalization project, accompanied by the ascent of capitalist consumption, together are likely to make our present century the most reactionary in history. In this book, the precise forces and processes behind this forecast are explained and assessed. With critical students of the international political economy in mind, as well as general readers interested in how our collective future might unfold, the chapters that follow aspire to illuminate what arguably constitutes one of the most important and certainly ethereal institutions of our contemporary world (dis)order. If we are to avoid the outcomes predicted herein, a critical, historically minded analysis of capitalist consumption now is essential.

Chapter previews

In Chapter 2, 'Power, Hegemony and the Institution of Consumption', we elaborate the nature of capitalist consumption's power – specifically, its role in the structuring of consciousness. Capitalist consumption, we argue, once institutionalized, has substantive implications both for everyday life and the globalization project. More than this, in 'developed' political economies at least, we argue that consumption now frames and contains hegemonic struggles. In 'developing' parts of the world, in the absence of democratic institutions and other relatively peaceful means of participation, once capitalist consumption is established, it potentially facilitates consensual rule – a means of governance effective in polities that have the cultural inclination and economic means to take part.

Chapter 3, 'The Birth of Capitalist Consumption', presents a history of consumption's institutional development in the West. Through an analysis of its birth in England (and maturation taking place over several hundred years) and its modern elaboration in the United States, this chapter identifies the precise dynamics driving both consumption's past development and its contemporary trajectories. Here we apply conceptual tools introduced earlier to consider consumption using a historicist methodology, taking care to relate the 'inside' of history (human consciousness) with the 'outside' (events, empirical forces and structural developments).

Among other findings, Chapter 3 reveals that the commodification of human relations tends to involve a concomitant rise in mediated abstractions. Capitalist consumption, we argue, both depends on these and, once institutionalized, it elaborates them. However, our history also reveals that the development of capitalist consumption usually faces substantive barriers: first, as a result of previously institutionalized ways of organizing society, and, second, as the outcome of similarly slow to change, affecting conceptual systems. Lastly, our history demonstrates that capitalist consumption's institutional development depends on the availability of wealth (needed, of course, to buy things) *and* on the presence of an existential vacuum. This latter condition constitutes the essential means through which the modern desire for commodities may develop to become a social 'norm' – a norm in which the use or intrinsic value of things becomes secondary to their purported psychological or symbolic importance.

In Chapter 4, 'Global Civil Society or Global Consumer Society?', we turn to a critique of in-vogue forecasts as to the almost voluntaristic unfolding of variously conceptualized progressive world orders. Given the historical dynamics generating the development of capitalist consumption, here we assess global civil society (GCS) and related prognostications. We find that GCS theorists have constructed a demonstrably faulty conceptual edifice – one so laden with unsubstantiated assumptions and hollow arguments that there is only one word that adequately describes the thought that lies behind the construction: delusional.

Having disassembled the GCS thesis (and related claims regarding the declining sovereignty of states), in Chapter 4 we also consider the potentials of another kind of 'GCS' – the emergence of a global consumer society. This, we argue, while more likely, also faces problems. In an increasingly interconnected world – one in which change and instability are becoming norms – the place-based conditions of daily existence, along with the ongoing centrality of the nation state, together make humanity's ongoing identification with a particular nation, religion, ethnicity or locale more rather than less likely. This, we argue, is probable despite and/or because of the transnational dynamics being fostered through the globalization project.

We conclude Chapter 4 by underlining yet another globalization project-generated and consumption-mediated development: the time needed to individually and collectively reflect and assess is almost certainly being reduced. In fact, the forces and processes identified in this and earlier chapters compel the unfolding of an international political economy in which instantaneous decisions and discontinuities of experience and consciousness are becoming routine. These, we argue, are not prescriptions for the construction of a transnational, progressive future – far from it.

In Chapter 5, '"Developing" Political Economies and Global Consumer Society', we return to Robert Cox's observation that capitalist consumption has been 'the dynamic behind market liberalization ..., and the driving force of economic globalization'.[46] We do this by assessing the institution's development and implications in India and China. Through a consumption-focused history of each nation, we find that the medium of capitalist consumption has emerged into an affecting but, among some at least, not yet reified component of daily life – variously influencing different classes and cultures in accordance with long-standing cultural norms, economic capabilities and, importantly, state policies. More generally, in these and other 'developing' political economies, we argue that capitalist consumption appears to be 'freeing' many through its elaboration of ever-more commodified, abstracted norms. As in the histories of England and America, existential questions have emerged alongside economic prosperity and fetishistic associations. Importantly, however, 'traditional' values and relatively non-abstract conceptualizations linger. This, we believe, constitutes a prospectively important window of opportunity.

In parts of the 'developing' world – at least among those who have escaped abject poverty – there exists the recognition that the globalization project is neither inevitable nor necessarily desirable. Moreover, in these places, perhaps for a limited time, the nation state generally is seen in a more 'matter of fact' light than it is in the West. Under these conditions, the neoliberal 'end of history' is still open to debate. Here, the capacity to respond to the globalization project critically, creatively and progressively through a resurgence of statist policies is at least imaginable.

In Chapter 6, titled 'Neo-Imperialism, Consumption and the Crisis of Time', we address contemporary US foreign policy in the context of, first, emerging challenges to the globalization project and, second, the conceptual implications of capitalist consumption. Here we argue that a post-9/11 neo-imperialist approach to world (dis)order developments has been influenced by consumption-mediated orientations emphasizing spatial reach and control to the neglect of historical reflection and duration. Washington-promoted strategies, countering both anti-neoliberal developments and the 'sensational' resistance of Islamic terrorism, entail a decidedly ahistorical and reactionary response. These, we demonstrate, constitute the predictable outcomes of a spatially focused (and time-neglectful) empire based not primarily on occupation but, instead, on the structuring of laws and regulations within 'sovereign' states and the reform of civil societies through a complex of affecting mediators – from property rights to contracts to consumption.

Through the globalization project, the priorities of never-ending growth and expansion, concretized through a mostly corporate (and US-facilitated) control over space, constitute the basis of much of the violence now so pervasive – a violence that's perpetrated on both people and our ecosystem. This dynamic, mediated and affected by capitalist consumption, marches on, leaving us little time to reflect or reconsider, (let alone reorganize) our collective priorities in a sustained, reflexive fashion. In this chapter, an important theme of the book is made explicit: that the ascent of a reactionary US foreign policy itself says something important about a still more general historical trend – the consumption-mediated, spiralling neglect of time.

Finally, in Chapter 7, our book's 'Conclusion', we rearticulate key arguments, emphasizing core tensions and historical contradictions stemming from our study. These, we argue, provide those interested in pursuing a progressive and reflexive agenda with opportunities to effect substantive change; change, we believe, requiring a number of prerequisite political, economic and cultural conditions to be defended or advanced. Among others, these include the resurrection of politics targeted at the nation state – the still sovereign and most influential level of global governance. What we call 'islands of resistance' – institutional, organizational and technological nodal points of critical, creative thought and reflexive, long-term action – are the foci of this prospective response. Following the work of analysts as diverse as Robert Cox, Harold Innis, Herbert Marcuse and Albert Schweitzer, in the context of the prevalence of both capitalist production and consumption, we stress that humanity's survival may well depend on a shift away from the immediate gratification of individuals towards the delayed satisfaction of state–civil society partnerships – not through some kind of Maoist repression of the former in favour of the latter but, instead, through a historical and dialectical awareness of both.

According to Cox, 'To change the system implies considerable sacrifice by present standards – a transformation of the idea of the good life and the good society.'[47] To do this, we first must come to terms with the saliency, attractiveness and, indeed, the power of capitalist consumption. This, precisely, is the subject of our next chapter.

2
Power, Hegemony and the Institution of Consumption

> Choose life. Choose a job. Choose a career. Choose a family, Choose a fucking big television, Choose washing machines, cars, compact disc players, and electrical tin openers.
> Choose good health, low cholesterol and dental insurance. Choose fixed-interest mortgage repayments. Choose a starter home ...
> Choose leisurewear and matching luggage. Choose a three-piece suite on hire purchase in a range of fucking fabrics. Choose DIY and wondering who you are on a Sunday morning. Choose sitting on that couch watching mind-numbing spirit-crushing game shows, stuffing fucking junk food into your mouth. Choose rotting away at the end of it all, ... nothing more than an embarrassment to the selfish, fucked-up brats you have spawned to replace yourself. Choose your future. Choose life.
>
> —Opening scene voiceover from 1996 film *Trainspotting*

What, specifically, is the nature of consumption's institutional power? More pointedly, what is the role of capitalist consumption in the contemporary globalization project? To answer these questions, in this chapter we introduce the three-dimensional approach to power developed by Steven Lukes and explain how the third dimension – the dimension that focuses on the structuring of consciousness – illuminates the hegemonic implications of consumption. Also, in the following pages, we explain key conceptual tools – in particular, a sociological conceptualisation of institutions and a communications studies heuristic device called conceptual systems – in anticipation of applying them to the histories and empirical examples presented later in this book.

Conceptualizing power

According to Lukes, the application of power involves at least three dimensions.[1] The first dimension is associated with students of politics called 'pluralists' and, in the field of international relations, 'neorealists'. Both schools understand power to be something demonstrable, something quantifiable through observable behaviour. For these theorists, individuals or groups exercise or resist power only when they *act*.

Students of the second dimension of power focus on the setting of agendas – the ability to determine 'the rules of the game'. In international relations, this perspective most often is associated with 'liberal institutionalists', theorists who generally work from the premise that historically developed structures – such as the regulatory conditions governing trade or the legal norms associated with state relations – warrant as much attention as does the one-dimensional focus on observable applications. Unlike proponents of the one-dimensional approach, for these analysts, the *absence* of explicit resistance does not necessarily mean that people are more-or-less content. Instead, inaction also may be the outcome of a set of conditions that don't allow prospective grievances to be expressed or heard.

Neither the one- nor the two-dimensional approach enables us to adequately address a concern raised at the outset of our book: acquiescence in the face of demonstrable global disparities. Following two decades of economic liberalization, the opening up of borders to capital and trade, and what has been called a transnational communications revolution, the 'developed' world now is characterised by summits of wealth dotted by a patchwork of poverty, and the 'developing' world by islands of affluence amidst seas of impoverishment.

Before we proceed, it should be pointed out that the one-dimensional view of power substantiates aspects of the Bush administration's foreign policy. For the White House, resistance in the form of protests or terrorism are portrayed as exceptions to some kind of global consensus supporting the 'free market' and Western interpretations of democracy. After all, if resistance only takes place through readily observable actions *and* if the majority of the world is not engaged in such activities, the one-dimensional view of power assumes that most support the globalization project. Whether or not the White House is correct is secondary to our main point here: the one-dimensional perspective insists that, in the absence of a quantifiable opposition, people are content. To bend a cliché, the anti-status quo exceptions prove the rule – the rule in this case being the legitimacy and righteousness of American leadership and neoliberal capitalism.

According to proponents of the two-dimensional approach, inaction in the face of injustice may be the result of structural conditions that limit or deter anti-status quo activities. Despite the relative nuance of this second face of power, it fares only slightly better than the one-dimensional perspective for one fundamental reason: it can't explain the *absence* of dissent among individuals and groups who do, in fact, have access to the mechanisms needed to resist.

In relatively wealthy liberal democracies, for example, where citizens (at least periodically through elections) are 'heard' by government officials, where they have the legal ability to organize, and where many have the wealth needed to 'vote with their pocketbooks', those who have the least (and, thus, also the most to gain) generally participate the least. For the one-dimensional analyst, these people must be either satisfied or lazy. Otherwise, wouldn't they do *something*? For students of the second dimension of power, in the absence of observable structural barriers, the first dimension of power constitutes, therefore, the only explanation left.

However, as Lukes points out, this conclusion may well be dubious: 'to assume the absence of a grievance equals ... consensus', he writes, 'is simply to rule out the possibility of false or manipulated consensus by definitional fiat'.[2] For proponents of the third dimension of power, the puzzle of limited dissent in the face of observable injustice is investigated differently. In this school of thought, inaction might be the result of social conditions and related 'common sense' norms that, in effect, deter or deny the *capacity* to resist. In other words, the absence of conflict may be the result of *a form of power that shapes consciousness itself.* Observable conflicts, from this perspective, may have been averted not because of structural barriers (as in the second dimension of power) but, instead, *as a result of the capacity of some to influence others' perceptions of reality.*

In short, the one-dimensional view of power understands acquiescence to be the product of satisfaction or apathy; the two-dimensional perspective understands that it could also be the outcome of 'the rules of the game'; the three-dimensional view, while recognizing that the first two exist, also theorizes non-participation as possibly the result of some kind of *non-consciousness.*

For one-dimensional analysts, a population's embrace of capitalist consumption and the inability of many to purchase commodities are choices made by informed, autonomous human beings. The fact that many want more – even when they already have more than enough to live comfortably – demonstrates a human nature characterized by insatiable wants. As for those too poor to take part in consumer society, either they only have themselves to blame (for not working hard enough in order to make more money) or they must be somehow content in their 'underdevelopment'. For the two-dimensional theorist, commodity consumption similarly is regarded as some kind of taken-for-granted norm. For those not engaged in the acquisition of things, in addition to the explanations tabled by one-dimensional scholars, two-dimensional analysts believe that readily identifiable barriers may be involved – barriers such as poor educational opportunities leading to limited job prospects that, in turn, restrict incomes and credit.

Both the one- and two-dimensional views of power are implicit in main-stream economic theory; the theoretical approach that constitutes the basis of IMF/World Bank 'development' policies, not to mention the dominant paradigm informing the policies employed by most states. For mainstream or 'neoclassical' economists, prices (or money values) are commonly used to measure, compare and, prospectively, improve the efficiencies of any given economy. Efficiency, of course, is the means to a particular end – the end being 'the maximisation of utility'.

For proponents of the third dimension of power, this mainstream approach to economics is an inherently power-laden project. While the first and second dimensional views assume that people naturally want to increase both pro-duction and consumption (and that, for the second dimensional theorist, at least, structural barriers might stand in the way), the third dimensional ana-lyst instead is compelled to pose a radical question. What if, logically and empirically, as an institutionalized way of thinking and acting, neoclassical/ mainstream economic theory itself socializes and normalizes a kind of intellectual myopia? What if mainstream economic policy *itself* frames and contains genuine human choice? What if, in effect, it *restricts* the presumed goal of neoliberalism itself – 'freedom'?

We can affirm these suspicions by briefly addressing two lines of inquiry. First, the use of money as the means of measuring or assessing 'development', 'progress' or 'utility' is demonstrably limited and problematic. Clearly, not everything is quantifiable nor, for that matter, is it analytically advantageous to measure everything. Without resorting to intellectual gymnastics, money simply cannot quantify what all economies need to function, at least over the long term: things such as a livable environment and loving relationships. In other words, when money is used as the primary means of assessing what is valuable, it soon becomes apparent that mainstream policies are handcuffed by their inability to quantify the largely unquantifiable.[3]

Another venue through which the unspoken (and sometimes oppressive) power of the neoclassical paradigm is revealed stems from its self-proclaimed mandate – the maximization of utility – which is, in fact, a term used as a proxy for the actual goal of mainstream economic policy: the maximization of production and consumption in the context of temporal and place-specific constraints. In effect, mainstream economists, international organi-zations and the vast majority of state policymakers, as a result of the institutionalization of the neoclassical paradigm, generally think and oper-ate through an altogether inter-subjective analytical framework. Efficiency is assumed to be necessary to enable people to produce and consume an ever-increasing quantity or dollar-value of commodities. Encouraging competi-tiveness and profit maximization through various policy measures and even cultural reforms thus become unquestionably 'necessary'.

Beyond the manifold problems that have arisen as a result of a way of thinking and acting that has no built-in concept of 'enough',[4] it soon becomes clear that power interests are served through this institution – vested interests primarily concerned with higher profits through greater efficiencies and more consumption.

By questioning the use of prices as measuring rods of value and the maximization of utility as a catch-all explanation as to why people (everywhere) should mould their lives around particular production–consumption norms, the third dimension of power reveals the logic behind the illogic. Environmental degradation, violent cultural disruptions, poverty for some and social injustice for others, all stem from or directly involve this arguably upside-down world in which political economy – 'the system' – seemingly runs humanity and not the other way around. 'Developing' nations, in this contemporary house-of-mirrors, are compelled to enforce property rights, produce or import cheaper products and, in urgent cases, submit themselves to strategic doses of neoliberal 'shock therapy', all in the quest to modernize and stimulate more production and consumption. As explained below, students of the third dimension of power do not begin with the premise that human beings, if given the opportunity, naturally seek to acquire things and live consumerist lifestyles. Whether people do or do not is as much (if not more) a matter of power relations structured (and occluded) through mediating institutions as it is a question of 'human nature' or the universalization of 'freedom'.

Another way to look at Lukes's three dimensions is to compare them in terms of the *mechanisms* used in exercising or resisting power. The one-dimensional view takes the world 'as it is'. Only quantifiable resources – from local election results to a military invasion – are worthy subjects of study. For the two-dimensional approach, codified procedures and regulatory conditions also can be important. The three-dimensional view recognizes both of these perspectives and their favoured mechanisms of power, but also seeks to identify what influences conceptualizations of what is feasible or unfeasible, realistic or unrealistic, imaginable or unimaginable. After all, if an aspiration is deemed unfeasible, unrealistic or, more profoundly, it cannot even be imagined, power probably will not be resisted.

The mechanisms through which the third face of power is employed include control over information, the communication of social mythologies, the ability to influence socialized norms and, even more fundamentally, the shaping of how people learn to process information and experience into what is known. These and other third dimension mechanisms directly influence what we will refer to as our *conceptual systems* – the means through which people come to conceptualize reality itself.

* * *

In the context of capitalist consumption, Lukes's analysis suggests that this institution almost certainly influences a broad range of thoughts and activities – from career aspirations to child-rearing choices to political approaches towards globalization. As Cox recognizes, consumerist thoughts and ambitions, perpetuated in most Western political economies after 1945, undoubtedly facilitated an ongoing and exploitative dominance of capitalists over workers.[5] The question, of course, is *precisely* how does it do this and what, specifically, are its effects?

Before answering this directly, the reader will note that in moving from a one-dimensional to a three-dimensional analysis of power, methodological difficulties arise. How, after all, can we assess something that cannot be readily observed or, indeed, doesn't even happen? Following John Gaventa's *Power and Powerlessness*,[6] we know that seemingly unobservable inequalities can, in fact, be measured. Indices such as growing or persistent economic disparities, the rising tide of physical and mental health problems, the measurable degradation of the earth's ecosystem, and many others, are quantifiable facts. In light of these – particularly as they are experienced by billions worldwide – inaction and inertia surely are not natural outcomes. Instead, what needs to be explained is the *absence* of action in response to these conditions. Indeed, the approach pursued in this book 'assumes that ... action ... by those affected *would occur were it not for power relationships*'.[7]

Beyond this position, based on what human beings logically would do when their livelihoods and health are threatened, we also need some method of tangibly demonstrating the third face of power. We need, according to Lukes, 'to justify our expectation that B would have thought and acted differently, and we need to specify the means or mechanisms by which A has prevented or else acted (or abstained from acting) in a manner sufficient to prevent B from doing so'.[8] In terms of our present study – in order to demonstrate the existence and significance of this third dimension of power and its applications *vis-à-vis* capitalist consumption – the right conceptual and heuristic 'tools for the job' are required.

Consumption as an institution

As mentioned in Chapter 1, a sociological institution can be defined as a historically constructed power-laden typification of habitualized thoughts and actions.[9] As with all institutions, consumption, as a shared way of thinking and acting, generally is experienced as an objective reality. This perception is largely a result of the fact that the consumption, as it is experienced and thought about in any particular place and time, largely pre-dates individual memory. All institutions constitute, in effect and paradoxically, a 'humanly produced, constructed objectivity'.[10] Most human beings, therefore, conceptualize consumption (as well as other institutions) in ways largely determined by others, particularly those from the past. Since we are born into an apparently universal and timeless complex of institutions, norms – such as those associated with consumption – generally are 'internalised', often appearing to be inevitable – the fruit of human nature or, from a common sense perspective, just 'the way it is'.

Although they are ongoing constructions (that is, the outcome of agency), once in place, institutions powerfully affect thoughts and perceptions. They, in effect, mediate and structure relationships, conceptualizations and consciousnesses.

Capitalist consumption, at least in relatively 'developed' political economies, constitutes something people take part in and think about in pursuit of more than just the physical necessities of life. Consumption also has become an important nodal point in the quest for meaning and identity. Of course, in the contemporary world, advertisers and marketers are key agents shaping these pursuits and their interests or, more generally, the interests of their clients (mostly corporations), are squarely aligned with the promotion of evermore consumption. As such, they obviously are fundamental to consumption's institutional development, particularly its widening reach and deepening influence.[11]

The recent history of China's turn to capitalism is an example of the often problematic nature and implications of establishing the institution of capitalist consumption and its subsequent mediation of power. In about 1979, socialist principles related to both production and consumption were radically reformed. Communist Party propaganda deriding capitalist consumerism was painted over with slogans such as 'Peasants Beam with Joy as They Get Rich', 'Get Rich by Working' and 'Have No Fear of Becoming Prosperous'.[12] Then, in 1982–3, the Party reverted back to themes and policies that deterred the 'decadence and "moral bankruptcy" of the capitalist West'.[13] While the state soon turned back to promoting consumption as a reward for hard work, as a means of stimulating workplace productivity and general economic growth (essentially, 'the maximisation of utility'), many Chinese remained reticent. Not only had decades of collectivist, anti-materialist policies left their mark on how people 'normally' thought and acted (a socialization not easily replaced by the allure of refrigerators and TVs), the political life of Chinese civil society was, for many years, fraught with predictable tensions. For example, farmers, who made noticeable profits and, as a result, were invited to receive public praise, often chose to stay home in fear of being criticized in their communities. Moreover, the PRC's *nouveau riche*, anticipating a possible state reversal, commonly joined the Communist Party as a kind of insurance policy against a prospective purge.[14] As Chapter 3 addresses, even in overwhelmingly capitalist contexts such as the United States, institutional norms related to consumption went through similarly anxious transitions. Just as there is nothing natural about consumerist lifestyles and ideals, the institution's ascendancy is rarely linear, typically provoking various forms of resistance as its history unfolds.

Institutions and how they mediate our lives almost always involve power struggles. Indeed, the globalization project itself entails a complex of international, national and local conflicts that, while sometimes explicit, are more typically implicit. Not only is contemporary history rife with such 'moments' of resistance, the institution of consumption – depending, in part, on its structural characteristics at any particular time and place – often shapes these, usually through its influence on norms of thought and activity.

For example, in many Western countries, the uncertainty, frustration and anger generated by aspects of the globalization project – stemming from its associated capital mobility, job-related uncertainties and 'race-to-the-bottom' environmental standards – often are expressed in ways influenced by capitalist consumption. Individualistic preferences rather than collective opposition, anti-social or self-destructive behaviours instead of progressive activities and liminal moments of consciousness centring on fashionable causes (for instance, the Live 8 'Make Poverty History' concerts in 2005), all entail ways of thinking and acting that bear some (not coincidental) resemblance to norms associated with consumption.

Among their other characteristics, these generally convey and perpetuate capitalist consumption's short-term, immediate gratification orientations – orientations that stand in sharp relief against both past and Third World-based movements that reference 'timeless' principles and the pursuit of long-term strategies. In this historical and inter-cultural context, one might ask if the suffragette, American civil rights and South African anti-apartheid movements could have possibly accomplished what they did had their participants focused on self-centred activities in anticipation of immediate results?[15]

While a here-and-now immediate gratification mode of dissent is most common in political economies where capitalist consumption has been well entrenched, the peoples of "developing" nations, while still relatively cognizant of collectivist historically entrenched ideals and strategies, are experiencing some significant generational changes. To again turn to the case of China, one-child policies in conjunction with rising incomes emerging in the context of a state-sanctioned promotion of capitalism has led to an unprecedented pampering of children through material goods. The freedom of children and adolescents to purchase *what they want* (as opposed to what the state or their family gives them) – a development often first experienced at McDonald's or some other fast food outlet – has implicitly sanctioned an individualistic, immediate-gratification way of thinking and acting, at least among a new generation of young, middle-class urbanites.[16]

But why is *this* institution so influential? Why, in relation to other institutions, is capitalist consumption analytically crucial if we are to understand the globalization project and the international application of the third dimension of power? Most obviously, consumption is something everyone does. Indeed, all living entities must consume to survive. In our contemporary political economy, some people don't work, some don't produce, some don't even reproduce, *but everyone consumes*. Consumption entails both observable behaviours (as demonstrated through the price system, displays of 'conspicuous consumption', monies spent on marketing, and so forth) *as well as* less observable (but equally influential) myths and socialized norms. As any advertising or marketing executive would concur, the institution's observable characteristics often are dependant on the less readily observable and *vice versa*.

Not only is consumption universally influential, its power implications can be gleaned from how people conceptualize their realities and act (or don't act) in the face of injustice and inequality. To illustrate this, let us reference an American study by Perri and Krueger.[17]

In the United States, income disparities have grown sharply since the 1970s. Nevertheless, from 1972 to 1998, these did not generate consumption inequalities. In 1972–3, the poorest 20 per cent of Americans made about 6 per cent of all income. By 1997–8, this bottom 20 per cent earned just 4 per cent. But rather than a drop in spending in line with this growing disparity, the poorest Americans consumed at the same rate they had 15 years previously. In other words, those least able to do so kept consuming, collectively accounting for more than 9 per cent of total spending in both 1972–3 and 1997–8.[18]

Perri and Krueger theorize that relatively impoverished Americans have kept buying for two reasons: easier credit and what they call income instability. The first is self-explanatory, to a limited degree, in that more people qualified for more credit at lower interest rates, in comparison to the 1970s. The second relates to general changes in the job market. In the 1970s, most employees held relatively stable positions, yet by the late 1990s many of these jobs, especially among the relatively unskilled, had evaporated, leaving legions in a state of employment flux. For brief periods at least, the incomes and prospects of many were good enough to provide them with the credit and optimism needed to keep spending. Income instability, rather than compelling people to 'save for a rainy day', instead encouraged more commodity purchases in light of the possibility of improving circumstances.

This conclusion raises questions, especially when we assess the study's findings in terms of the three dimensions of power. For one thing, why would the poorest Americans keep spending, even in the face of declining incomes, job insecurity and mounting debt? In 1990, US consumers owed $3.55 trillion. By 1999, this figure had increased to $7 trillion.[19] Today, for the first time since 1945, the average American has no savings (see Illustrations 2.1 and 2.2 below). Cheap, widely available credit and longer working hours have enabled most to keep spending.

Never mind the one- and two-dimensional myth of rational *homo economus* and the cliché that the glass, for the 'insatiable consumer', is always 'half-full' (instead of, for some, nine-tenths empty!). Something quite remarkable and powerful is at work. The question, of course, is what? Why the optimism and/or the preference to spend borrowed money instead of cutting back?

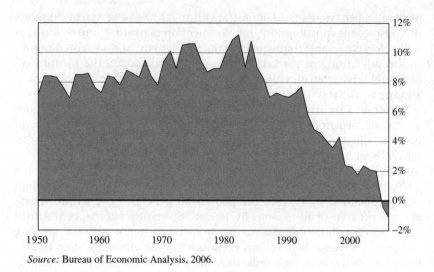

Source: Bureau of Economic Analysis, 2006.

Illustration 2.1   US personal savings, as a percentage of disposal income, 1950–2006

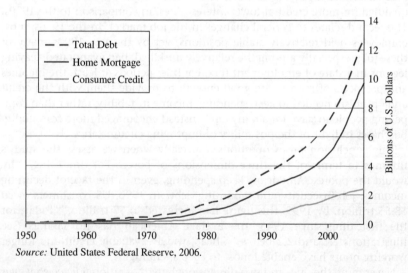

Source: United States Federal Reserve, 2006.

Illustration 2.2   US household debt, 1950–2006

Why, given the opportunity (such as a temporary job), do people act in ways that seem antithetical to their own experiences and apparent long-term interests?

Rather than assuming, as do Perri and Krueger, that Americans are prone to anticipate better times ahead and thus 'naturally' choose to live in debt, we should ask instead *might there be less visible, sociological forces at work?* Perri and Krueger believe that, given the opportunity to spend money they don't have today (but hope to have tomorrow), people innately will want to buy things. But, as the third face of power suggests, the reluctance of most to decline more credit and stop buying points to another dynamic at work – one difficult to observe but verifiable nonetheless.

In this case, we might ask what compels experienced, thinking human beings to act in ways that demonstrably run against their long-term (and perhaps even short-term) interests? The answer might be the prevalence of a powerful, mediating institution – capitalist consumption.

In a British study, materialistic (that is, consumerist) values are shown to be key predictors of compulsive shopping.[20] According to a study conducted at Stanford University, almost 24 million Americans have 'compulsive shopping disorder' – an affliction characterized by an 'out-of-control spending' that 'rips apart relationships and plunges consumers into overwhelming debt and bankruptcy'.[21] In another US study, not only are compulsive shoppers drowning in debt, the majority also are substance abusers and/or have anxiety disorders and/or eating disorders.[22]

Whether spending beyond one's means leads to such problems or these problems lead one to shop (or, more likely still, both are related to broader cultural variables), the point we need to underline here is that, even if a culture is overwhelmingly optimistic, falling into more debt with little or no tangible prospect of escape rarely constitutes the act of a rational, logical individual. We know that most Americans historically have been notoriously frugal consumers – at least until 1945. And, as our history in Chapter 3 demonstrates, today's free-spending consumer is far more a social construction than he/she is the straightforward outgrowth of more wealth-enabling 'innate' consumerist inclinations to take flight. The fact that the insatiable and increasingly debt-laden consumer is a social construction (and one that tends to be self-perpetuating) is affirmed by the fact that, in the United States at least, the average credit card debt among young adults (people 25–34 years old) increased 55 per cent between 1992 and 2001. For Americans 18–24, this debt load more than doubled.[23]

The capitalist dynamic and the mediation of change

Consumption's saliency stems less from its functional importance for capital than its status as a dynamic kind of cultural mooring. Indeed, virtually all institutions entail useful references or norms that help people make sense of existential queries and social uncertainties. Arguably, this is why institutions as seemingly diverse as religion and consumption resonate in a diversity of cultures from one generation to the next. What makes capitalist consumption such a unique institution is also what makes it strategically important.

All institutions, to repeat, are seemingly universal and timeless mediators of relationships and interactions. Ways of thinking and acting in several religions, for example, have changed very little over the centuries. Male dominance, although variously structured through patriarchal norms, pre-dates capitalism. Contemporary consumption, while similarly 'natural' and pervasive, differs from other institutions in that *it is explicitly characterized by a state of flux.* Like others, consumption is about continuity but, uniquely – because its economic *raison d'etre* is about turnover and 'what's new' – *capitalist consumption is an institution that reifies change itself.*

The conservative yet radical implications of this unique institution are based both on the conservative or mooring implications of all institutions (as discussed above) as well as capital's systemic compulsion to grow.[24] Modifications to consumption generally are implemented most directly by both buyers (consumers) and sellers (often corporations), and indirectly by nation states. Corporations and states have mobilized various organizations and technologies – as well as other institutions (such as the law, education and religion) – in the task of changing the institution in some parts of the world and deepening its influence in others. In relatively 'developed' economies, this generally has involved new efforts, through technology, to entrench already-consumerist ways of thinking and acting – ways of thinking and acting that developed over hundreds of years of inter-generational change, as explained in Chapter 3. As for 'less developed' areas of the world, efforts continue to widen capitalist consumption into previously under-exploited and geographically distant markets.

In this compulsion – this drive to sell more commodities through the widening and deepening of capitalist consumption – a fundamental dynamic emerges: capitalism drives forward the development of new forces of production and, thus, it systemically requires an ever-increasing amount of consumption. This, in turn, leads to the usually problematic reform of more than just the ways in which consumption itself is conceptualized and practised; it also generates reforms to a broad range of other, sometimes more conservative, institutions. This, of course, is not a result of institutions themselves being either open to change or obstinately against it (as this would imply a reified conceptualization of institutions). Instead, vested interests, defending shared ways of thinking and acting, consciously or unconsciously enable or resist such reforms.

Our main point here is that capitalist consumption – particularly among those with the capacity to change in step with the globalization project – has proven itself to be a remarkably influential institution, mediating the tumultuous changes now characterizing the contemporary political economic (dis)order. With the notable exception of the relatively well educated, middle-class cadre leading al-Qaeda,[25] capitalist consumption, if accepted, has made change itself more manageable, not only for capitalists seeking more consumers but also, socially and psychologically, among most who have (or prospectively have) the wealth needed to take part. While clearly there are limits to how fast consumption ideals and practices can be modified in any particular place and context (limits, that is, to how relations of production can change in response to this dynamic), capitalist consumption nevertheless has come to bear an enormous institutional responsibility; today, it must do more than just stoke an ever-greater demand for commodities – *it also must frame and contain resistance itself.*

Let us elaborate this point in the context of neoliberal globalization.

Over the past quarter century, rather than a wholesale retreat of the state from political economic life, states have been structurally recast. The neoliberal state – reformed through both internal and external pressures – has become the arbiter and guarantor of 'individual' (especially corporate) rights and freedoms. Of these, rights and freedoms involving private property, contracts and 'consumer sovereignty' have taken precedence. The contemporary proliferation of oppositional movements and discourses that focus on such rights has not been coincidental. Through both the general application of neoliberal economic policies (itself facilitated, if not legitimized, by neoclassical economic theory) and the promulgation of capitalist consumption (especially following the collapse of the USSR), an emphasis on the rights and freedoms of the individual has been ascendant. Arguably, this political-cultural shift, facilitated by (and itself facilitating) the ascent of relatively fragmented oppositional movements (i.e. the decline of organized labour and the rise of NGOs), has been a cornerstone of the mushrooming of inter- and intra-state inequalities and injustices.

Almost everywhere the state now is mandated to maintain, if not to promulgate, the rights of individual producers and consumers (especially *corporate* producers and consumers) rather than the Fordist/Keynesian recognition of the reproductive needs of capitalism *in toto*. The neoliberal globalization project thus has been accompanied by the retreat of the managerial welfare state, *not the state itself.*[26]

Not surprisingly, this neoliberal state, in its structural empowerment of capital, has fewer 'off the shelf' resources available to it – resources needed to buffer the deleterious implications of globalization and maintain the infrastructures that keep the project going. In this political-cultural climate one would think that the maintenance of popular consent would be increasingly difficult. As states – partly as a result of their own actions (such as signing on to trade agreements and other such arrangements) – now claim to be unable or ill equipped to redress a litany of globalization-related problems, publics in both 'developed' and 'developing' countries could be forgiven for dismissing their variously cast political systems as shams.

According to the Pew Research Center for the People and the Press, which conducted opinion polls among 54,000 people in 44 countries in 2002 and 2003, majorities in *every* country surveyed believed that their 'way of life' needs some form of government protection. Many also claim to dislike the quickening pace of modern life yet, simultaneously, said that they support globalization.[27] These and other indicators of public sentiment demonstrate a growing acquiescence to historical developments – a kind of mixed or confused antipathy to politics rather than exuberant support or defiant resistance. Of course the latter extremes are present: American state officials generally represent the former and al-Qaeda the latter.

As the World Trade Organization (WTO) states in the first paragraph of its charter, its goal is to stimulate 'a large and steadily growing volume of real income and effective demand'.[28] It is this focus on growth and consumption that is the *raison d'etre* of the globalization project while, paradoxically, nation state capabilities concerning capital's own reproductive needs have been marginalized. Prosperity and consumption, we argue, both satisfy capital and generally pacify people. At a surface-level, as the Pew surveys reveal, those who anticipate that globalization will 'deliver the goods' tend to accept it as an inevitability. Beyond this, we believe that the widening and deepening institutionalization of capitalist consumption has an important influence on the normalization of an ahistorical, acritical mindset.

Consumption and hegemonic order

Gramsci recognized that as long as a political economic system delivers what most believe to be fundamental rights and essential goods, resistance movements (and the sustained collective consciousness they need to be successful) generally can be contained. Resistance, expressed in various ways, may well trigger significant reforms. However, reforms that in various times and places threaten status quo interests – such as civil rights, workplace empowerment or, more radically still, challenges to the building blocs of capitalism itself such as private property – are rare. However, the capacity of a political economic system to 'hear' dissent and subsequently change, at least marginally, constitutes more than just a safety valve for ruling class interests; it's also the very hallmark of any hegemonic order. For rule through consent to take place, sporadic resistance must be tolerated and occasional (but limited) reforms need to take place. Otherwise, the system's (and the ruling class's) legitimacy cannot be maintained. Rule through consent, in such circumstances, then will be replaced by the less efficient and relatively tenuous method of rule through coercion.[29]

Consent is not entirely a means of control and deceit. People can – and sometimes do – participate in the crafting of successful reforms. The history of hard-won gains – from the 40-hour workweek to women's suffrage, from human rights legislation to environmental and workplace safety regulations – all involved acts and laws passed through various democratic bodies. But, then again, there are limits to the extent to which large scale and potentially revolutionary challenges can be tolerated. 'Democratic' expressions of dissent, funnelled through sanctioned channels, typically provide status quos with at least some freedom to apply limited coercion in defence of 'public safety', property rights and 'law and order'.

As with the third dimension of power, hegemonic rule involves the capacity of a ruling class (or an elite or, more generally still, the status quo) to contain the subordinate masses through the enculturation of 'common sense' ways of thinking and acting.

To take this a step further, hegemony involves a *process* through which both rulers and ruled get something tangible, both material and psychological, out of their capacity to participate. Hegemonic (consensual) rule thus can only take place when the dominated take part; *when they, in effect, become co-authors of their own oppression.* But, as in the first dimension of power, this does not necessarily mean that the ruled want to be ruled. Nor, as in the second dimension, does it necessarily imply that the oppressed are without the means of organizing and expressing their dissent. Instead, having the means to resist in terms of rights, periodic elections, a 'free' press and other such nodes of resistance constitute structural conditions that can accommodate the third dimension of power.

Capitalist liberal democracies are generally hegemonic due, in part, to their legitimacy in the minds of the majority. Their rights, their legally defined freedoms, their capacity to accommodate dissent and, in some cases, substantive change, all are important. As for the role of the third face of power specifically, the actual stability of such systems entails the *absence* of large-scale and sustained anti-status quo movements. In sum, a hegemonic order is in place when genuinely counter-hegemonic movements are more than just absent; such orders are in effect when these are largely *unimaginable.*

Capitalist consumption has become an important medium in the process of winning and maintaining this consent. In relatively wealthy political economies, commodities and the act of consuming (i.e. buying and using goods and services) tangibly remind us why we conform, why we work to earn more money, and why we generally respect private property. As addressed in Chapter 3, in both the West and now in 'developing' countries, an important step in this development has been the successful compelling or enticing of labour away from the workplace and towards the marketplace as their primary loci of meaning, identity and even political action. A core element in this ongoing history is, to repeat, the visceral experience of consumption. But more than this – and a point that cannot be overstated – capitalist consumption itself constitutes a means through which individuals *themselves* exercise power – at least power framed in the context of their own consumerist choices.

Buying things tangibly reminds the encultured worker/consumer of two things: *first*, that the system, as it is, can furnish us with 'stuff' – comforts, sensations, sedations. And *second*, through our pocketbooks, we possess the potential to improve our material circumstances and, in some cases (such as the contemporary preference for 'green products'), consumer choices can generate substantive change.

More abstractly, contemporary marketing is replete with messages equating personal betterment, private liberty and even freedom itself with consumer choice. The reasons why modern and neo-modern cultures buy into this – why people in the relatively 'developed' world abstractly accept the association of consumer autonomy with real political power – involve a complex of historical, social and psychological factors addressed below. At this stage of our book, it is enough to point out that capitalist consumption generally has institutionalized an inherently contradictory understanding of 'freedom'. As Barber stresses, the freedom of the private consumer 'seals off the real public consequences of private choice'.[30] Freedom to buy and drive an automobile, for example, inadvertently imprisons the owner in a world that is dependent on dwindling energy reserves and one that is largely indifferent to the long-term and collective consequences of environmental collapse. He further explains that

> The consumer ... is radically individuated rather than socially embedded, and less rather than more free ... She is permitted to choose from a menu of options ... but not to alter or improve the menu or the world. In this, the dynamics of consumption actually render the individual more rather than less vulnerable to control, much in the way that the infant, for all its sense of power, is actually powerless in a world from which it cannot distinguish itself.[31]

Having recognized this, consumer boycotts have, at times, affected progressive change. In the 1950s, the civil rights movement called on Americans stop shopping at Woolworth's in response to its policy of not serving blacks at its lunch counters. Later, non-union farms were boycotted in line with Cesar Chavez's exposure of how California's grape industry treated its immigrant workers. Internationally, consumer pressures on corporations and governments to isolate South Africa certainly facilitated the end of that country's apartheid. More recently, 'good' corporate behaviour is being supported by consumers and investors. So-called socially responsible investment firms provide at least indirect incentives for companies such as Costco, Ben & Jerry's and even Pepsi to be 'environmentally-friendly' or provide workers with 'liveable' wages.[32] The fact that such developments generally perpetuate broader systemic injustices and 'externalities' (such as global warming) is secondary to the fact that consumers can and do experience some amount of discernable power. The hegemonic implications of this latter point should not be forgotten.

Through consumption, the capitalist system rewards compliance and, potentially, empowers its participants. In such circumstances, when capitalist consumption provides most of us with so many seemingly and actually beneficial things, why would anyone want to sacrifice or risk what they have (*or* one day might have) to overthrow it? Institutions such as capitalist consumption thus facilitate a *pragmatic* form of quiescence – one based on conviction and consensual relations. For those with the means – or at least the prospective means – to improve their material conditions, capitalist production relations, institutionalized through the wage labour contract, potentially provide the resources needed in the idealized world of commodity consumption. In fact, anyone with enough cash or credit can consume almost anything they want. The enormous productivity of capitalism and the freedom to buy and possess things for those with the resources to participate are very real. Also real, at least for some, is the freedom to make money and thus take part in society as consumers. Because of these experienced or witnessed realities, consumption, as an institution, legitimizes what may be an otherwise insecure or unjust existence. It is for this reason (among others) that historical periods characterized by sharp declines in consumption, or in times when the material conditions of life shatter even the prospect of consuming, hegemonic orders *then* may come under assault, as in Western Europe in light of the 1930s Great Depression.

* * *

The US military's occupation of Iraq has not triggered the kind of mass and sustained protest activities experienced 40 years ago in response to the Vietnam War. Unlike so-called low intensity conflicts that garner only sporadic news coverage – such as America's ten-year effort to overthrow the Sandinista regime in Nicaragua or its 15-year counter-insurgency war in El Salvador – the Iraq disaster has been covered extensively (although less than truthfully[33]), culminating in the defeat of the Republican dominated Congress in 2006. Yet, as of 2008, the war continues and the demonstrations, sit-ins and street riots that compelled the Nixon administration to withdraw from Vietnam have been relatively non-existent. A question we might ask is *why*? What, over the past four decades, has changed in American political culture?

Generally, in light of the third dimension of power and the mediating role of capitalist consumption (along with other media shaping conceptual systems), the common sense of most contemporary Americans has changed. After 9/11 and in the context of globalization's apparent inevitability, there seems to be no retreat from foreign entanglements, including wars. Capitalist consumption, alongside free-trade agreements and the Internet – making inexpensive goods and services available to most in relatively 'developed' parts of the world – not only renders the globalization project 'natural', for many it also appears to be desirable. More importantly, consumption mediates the reification of individualism and the myth of the sovereign consumer, and both are experienced through everyday spending. This, in turn, deepens Americans' (and others') short-term, 'me-first' inclinations. Sustained and collective responses to international crises thus have become more difficult.

The point we want to underline here is that consumption now stands as a pervasive, entrenched institution whose unintended political consequences have included the fragmentation and displacement of dissent. Furthermore, in light of the globalization project, consumption's mediating influence arguably has made it easier to mobilize consent. Let us extend this argument through the use of three analogies – consumption as a carrot, a stick and a treadmill.

Carrots, sticks, treadmills and common sense

As the *Oxford Dictionary* reminds us, the carrot is a vegetable commonly used as an incentive, a means of persuasion, particularly as a stimulant to a typically stubborn beast of burden – the donkey. In tracing aspects of the history of consumption, and as we assess various forms of resistance to globalization, this analogy underlines what generally has been forgotten: the development of both the compliant workforce and the consumers needed to keep capitalism going almost always involves resistance; a resistance that entails everything from the persistence of cultural norms (such as frugal spending habits) to organized expressions of anti-consumerism (as represented today by a range of agents, from 'culture jammers' to al-Qaeda). As in the past, dampening and containing this resistance has involved the carrot of consumption – consumption as a tangible reward for conformity and the belief that 'the good life' of consumption *really is the good life*.

Of course such carrots are not the only tools impelling people to buy into consumerist lifestyles. All societies employ sanctions against non-conformists and the metaphorical 'stick' is close at hand. Again according to *Oxford*, a stick is the 'shoot of tree cut to convenient length for use ... as a bludgeon' or a 'cane used in punishing'. Alongside the globalization of capitalist production and the wealth it generates, a significant number of people are being left behind. For those hundreds of millions now having little prospect of participating in consumption (beyond consuming what is needed merely to survive), their role in the global market system involves the task of producing goods for others. For the Bangladeshi picking through garbage in search of sellable scrap, for the sweatshop worker toiling in a factory on the outskirts of Nairobi, for the 'wetback' maid cleaning condos in Houston, the carrot of consumption is an incentive dangled in front of someone else. It is in light of such disparities that consumption is a kind of stick – a weapon used to compel a sea of humanity to organize their survival around the needs, desires and profits *of others*. For these, the donkeys of global capitalism, there is no consumerist Utopia on the horizon – only the sting of the whip, represented by the daily threat of not having enough to live on.

As for those living in relatively wealthy parts of the world, beyond tangible threats such as poverty, homelessness and even incarceration if they dare not conform, social-psychological punishments face those who refuse to take part. As social relations become evermore mediated and abstract, traditional communities, identities and meanings have, for the most part, been replaced by commodified associations (see Chapter 3). In this transformation – stimulated most forcefully by advertisers and marketers – there is little imaginable alternative but to conform within the parameters of consumerist identities or acquisition-focused meanings.

A final analogy can be drawn from the notorious device called the treadmill (see Illustration 2.3). Dating from the late eighteenth-century England, the treadmill was used to instil compliance and channel the labour of that country's burgeoning prison population. Stationary and unable to escape, the incarcerated typically 'climbed' the equivalent of 12,000 stairs a day. As one report filed in the early part of the nineteenth century put it, through its employment 'the prisoners are subject and accustomed to a fixed and

Source: The National Archives, UK.

Illustration 2.3   Treadmill at Pentonville Prison, North London, 1895

certain degree of labour and restraint, *by which they become more subdued and tractable'*.[34]

More than just a means of exhausting and disciplining – sapping energies that otherwise might be applied to rebellion – treadmills used human beings (again, as with donkeys) to power pumps and mills. Just as contemporary consumption is both an incentive and a means to discipline the rebellious, the prison treadmill was simultaneously a fuel and a stick. Oscar Wilde, while in prison in 1895, was subjected to work on one and wrote about it in his *Ballad of Reading Gaol:*

> We banged the tins, and bawled the hymns
> And sweated on the mill,
> But in the heart of every man
> Terror was lying still.

* * *

While hegemonic order implies consent, to repeat, this is consent backed by coercion. People are free to acquire the goods and services they want but, to exercise this freedom, one rule is universal: they *must* have money. As such, most must work for a wage. If someone is unable or unwilling to play by these rules, they are no longer free to take part.

C. Wright Mills put the relationship between money and freedom as such: 'Whatever else it may mean, freedom means that you have the power to do what you want to do, when you want to do it, and how you want to do it. And in ... [capitalist] society the power to do what you want, when you want, how you want, requires money. Money provides power and power provides freedom.'[35]

The widespread refusal or inability to participate in this pecuniary world would constitute the death knell of capitalism. Without rule abiding, paying consumers and, by extension, without private property itself, there would be little reason to sell one's labour for a wage. Indeed, a broad range of institutionalized nodes of participation and, thus, media perpetuating system operability and legitimacy – from property rights to voting to free speech – entail rules, norms and codes of conduct. The citizens, workers and consumers of liberal democracies are free but only if they exercise these prescribed freedoms in the context of specifically structured conditions. Those straying outside the status quo invite social ostracism, state-imposed fines, private litigation and perhaps even jail time. The stick must be close at hand.

As the carrot, stick and treadmill analogies illustrate, the freedom to consume is not all that 'free' after all. Like all institutionalized norms, capitalist consumption mediates how we think and act. Consumption frames and contains as much as it liberates.

It is worth recalling that Gramsci's concept of hegemony was based on Machiavelli's *The Prince* and it draws upon the distinction between force and fraud in the operations of what Machiavelli believed to be the ideal state. The consensual component of hegemony, for Gramsci, thus can be interpreted as a sophisticated kind of fraud. The freedoms and participatory opportunities that characterize liberal democracies are indeed 'real' but, then again, they are not.[36] Through institutions such as consumption, consent is simultaneously voluntary and engineered; it is engineered by logistically 'delivering the goods' *and* through the perpetuation of common sense ways of thinking that situate acquisition and consumption as primary goals of life. As a once popular bumper sticker put it, *The One Who Dies with the Most Toys Wins.*

By 'common sense', we are not referring to some kind of objective compass upon which rational decisions are made. Instead, the common sense of any particular place and time is largely constructed; it is inter-subjective, enabling people to 'understand' what they experience despite pervasive inconsistencies. For example, 'money can't buy you happiness' is common sense, but so too is the assumption (continuously propagated by advertisers and marketers) that commodities solve problems. Feeling lonely? A new car will attract a potential mate; Seeking career advancement? A new suit should do the trick; Looking for friends? A brand of beer will do wonders for your social life.

Because of its axiomatic and seemingly universal characteristics, common sense is difficult to either promulgate or disrupt. All-encompassing references to the rights of the individual, the vagaries of Big Government, or the happiness that comes from consumption do not have to be explained – they're just 'the way it is'.

Common sense resonates with people because it helps us make sense of our lives. Having said this, this same common sense, through its daily elaboration, may also serve to internalize an individual's subordination. While 'consumption is the means to happiness' maintains some workers' compliance (and, more generally, keeps capitalism ticking), knowing that 'money can't buy you happiness' simultaneously dampens anger in the face of material inequalities.

As Michael Mann demonstrates in his essay, 'The Working Class', working class consciousness (in Britain, at least) is characterized by inconsistencies, cynicism and a generally fatalistic outlook on life.[37] In line with the third face of power, rather than the absence of opposition to the status quo, common sense ways of thinking more accurately reflect and perpetuate disparate values, the marginalization of ideals and, related to these, *a general absence of feasible alternatives*. For most, realistic and imaginable options to the status quo are not worth pursuing (let alone pondering) because – to borrow Margaret Thatcher's infamous reasoning – 'there is no alternative'.

But where does common sense come from? The short answer is that it comes from all of us and, more specifically, from the institutions we use to structure and mediate relations with one another. Because institutions generally transcend personal biographies, they are seemingly irrefutable. As such, the power of an institution in daily life and its subsequent influence on common sense directly involve its *literally unquestionable* status. As long as it operates under the 'radar screen' of critical inquiry, the institution's role and influence generally continues unabated.

Conceptual systems

Students of the first and second dimensions of power tend to simplify the relationship of information and experience to knowledge, *the relationship of what is communicated with what is known*. At its extreme, their position is a throwback to the classical empiricists who argued that people understand their lives and worlds as a result of what they accumulate through their senses.

For Bacon, Locke and others, human beings acquire knowledge through innate information-absorbing capabilities. However, there are significant problems with this position; for one, if it is true, people would have a difficult time comprehending information in the *absence* of a relevant education or experience. Indeed, the problem facing empiricists in conceptualizing the relationship between information and knowledge can be summed up in the difficulties they have answering the following question: if what is known is dependent on what information already has been absorbed, how can new information (that is, a new experience) be interpreted 'reasonably'?[38]

To understand how we make sense of information without having some previous exposure to it – while also rejecting the tautology that we know what we know because, in essence, we already know it – it has been proposed that people *learn* to interpret information in particular ways. Rather than understanding the mind to be some kind of information-absorbing sponge, instead, *people learn how to select and process information and experience into knowledge*.

The information we receive and the experiences we live – whether it is a lesson taught by a grandparent, a commercial heard on the radio, a skill learned at a job or the sensation of buying one's first home – do not always become an ingrained part of our 'reality'. Indeed, the history of capitalist consumption is rife with examples that illustrate this point. In both the West and in 'developing' nations, marketers and advertisers frequently make appeals that are misinterpreted or fall on deaf ears precisely because people do not have the capacity to make sense of the message, at least not in the way it was intended. When aiming to sell new things (or, more ambitiously, lifestyles) to people, the ad or marketing campaign, can never stray too far from where the audience already lives, metaphorically speaking. It is in this sense that the institution of consumption both reflects and modifies – it *mediates* – the ways in which cultures and sub-cultures think and act.[39]

To see how the institutionalization of capitalist consumption works – and sometimes doesn't work – our first step must be to recognize that all human beings are social animals who are socialized through a range of media (broadly defined) – specifically, technologies (including techniques), organizations and institutions. Through this mediated socialization, we all develop what can be called *conceptual systems*. These are what all human beings use to process information and experience into what we know to be 'reality'.

At any particular moment, our senses are deluged with information and, from the moment of birth, we are involved in the task of learning how to manage and make sense of it all. What is relevant and new must be sorted out from what is seemingly irrelevant and routine. In this way, human beings learn to cope with an incalculable number of sights, sounds, odours, tastes and textures. The alternative to this socialization and the structuring of conceptual systems would be madness.[40]

To communicate anything, from a simple desire to a complex message, the people involved must share similar references and associations or, at the very least, some pre-existing familiarity with what is being conveyed. If, however, people do not share a common language, mutual cultural references, and so forth, information may be communicated but little (if any) will be understood. As we are socialized – a process that is especially affecting in the first years of life – our conceptual systems become more entrenched. As we learn to mediate information and experience in terms of our families, cultures and political economies, we also learn to sort out what information is 'good' and what information is 'bad', what behaviours are 'rational' and 'irrational', what thinking is 'realistic' and 'unrealistic'. Information and experience, therefore, are funnelled and filtered into what we know using learned, intersubjective, power-laden conceptual systems.

As James Carey explains, 'Knowledge is not simply information. Knowledge is not given in experience as data. There is no such thing as information about the world devoid of conceptual systems that create and define the world in the act of discovering it.'[41]

Different relationships have different qualitative implications – implications that reflect and affect structured conceptual systems. In evaluating how different experiences and interactions are interpreted and, in turn, shape conceptual systems, a distinction should be made between those involving communications that are *relatively direct* and those that are *relatively indirect*. At the core of this difference lies the relative (but not absolute) importance of face-to-face relationships in the formation and shaping of conceptual systems. The essential roles played by what sociologists call our 'significant others' during infancy forever impress upon us the need for some amount of intimacy in our more meaningful relationships. This usually involves some time in the physical proximity of another and this intimacy can be sustained, at least temporarily, even if the other person moves far away. The accumulation, over time, of relatively direct relationships and experiences constitutes the bases of our ever-mediating conceptual systems and, gradually, our identities and sense of meaning.[42]

This is not to say that thousands of hours of watching television, reading books and surfing the Internet do not have varied and sometimes significant effects on conceptual systems (as most students of cultural imperialism, for example, would assert). Nor is it to say that those optimists who believe that a progressive global civil society will be upon us one day are entirely naïve (perhaps they are not, but this discussion will have to wait until Chapter 4). Instead, we are arguing that our relatively more mediated relationships are limited in their potential to directly shape conceptual systems and thus interpretations of what is feasible, realistic and imaginable.

Conceptual systems and the impact of capitalist consumption on them (and *vice versa*) will be addressed through mostly empirical examples in subsequent chapters. Our point in raising them here is to underline the importance of conceptual systems in the context of both common sense and the hegemonic process. Hegemonic rule involves the socialization of people through the institutions of everyday life. From birth, people are influenced most significantly by their primary caretakers, and then by their most intimate relationships. Parents, friends, teachers, lovers, employers and many others, all shape the conceptual systems we develop and apply to make sense of things, forge identities and find meaning in our lives. But, to repeat, *all of this takes place and involves the mediation of institutions that are, for the most part, seemingly timeless, universal and apolitical.* Our parent's religion, our teacher's expectations, the ways in which our acquaintances express care and anger, all are influenced by and are negotiated through predominant institutions including, of course, consumption.

Through capitalist consumption, parents routinely demonstrate their love through purchased gifts, employers express their satisfaction through cash, spouses convey affection by spending money on one another. Through commodities and the price system, our identities and the meaning of life (and even love) are directly associated with what can be bought and sold. Goods and services are sought, purchased and exchanged to communicate intimate and important messages, not only to others but to one's self also. Just as the professor buys and wears a particular jacket to tell himself and others that he is 'a professor', the food he eats, the car he drives and the way he furnishes his home typically involve much more than just utilitarian needs – they mediate his identity and tangibly represent what is meaningful in his life.

Over time, our conceptual systems tend to ossify. Having internalized consumerist identities and meanings, the shared institutions used in this process (including family, courtship, the price system and many others) not only live, they live on. *It is through this historical and biographical process that capitalist consumption has been structured into the third dimension of power – directly influencing how we process information and experience into what is realistic, feasible and even imaginable.*

Hegemonic framing

Power in the international political economy involves more than just what is readily observable. Particularly where disparity and injustice are demonstrable, we would do well to investigate why people don't act and, when they do, why these rebellions – at least in the context of contemporary globalization – are rarely collaborative and sustained. As outlined above, consumption, as one of many institutions mediating the third dimension of power, is more than just a neglected nodal point of the hegemonic process, its unique characteristics – specifically its role in prospectively normalizing *change itself* – makes it extraordinarily important. Through its conceptualization and practice, consumption facilitates an awkward, if not tenuous, stability. Capitalist consumption, in effect, provides people with a kind of cultural-psychological ballast. It grounds, however temporarily, our lives through a purposeful pursuit and material realization of meaningful things and activities.

If, as Gramsci recognized, rule through consent involves liberal democratic institutions, what hope is there for a generally non-coercive international order where, domestically and internationally, these institutions are not in place? How might the peasant in Kenya or the worker in Jamaica consent to a decision made through the WTO if he had little or no perceivable influence in that organization's ruling? Without the means to participate and in light of associated disparities, the legitimacy of the globalization project is strained and sometimes disabled. Coercive measures then come to the fore; prospectively, globalization and the vested interests behind it are de-legitimized.

Consumption, however, provides the largely undemocratic globalization project with a semblance of needed consent. As discussed earlier, capitalist consumption prescribes upon the individual the right to buy goods and services and the freedom to own commodities. Consumption, in this regard, is (formally speaking) a participatory institution. Just about anyone with money can take part and, in so doing, exercise control over at least some aspects of their lives (indeed, as C. Wright Mills would argue, in capitalist society, more money buys more freedom). Capitalist consumption, despite the restrictive rules and norms it entails, conceivably gives people in undemocratic systems – compelled to accept the decisions of foreign executives and international bureaucrats – a modicum of power. Thus, capitalist consumption gives people tangible reasons to acquiesce – enthusiastically or fatalistically – rather than to resist.

But having recognized the mediating and potentially consent-building role of consumption, tensions and outright contradictions persist. While the dynamism of capitalism compels ongoing reforms to the institution, there are limits to how fast and to what extent consumption ideals and practices can be modified in a particular locale. The reasons for these disjunctures can be broadly labelled as 'cultural' in that people, through a complex of established conceptual systems and mediating institutions, may resist change. Such bottlenecks also can be classified as 'economic', in that people may not have the material means to participate in capitalist consumption. Nevertheless, through its institutionalization of change and participatory proclivities (especially among those minimally affected by cultural and economic barriers), consumption may well be the mediator *par excellence* enabling globalization.[43]

Once in place, however, capitalist consumption and other institutions may themselves constitute the bases of problems. It is, after all, the relative autonomy of those participating that facilitates rule through consent, and such 'voluntary' methods of rule, particularly in lieu of cultural or economic problems, can be fragile. Most are not choosing to play by the rules of capitalism and pursue consumer lifestyles because they have been formally ordered to; they consent to take part because they are getting something out of it (material comforts, identities and meanings) and because they are being socialized to see few (if any) realistic alternatives. Here we see the antipathy many feel towards globalization being contained through the *individualistic* power that the institution implies. *Divide et impera*, indeed.

* * *

In 'The Working Class', Mann arrived at some notable conclusions. Mann's analysis of British workers found that their anti-status quo perspectives were shaped less by philosophical principles than populist concepts and everyday experiences. He also found working class people to be much less interested in having consistent value systems than middle-class individuals.[44] While different surveys in different countries consistently portray strong normative commitments to the status quo among the upper and middle classes, others typically demonstrate cynicism and resignation. The alienated masses in relatively wealthy and democratic countries, particularly in the context of a post-Fordist decline of class consciousness, have tended to demonstrate their frustrations by turning inwards. As Mann explains, inaction in the face of inequality is not the result of contentment, nor is it entirely the outcome of structural exclusion: it is also the result of a life and mindset in which ideals are secondary to one's physical-psychological survival.[45] If coping with such realities involves trivial acts of vandalism (such as an assembly line worker throwing a marble into a car door), substance abuse (whether it is alcohol, prescribed medications or illegal drugs) or taking on more and more ultimately self-destructive debt, so be it. From a ruling class perspective, such acts not only are preferable to some kind of organized class-based resistance, the more divided and self-centred people are the less threatening they become. Quite possibly, such individualistic expressions also reflect a working class open to the appeals of marketers and advertisers reflecting and deepening a search for meaning and identity through the marketplace.

In this chapter, we have argued that a third face of power is at work, influencing both everyday life and the globalization project. Herein we have addressed consumption as a power-laden institution. Through daily interactions and discourse, this institution (along with others) not only mediates the socialization of most in 'developed' countries, it is now mediating the cultural transformation of many in 'developing' parts of the world also.

Depending on the place and time, different institutions are structured and used in different ways to shape parameters of acceptable behaviour and thought. Moreover, the common sense that people employ to deal with life's mysteries and injustices is contingent on these historically constructed institutions. This is not to say that the more general mode of production (for example, hunter–gather society, feudalism or capitalism) is not a profoundly influential context shaping how people structure these predominant institutions. Nor is to say that different people in different political economies do not act and think in different ways. Different people are influenced, particularly through their respective socialization experiences, by disparate institutional media.[46]

Nevertheless, capitalist consumption has become a dominant institution shaping the thoughts and activities of both the globalization project's status quo and many of its detractors. In fact, consumption does more than just mediate: *it now frames and contains hegemonic struggle itself.* Among the world's relatively wealthy, consumption directly influences the conceptual systems used in the process of constructing reality. Religious holidays, especially Christmas, have become consumerist orgies; schools now emphasize individual achievement with the end-goal of acquiring the means to accumulate commodities; advertiser-financed mass media celebrate consumerist lifestyles, especially through their representations of the rich and famous; states, mainstream economic theorists and international organizations define economic progress in terms of greater efficiencies, facilitating more production and consumption; stock markets rise and fall based on the latest consumer confidence surveys; even parents equate love with commodities by rewarding children with purchased goods and services.

In *Trainspotting*, a film about Glaswegian working class heroin addicts, the opening scene's voiceover (reprinted at the beginning this chapter) facetiously exhorts the audience to choose 'life'. Never mind that this life now is defined by the acquisition and consumption of commodities (from dental insurance to starter homes, from leisurewear to junk food); this 'choice' constitutes *the* common sense framework of any normal person's 'future'. While *Trainspotting* refers to arguably the most time-wasting of hobbies – standing by railway tracks recording car numbers in the hope of logging as many trains as possible – it's also a metaphor for the life-wasting scourge of heroin addiction (the narrative focus of the film). However, the movie (and the novel it is based upon, by Irvine Welsh) also stands as a critique of consumer culture. Through the hegemonic framing of 'choice' itself, lifetimes also are wasted aboard the now ubiquitous consumer treadmill.

Hegemonic consent for the globalization project can't emerge through underdeveloped or non-existent democratic and related participatory activities. These, after all, take too long to construct and sometimes constitute too great a risk as elections might put anti-status quo governments into office (as demonstrated by the Palestinian election of *Hamas* in 2006). The participatory and 'empowering' characteristics of capitalist consumption instead will need to play a more central role. Yet, having said this, as explained above, consumption also involves a number of economic and cultural tensions. Indeed, as we will see in later chapters, capitalist consumption's institutionalization itself may entail some potentially explosive contradictions.

3
The Birth of Capitalist Consumption

> Today we dare not wait until men in their own good time get around to wanting the things; do we permit this, the machine flies to pieces. The wind blew and so the windmill went around. Under the new order, the windmill goes around and so the wind must blow. It is becoming a matter of general remark that the economic emphasis is changing; it is shifting from how to make things to how to dispose of things that are made so that the machine can be kept in constant operation. The problem before us today is not how to produce the goods, but how to produce the customers.
>
> —Samuel Strauss[1]

In this chapter, we present a history of the institutionalization of capitalist consumption in the West. Our goal here is to use history as a resource – a resource containing demonstrable patterns and tendencies that can be used to illuminate contemporary developments around the world. Rather than a comprehensive overview, the task at hand is to outline how capitalist consumption emerged and, in so doing, identify the dynamics behind contemporary trajectories.

Implicit in what follows is a particular approach to historical development. Beyond identifying the influential actors who promoted capitalist consumption, or the systemic pressures impelling its institutional development, we utilise what can be described as a 'historicist' methodology. In keeping with the three-dimensional view of power, this approach compels us to focus on more than just readily observable actions and discernable pressures; it also assesses the structuring of consciousness or, to use the term introduced previously, conceptual systems.

Historicism concentrates on the connections between structured relationships and the ways in which people think (and, thus, act). Furthermore, in the words of R. G. Collingwood,

> [t]he historian [or historicist social scientist] ... makes a distinction between what may be called the outside and the inside of an event. By the outside of the event I mean everything belonging to it which can be described in terms of bodies and their movements ... By the inside of the event, I mean that in which it can only be described in terms of thought ... The historian is never concerned with either of these to the exclusion of the other. He is investigating not mere events (where by a mere event I mean one which only has an outside and no inside) but actions, and an action is the unity of the outside and the inside of an event ... *[H]is main task is to think himself into this action, to discern the thought of its agent.*[2]

It is with this in mind that we sketch our history, taking care to identify consumption's institutionalization in the thoughts and activities of people both past and present. Our focus here is pre-nineteenth-century England and developments based in the United States over the past two hundred years.[3] Of particular interest in what follows is a general pattern associated with the ascendancy of capitalism and related developments: as societies become more complex – characterized, among other things, by an elaborated division of labour and the growing commodification of relations – identities and meaningful activities tend to become more abstract; that is, they become increasingly mediated by an array of affecting technologies, organizations and institutions. In such circumstances, the potential for capitalist consumption to become institutionalized – and thus directly integrated into conceptual systems – increases, leading to some significant implications in the realm of Lukes's third dimension of power.

At the end of this chapter, we summarize our findings in terms of two fundamental indices of human existence and, indeed, power itself – space and time. With references to contemporary developments related to the globalization project (which we pursue in Chapter 4), herein we address the following question: *what does the past tell us about the present and future of consumption and its mediating role in the international political economy?*

From feudalism to capitalism: Existential implications

The seeds from which the institution of capitalist consumption emerged first were planted in the soils of early capitalism. The capitalist modes of production and consumption, born centuries ago, constituted a revolutionary break from all pre-existing ways of organizing human relationships. Indeed, the birth of the modern world order – with its core institutions such as private property, the wage labour contract, state sovereignty among others – has wrought such profound changes to how humanity lives *and thinks* that even a cursory overview reveals significant insights.

In pre-capitalist Europe, most people had access to their own means of subsistence. Power relations, and disparities generally, involved socially entrenched customs and obligations. For the vast majority, labour activities could be classified as 'unfree'. As serfs (or previously and elsewhere, slaves or members of a particular caste), people were born into explicitly exploitative circumstances from which they had little or no means of escape. More than five hundred years ago, in England, things began to change. At this time and place, relationships became increasingly commodified, beginning with the compulsion among people to sell their labour as a commodity in order to acquire the monies needed to buy other commodities.

Prior to this development, uniquely in England dating from 1066, land was formally controlled by the monarch who parcelled it out to approximately fifteen hundred feudal lords. They, in turn, subinfeuded these holdings to about eight thousand sublords. Through tradition and customary law (law set by precedent or, more usually, 'the way things have always been' according to living memory), the bottom of the social hierarchy – serfs – had access to arable lands. The power dynamic between lord and serf entailed efforts by the former to extract surpluses from the latter in a manner that enabled serfs to reproduce themselves and, in so doing, reproduce the political economic order. While the lord–serf relationship was contradictory (in that their fates were fundamentally intertwined yet, also, at odds), the structural conditions and dominant media influencing feudal relations delimited the capacity to imagine other ways of organizing society, let alone pursue substantive change.

When compared to our contemporary political economy, this pre-capitalist order was both relatively stable and *explicitly* unjust, not to mention economically and culturally (again, from today's perspective) stagnant. In a system in which a dynamic compelling the growth of either production or consumption did not exist, endogenous forces propelling radical reform were absent.

So what changed? What could have upended this way of life, setting forth a train of developments leading to the dynamic world of capitalist production and consumption? The initial push came, quite literally, from death. In just two years, following the bubonic plague's infestation of England, more than half the domestic population died. Economically, lords and sublords suddenly had a much smaller pool of labour to draw upon while serfs, as a result of this shortage, became more mobile, some migrating to relatively attractive manors and even drawing, for the first time, wages for their work. By the mid-fourteenth century, in England, the explicit inequalities characterizing serfdom largely were eclipsed.[4]

The capacity of lords to exploit the serf-cum-peasant had been curtailed, *compelling* the former to re-think and re-organize traditional political economic relations. While demographic crises triggered similar struggles throughout most of Europe, the English experience uniquely laid the foundations for capitalism's eventual ascent. Simply put, lords and serfs in different societies had varying organizational and, indeed, psychological capabilities which directly influenced outcomes – permanently dissolving the power structures holding feudalism in place *or* (in much of Europe) re-casting these structures through mostly coercive mechanisms. In noting such radically diverging histories, Robert Brenner explains that the 'crisis was accompanied by an intensification of class conflict inherent in the existing structure, but with different outcomes in different places ... [T]he contending agrarian classes and their relative levels of internal solidarity, their self-consciousness and organisation, and their general political resources – especially their relationships to the non-agricultural classes ... and to the state' – generally set the structural parameters of what followed.[5]

The key difference between English serfs and others, particularly their colleagues in other parts of Europe, was the size and relative complexity of local towns. Through long-standing inter-dependencies forged in village political economies, the solidarity of the English serf/peasant was well established at the time of the plague. In response to efforts by lords to re-establish past 'unfreedoms', this sense of community became more explicitly political. Elsewhere, especially in Eastern Europe, the rural political economy was more individualistic, collaborative practices were limited and there existed little tradition of collective struggle against the lords for access to the commons.[6] However, throughout most of Western Europe, particularly in England, the culture of serfs and peasants was inundated with village-based institutions that constituted nodal points of a conscious resistance. Serfs and peasants who, more often than not, lived in ancestral villages with their extended families, held strong community-based class loyalties. 'It was on this basis', writes Brenner, that peasants 'were able to limit ... the claims of the aristocracy and, ultimately, ... dissolve serfdom'.[7]

Increasingly, from this point on, the lord's relationship to his agrarian workers became, through various media – the law in particular – a site of conflict rather than stability. An open effort to regain lost political power and economic surpluses ensued, as did the struggle among peasants to retain both age-old rights and newfound privileges.

Previously, conflicts over land – particularly its use and who had access to it – centred on the question of *possession* rather than ownership. Because almost all lands were used in accordance with disparate and sometimes conflicting local customs, disputes concerning the right to live somewhere or work a piece of land often involved violent conflict. In the case of freeholders,[8] the monarch's representative was the ultimate adjudicator of 'common law'. In England, references to land 'owners' appeared in legal texts for the first time in 1491 and, over the course of the next century, possession was largely replaced by state-enforced references to land as private property. As D. J. Seipp writes, 'old debates were phrased in new ways. Conflicts were no longer between holders of rights of common and "the lord of the manor" or "he who has the freehold". Now the protagonists were the commoner and the "owner of the soil" or "owner of the land"'.[9]

While, by the end of the sixteenth century, custom still constituted *the* law, it was no longer taken for granted; customary practices and relationships – sometimes constituting bottlenecks for lords seeking higher rents or new sources of revenue – had to be proven by claimants (usually peasants). Moreover, an act of Parliament could override them. As a distant authority (the monarch) progressively transcended living memory and experienced precedent, the legal principles that mediated daily life, and more generally the power relations that governed the English political economy, became even more abstract. Importantly for the history of capitalist relations and capitalist consumption, communal interests based on corporate needs and shared experiences increasingly were pushed aside in favour of individual property rights and previously unimagined insecurities.[10]

Facilitating and facilitated by this dramatic re-organization was the renting out of large tracts of land to 'leaseholders'. Through the employment of workers hired for a wage, leaseholders farmed to make a profit. The rents charged (by 'freeholders' who, in turn, paid lords with services, produce or money) were based on what the market could bare – that is, the highest fees possible – rather than customary rates. According to Ellen Wood, this established a dynamic in which leaseholders were compelled to increase efficiencies – to get more for less out of agrarian workers. Because their tenure on the land was insecure (based, as it was, on their ability to pay in the context of a competitive marketplace), 'uncompetitive production could mean outright loss of land'.[11] Now that *access to* land (the means of survival) was no longer a customary right (as it now lay in the hands of 'private' interests), the logic of capitalism and its compulsion to grow was established in daily relations.

Some lords asserted property rights directly. By renting out lands, lords nullified customary access, compelling some peasants to work for a wage. More generally, this further institutionalized capitalist norms and relations – norms and relations propelled forward by two developments: the enclosure movement and the restructuring of market exchange activities.[12]

The explicit power of the feudal lord over his serf, pushed back in the aftermath of the plague and subsequent anti-poll tax revolts, thus was re-established by the end of the fifteenth century in the guise of new political economic structures and identities mediated through institutions. For example, enclosure – the conversion of arable common lands into fenced pastures for sheep farming – spanned more than two centuries. Despite, or perhaps because of, its direct assault on customary rights and the concomitant ascent of private property, conflicts over how rights were conceptualized and put into effect continued well into the eighteenth century.

According to C. E. Searle, it was only then, at the twilight of the struggle, that 'a wholesale transformation occurred in the conception of the rights of landownership':

> There was a perceptible change in ideas relating to property from a belief in the 'limited and not always saleable rights in things' to notions of 'unlimited and saleable rights to things'. Landowners were no longer prepared to countenance any constraints over their rights to the complete control of, exclusive benefit from, and total freedom to alienate their property.[13]

By 1630, up to half of all English peasants were compelled to work for a wage.[14] After 1650, farmers actively sought and applied new production methods in order to reduce costs and improve efficiencies, particularly costs and efficiencies concerning labour. Larger, more productive farms gradually drove smaller, less efficient holdings out of business. By the early nineteenth century, in stark contrast with much of the world, England had no more peasants – the country had been fully proletarianized.[15]

This formal and psychological distancing of people from the land (to repeat, their chief means of survival) generated both resistance and, over time, modified conceptual systems. England's peasantry-cum-proletariat were compelled, over the course of generations, to reform their everyday thoughts and activities. The individual and short term came to dominate the collective/corporate long term. Beyond the unpredictability of one's material circumstances, the transition towards capitalist social relations also involved rising existential insecurities. Place of birth, family trade, communal traditions became secondary, if not irrelevant, as people were compelled to sell their labour in exchange for a wage and, over time, emigrate to urban centres in search of contracted work opportunities.

The decline of community, the ascent of the impersonal

Similarly significant changes, with important implications for conceptual systems, took place in the realm of consumption. In the mid-sixteenth century, England had up to 800 marketplaces, each serving up to 600 people (more in urban centres, especially in London). Reflecting long-standing norms, these markets were held to exchange mostly agricultural products. As with feudal relations, generally they were regulated through explicit references to tradition. Sellers in these seemingly timeless markets were almost always the direct producers of the foods or goods being sold (the latter included butchers, bakers and brewers). Indeed, their local character and small size ensured an intimate familiarity among buyers and sellers, with such face-to-face, long-term interactions usually facilitating fairness and trust as social norms (see Illustration 3.1).

Source: Bibliothèque Nationale de France.

Illustration 3.1   A medieval market (n.d.)

The importance of this corporate harmony for the reproduction of social-economic relations was underlined by the presence of officials responsible for collecting tolls, testing bread, and verifying the quality of goods in relation to prices. In addition, market courts, overseen by the local Justice of the Peace, resolved outstanding disputes. These sometimes involved claims that a seller was not charging a 'just' price. This fair or just price was a 'common estimate' and, unlike the competitive capitalist norm of charging what-the-market-will-bare (theoretically the outcome of the so-called law of supply and demand), the primary function of the pre-modern marketplace was to ensure that adequate supplies were available at prices people could afford.[16]

Additional but secondary sites where sellers and buyers met were village shops and seasonal fairs. The latter provided more specialized goods while shops generally were little more than the homes of local craftsmen.

It is important to note that in markets, fairs and shops non-monetary forms of exchange were normal; people knew one another and bartering or exchange through reciprocity was routine.[17] In sum, writes John Lie,

> [e]xchange relations operated in open face-to-face interactions of direct producers and buyers. People could literally see what was happening – they knew who traded what with whom and for how much ... Prices and out-puts were determined ... by social norms and the vagaries of production. The 'freedom' to trade referred to the right to trade inside the marketplace and follow its rules and regulations.[18]

Up until at least the seventeenth century, not only did buyers and sellers know one another, they knew about the goods and services they acquired, including how and when they were made. In this pre-modern era, most worked as members of local, largely self-sufficient communities. People gen-erally laboured when they needed to and mostly in order to exchange their products with others who they knew personally. Thus, at this stage in Western history, consumption constituted a relatively straightforward activity. Through reciprocity, bartering or monetary exchange, people acquired things that were clearly useful, that is goods and services that satisfied mostly utili-tarian needs. As such, and in the context of a society in which almost everyone knew the biographies of what they consumed, the price of some-thing (its 'exchange value') was generally a function of its tangible usefulness (its 'use value').

But like the growing insecurities people experienced as they became waged workers – now 'free' to sell their labour through contracts – changing market relations had social-psychological effects. Along with capitalism's production-based efficiencies came a dramatic rise in the number of com-modities for sale. With this productivity, more timely, impersonal and money-based transactions emerged. Prices set by supply and demand calculations became the norm, replacing the previous conventions of 'just pricing' and 'fair distribution'. These reforms triggered the emergence of a concomitant existential isolation among increasingly competitive market-place participants.

Paradoxically, however, the economic sector that displaced so many English peasants and fuelled the rise of capitalist agriculture – the woollen cloth industry – also limited the geographic scope of developments related to the institution of capitalist consumption, at least initially. The early market for cloth was mostly overseas, primarily in Holland and Germany, and the pri-mary beneficiary of the export's success was the city of London. Its location on the Thames (and the river's accessibility to sea traffic), its geographic location at the hub of ancient (but limited) roads and the absence of crown-imposed import regulations 'meant that international trade was as easy as inland trade over a short distance'.[19] From the mid-sixteenth to the mid-seventeenth century, London's population grew from 120,000 to 375,000, and by 1750 the city was occupied by 650,000 residents, becoming the largest and fastest growing city in the world.[20] This growth in wealth and population, financed overwhelmingly by cloth exports, stimulated more than just agricultural efficiencies; it also generated new (mostly local) markets for other fledgling industries.

The majority of urban consumers – the wage-earning working class – had limited incomes. Nevertheless, they constituted an important but limited market, buying mostly staple goods such as bread, beer, coal and clothing.[21] From around 1700, a broad range of mid-strata jobs and mid-level income earners emerged. This new middle class was represented by an array of occupations, from merchants to lawyers, from entrepreneurial craftsmen to skilled tradesmen. In eighteenth-century London, for the first time, specialist retailers outnumbered producers selling their own wares.[22]

To repeat, overseas trade was the primary stimulant of these London-based developments. Because of this and the dependency of the monarch on wealth generated through international commerce, projects aimed at developing domestic transportation and commercial relations were neglected. It was in this context that an opportunity arose for a new kind of retailer – the travelling merchant. According to Lie, 'The beginning of many industries, including the leading sectors of the industrial revolution, can be traced to simple commodity production for the local market region, which was expanded by [travelling salesman known as chapmen] ... Chapmen provided the connection not only between producers and consumers but also among producers.'[23]

By the eighteenth century, England's domestic commercial infrastructure had been disparately carved out by the regular travels of chapmen who specialized in the sale of cheap commodities to the relatively poor. Beyond establishing domestic markets for cotton and iron goods, these salesmen forged long-standing relationships with customers and provided many with credit. As in the traditional marketplace, recurrent contact led to good will and trust. Here we see the lasting importance of long-term relationships and personal exchange relations amidst (or in light of) the decline of England's traditional economy. Even the prices charged by chapmen remained largely set by communal expectation rather than what-the-market-will-bare calculations. Ironically, the success of these networks of door-to-door salesmen marked the twilight of the old town marketplace and its transparent rules and regulations.[24]

Capitalism and the mediation of relations

Before proceeding with our history and its implications for contemporary consumption, let us pause to underline an important trend, one found not only in the past but also today in the contemporary history of globalization.

Accompanying the rise of capitalism, we see a quantitative growth in the division of labour, the elaboration of increasingly complex methods of generating wealth and, crucially, the proliferation of mediated social relations. The structuring of capitalist relations through laws and regulations backed by the state facilitated the drive to produce more with less, particularly efforts to get more for less out of workers. Today, similar developments involving radically re-structured relationships, muscularly enforced by states, are essential components of the globalization project. As in the past, two mediating institutions accommodate these developments: private property and the wage labour contract. The former enabled (and still enables) nature and human relationships to be re-framed in terms of individual rights (rights that, by definition, exclude others). With private property (or now 'privatisation'), the commons of the past (or the statist enterprises and services of the present) could be exclusively 'owned' and its use converted to ventures focused primarily on the extraction of surpluses leading to privately held profits.

At the dawn of capitalism, this transformation most infamously involved enclosure and sheep farming. Today, in various parts of the world, the extraction of raw materials (such as oil) or the ability to make investments in activities previously unexploitable (involving enterprises engaged in a broad range of commercial pursuits, from selling water to genetic engineering) also constitute the institutional expansion of private property. As for the wage labour contract, hundreds of years ago it provided textile manufacturers, coal mining entrepreneurs and other emerging interests with the labour force needed to practice capitalism and build and maintain the local and then the national political economy's infrastructure. As with similarly affecting institutions, over time, private property and the wage labour contract became shared, power-laden ways of thinking and acting. But rather than a smooth transition from feudal institutions into capitalist (and today, rather than the straightforward and peaceful transformation of traditional economies and public sector responsibilities into neoliberal 'opportunities'), capitalism almost always entails the use of coercive measures. Individuals and communities, facing destitution – in England 500 years ago and in other parts of the world today – were and are *compelled* to sell their labour for a wage, becoming, in effect, both commodity producers *and consumers*.

As the history of English capitalism demonstrates, this radical re-ordering of social relations took place slowly (and painfully) for at least two interrelated reasons. First, institutionalized ways of acting and thinking are generally difficult to change – they are, in fact, typically conservative structures (see Chapter 2). Second, people often resist those changes they *perceive* to be against their interests. More specifically in relation to capitalist consumption, its institutionalization involved two prerequisites. The *first* was the growth of wealth or, in slightly more technical terms, the production and distribution of the surpluses needed to enable people to buy more commodities. The *second* was the presence of a vacuum of identity and meaning – an existential vacuum into which new commodity-based identities and meanings could be successfully promoted, acquired and, eventually, normalized.

As mentioned above, by the end of the seventeenth century, only a minority of the English population possessed the wealth needed to purchase goods and services beyond staples. Indeed, the rapid growth of urban centres, especially London, was critical for an elaboration of capitalist production and consumption, at least in a concentrated area. Here, as with the emerging middle classes in contemporary Mumbai, Mexico City or Manila, capitalist consumption initially developed among a relatively exclusive population. Traditional exchange relations – based on long-standing familiarity and inter-personal interactions involving custom and trust – were eroded and subsequently replaced by anonymous seller–buyer relations involving money. Nevertheless, non-monetized forms of exchange tended to persist, particularly among the poor. But as capitalism grew – as people were compelled to re-locate to find work, as relationships became increasingly mediated through contracts, as competition eclipsed cooperation – taken-for-granted relationships and long-standing identities faded. Consequently, a kind of social-psychological vacuum emerged and into the void, through the efforts of retailers, marketers and advertisers, identities and meanings associated with capitalist consumption were introduced. Through this process and the mediation of a broad range of complementary institutions, organizations and technologies, capitalist consumption became a 'normal' way of thinking and acting, engrained into conceptual systems.

Competitive consumption and the new bourgeoisie

In England, by 1700, traditional social relations were well on their way to being replaced by a more dynamic, individualizing order – one in which pecuniary gain came to dominate society. Instead of direct producers selling their outputs to customers, middleman merchants and specialized retailers emerged.[25] As local markets gave way to regional and, later, national ones (eventually facilitated through canals and railways), retailing became more a branch of wholesaling than direct production.[26] Crucial to this history, as well as to the assessment of developments and capacities related to consumption and globalization, is the need to understand the complementary (and sometimes oppositional) ways of thinking that accompanied it.

In most cultures and times, after attaining a certain level of wealth, elites typically put their riches on display as a means of conveying status; in keeping with this trend, as the early years of capitalism began to transform the feudal agrarian economy, the nobility of the Elizabethan era reached new heights of grandeur in their lifestyles and spending habits. Faced with political

Source: The Ashmolean Museum of Art and Archaeology, Oxford, UK.

Illustration 3.2   Elizabeth I, 1533–1603

challenges, such as maintaining the loyalty of the masses in relation to the emerging merchant class, Elizabeth used her unparalleled wealth to demonstrate the monarch's unchallengeable power. This involved, among other things, elaborate ceremonies and wardrobe (see Illustration 3.2). In response to such displays, a kind of conspicuous consumption 'arms race' was initiated in which the use of wealth to purchase and exhibit commodities became an explicit means of communicating one's position relative to others.

Previously, the elites of England were preoccupied with the maintenance of their social position through an emphasis on familial history and hierarchical traditions. Now, in a period of intensified competition involving the monarch's demonstrative use of wealth and individual fortunes generated through foreign trade and capitalist methods, elite resources increasingly were funnelled into here-and-now activities. Individual short-term concerns thus, for the first time, began to outweigh the long-term interests of the family corporation. Indeed, some argue that this period marks the beginning of the contemporary interest in fashion over tradition – the cultural preoccupation for purchasing and displaying *new* commodities as indices of status and success.[27]

For a time, following the example set by Elizabeth, it had been mainly nobility who used wealth and fashion to indicate superiority. By the eighteenth century, however, this practice spread to the middle class. Total spending in England at the end of the seventeenth century was 10 million pounds or 10 pounds per household. By 1770, it increased to 30 million pounds or 25 pounds per household. Just three decades later, in 1801, total sales amounted to 90 million pounds or 40 pounds per household. Adjusting for inflation, comprehending the poverty of most workers and peasants, and recognizing that the nobility could not have accounted for much of this extraordinary rise, the eighteenth century clearly constituted something of a consumption boom for the new bourgeoisie.[28]

Burgeoning demand was brought about by more than just wealth – it also constituted a 'new habit of mind and pattern of behavior' whose 'aesthetic and stylistic considerations [began to take] ... precedence over utilitarian ones'.[29] Commercial interests responded with whole new categories of goods such as potteries, watches and furniture whose purchase and display increasingly took place for the sake of novelty, style and identity. Accompanying this turn was the cultural movement, Romanticism, emphasizing humanity's uniqueness and the potential for individual enlightenment through experience, travel and thoughtful consumption.[30]

The new middle class; capitalism's production of an ever-growing number of commodities; and the political economy's general need for a new workforce of accountants, lawyers, administrators, clerks and the like entailed a further concentration of people in towns and cities. The push or compulsion among this middle strata to use their new found wealth to purchase goods for status, pleasure and identity was rooted in the accompanying emergence of a kind of social-psychological vacuum. With no historical or contemporary reference points, how was this new class suppose to think and act? As with wage labourers, following the violent tumult of primitive accumulation, the bourgeoisie's forefathers and mothers were stripped of their long-held identities and meaningful relationships. No longer, for example, were surnames the mark of the family's trade (such as Barber, Miller, Sawyer) or place of residence (for instance, Walsh, Hill, Ford). Through the individualization entailed in the wage labour contract, the need to commodify one's labour in order to buy what was needed, and the demand for a workforce possessing new or limited skills (not to mention the relocation of countless migrants away from traditional communities to relatively heterogeneous cities, and the anonymity this entailed), previously unimaginable questions arose (at least subconsciously).

Don Slater explains that

> In a post-traditional society, social identity must be constructed by individuals, because it is no longer given or ascribed, but in the most bewildering of circumstances: not only is one's position in the status order no longer fixed, but the order itself is unstable and changing and is represented in ever changing goods and images ... Goods can always signify social identity, but in the fluid processes of post-traditional society, identity seems to be more the function of consumption than the other, traditional, way round.[31]

Developments affecting both consumption and religion were influenced by these conditions. Dating from the eighteenth century, Christianity emerged to become something of a lifestyle marker for the so-called middle orders. Weekly attendance at church became the norm among the relatively well off, in contrast to the working class and their general agnosticism and even antipathy.[32] Wealthy families even purchased pews and funded religious schools.[33] By 1800, the religious fervour of the predominantly Protestant middle class and its promotion of bible reading in the home motivated an almost universal bourgeois literacy – an ability to read that was remarkable in contrast to the majority who were mostly illiterate.[34] While hundreds of grammar schools were established in the seventeenth century teaching Latin and Greek, it was only in the eighteenth century that these and a large number of new free and fee-paying schools began to teach English, as well as mathematics, geography and history.[35]

With middle-class literacy, reading became a popular recreational activity. Newspaper reading increased dramatically in the eighteenth century, while novels, religious tracts and poetry also became commonplace pastimes.[36] This literacy, coupled with the search for individual and collective identity, constituted a receptive mindset for commercial interests. Beyond its use by advertisers to engage prospective customers, the *practice* of reading itself modified conceptual systems. More specifically, through the act of silent reading and solitary discovery, *individualism* itself was implicitly encouraged – a way of thinking that facilitated commercial and liberal ideals concerning the development of private faculties and individual empowerment.

The commercial newspaper and its sale of 'today's news' was a key nodal point in the mediation of these emerging middle-class realities. Every day the newspaper implicitly but powerfully told its readers that change itself was normal. Previously, the pre-modern mindset had little or no sense of history as a cause-and-effect, progressive process; temporally, the past and present were rarely segmented and, spatially, society was hierarchical and communal. But now the question 'what's new?' and the rise of fashion (both in the realm of things and ideas) marked a sharp break from past conceptual norms. At least among the middle class, the date on the top of each newspaper linked them together as a community of readers – an abstract community of strangers sharing an increasingly mechanized sense of time. Life came to be characterized by a predictable 24-hour news cycle in which what is new itself became a valuable commodity.[37]

The fact that individuals consumed the news in privacy – or, as Hegel famously put it, in 'the lair of the skull' – significantly influenced conceptual systems. Daily newspaper reading, in particular, became simultaneously a shared *and solitary* ceremony. Papers, bibles, novels and other publications commonly read in silence facilitated the paradoxical rise of this new kind of community – a community, to repeat, of anonymous individuals. The literate resident of London possessing 'disposable income', in his search for identity and meaning, used reading, perhaps unconsciously, as a way of 'connecting' with others.[38] While Protestantism constituted a significant step away from the hierarchy of traditional society, the commercial newspaper (and its advertising, of course) ultimately solidified a new social order in which individuals and their here-and-now desires prevailed.

In the history of now 'developed' political economies, over the course of generations, people, struggling to survive or succeed in a competitive system, radically reformed their conceptual systems using a broad array of affecting media. Beyond the sudden, unprecedented availability of clothes, furnishings, foods and the like, the purchase and possession of innumerable things became the means of telling the world *and oneself* 'this is who I am'. At long last, the institution of capitalist consumption was born.

Temporal transformations and working class life

With the availability and eager acquisition of commodities, in the eighteenth and nineteenth centuries a new middle-class culture emerged in which industry, integrity and individualism were idealized. In this political economy – one increasingly mediated by contracts, property rights and money – these qualities came to be both culturally valued and prospectively profitable. However, too much individualism – at least in terms of an individualism that ignores the rule of law – would be counter-productive.

To maintain this new and somewhat paradoxical order, various dimensions of power were exercised. State coercion reflected the first face of power. The power to structure 'the rules of the game' constituted the second. Lastly, techniques constituting the third dimension of power were employed. For instance, England's first elementary schools were established not coincidentally just after the French Revolution. Also after 1789, a spike in church building took place. These and other developments were shaped, in part at least, by an explicit ruling class interest in teaching the masses how to think and behave.[39]

Following E. P. Thompson, one way to appreciate the potential and actual resistance among workers (and thus, perhaps, to better comprehend contemporary responses to the globalization project) is to assess their consciousness and activities in terms of 'traditional' versus 'modern' notions of time. Under feudalism, a relatively organic, seasonally sensitive understanding of time was dominant. In the winter, for example, when the days were shorter and fewer chores had to be completed, life flowed more or less in tune with the dominant context of nature. People were linked to past and future generations through the intimacy and relative permanency of extended families and local communities. Capitalist social relations – particularly the demands placed on people through wage labour contracts and their remuneration based on time – subsequently divorced life from ecology and culture from tradition. Beginning about five centuries ago, vested interests engaged various institutions, organizations and technologies in the task of transforming established or 'fixed' work-rhythms into those that could be explicitly measured by time, marking the beginning of a cultural shift from the predominance of cyclical time to linear time.[40]

In sum, the capitalist dynamic – its compulsion to increase economic efficiencies and surpluses through the exploitation of waged labour – involved at least two problematic tasks: *first*, ending people's 'traditional' access to lands and other communal rights and, *second*, eliminating the seemingly ageless norm of task-oriented occupations.

Before capitalism, relatively unstructured temporal norms and cyclical work habits engaged people as members of inter-dependent communities whose daily routines involved little demarcation between 'work' and 'life'. With capitalism, however, work was no longer just part of what was done as one 'passed the time of day'. In this emerging political economy, time itself became money. In the words of Thompson, now 'the employer must *use* the time of his labour, and see it is not wasted: *not the task but the value of time when reduced to money is dominant*. Time is now currency: it is not passed but spent'.[41]

This transformation, taking place over generations, employed new mediating technologies such as mechanical clocks as means of synchronizing and disciplining labour. It also involved organizations such as those established through the English poor laws as well as a number of institutional third-dimension-of-power changes that went well beyond state-directed regulations. An example of the latter can be found in Baxter's *Christian Directory*, first published in London in 1673, and its warning, 'Let the time of your Sleep be so much only as health requireth; For precious time is not to be wasted in unnecessary sluggishness ... [Q]uickly dress you ... and follow your labours with constant diligence.'[42]

As one observer put it, writing in 1842, 'The manufacturing population is not new in its formation alone: it is new in its habits of thought and action, which have been formed by the circumstances of its condition.'[43]

Indeed, a 'conscious' working class and its sometimes militant organization were born in response to these changes, guided by its shared memory of past rights and privileges. By the early nineteenth century, these historic ideals, although largely eradicated in practice, were reproduced through working class unions, educational movements and periodicals as well as 'intellectual traditions, ... community patterns, and a working-class structure of feeling'.[44] Arguably, the general *absence* of the institution of capitalist consumption among England's impoverished workers played its role – impelling many in the working class to find identity and meaning through their relationships with one another and by referencing the past rather than the here-and-now.

For the working class, until the twentieth century, capitalism's growth was accompanied by long hours and low wages. Under these conditions, the urban worker typically was limited in his/her ability to perform even sub-sistence tasks. As Ursula Huws suggests, one way of summarizing the history of capitalism is to trace it as the gradual replacement of tasks performed communally and at home with things made by private interests for money. In the seventeenth century, most homes and villages were engaged in a broad range of self-sufficient activities, including brewing, dairy-work, the care of livestock, spinning wool, crafting furniture, making soap, candles and many others.[45] But through the process of primitive accumulation, not only did the need for wages make most of these time-consuming activities untenable, emerging mass production techniques reduced the time and cost of manufacture, making many homemade goods uneconomical. Community interdependence and self-sufficiency thus were replaced by individualism and dependency. Timelessness was replaced by efficiency.

Commodity fetishism, electricity and the department store

For both the bourgeoisie and working class, the skilled and creative tasks performed in the home gradually were replaced by commodity consumption. By the eighteenth century, at least in urban centres, shopping itself became an essential part of housework (a development that further entrenched the need for a wage). Skills and craft traditions, passed down through oral forms of education, eventually gave way to a complex division of labour involving specialists and new technologies. Industries emerged and the consumption demands of a growing workforce facilitated a dramatic growth in retailing.[46] Beyond the manufacture and availability of goods designed to serve practical and, increasingly, social-psychological needs, an important new technique was employed in the task of selling commodities: impersonalized sales.

In the decades around 1800, entities that looked like the modern store began to appear in London, Paris and other Western cities. It was at this time that delineations between households and shops emerged as retailers, trying to attract more trade, de-personalized their businesses to attract the patronage of strangers. Previously, shopkeepers sold goods directly from their homes, but in the emerging effort to sell to strangers – a task not altogether feasible when retailing from one's abode – sellers established separate spaces to conduct business, usually on the main floor of residences with storefront signs that, in effect, invited passers-by to walk in.[47]

As shopkeepers came to know customers as strangers rather than familiar clients, another development took form: the use of fixed, non-negotiable prices for goods and services. Rather than negotiating the price of every item (thus maintaining the importance of familiarity), buying became a more mechanical, impersonal transaction. The patron coming in off the street, taking part in the new 'dropping trade' (as it was called), knowing that the price she would pay was the price everyone paid, had less apprehension doing business with someone she did not know.

Through the impersonalization of what had become an essential task, the commodities purchased were physically and psychically removed from the people who made them and the conditions of their manufacture. Money, rather than familiarity, became *the* medium of exchange. In the absence of buyers knowing the biographies of commodities, a new level of abstraction arose.

In the new economy's focus on selling things rather than maintaining relationships, retailers could more easily associate what they were selling with qualities or meanings that had little or nothing to do with the commodity itself. In the eighteenth century, in the context of this distancing of production from consumption, for an eager middle class seeking identity and meaning, promotions vaguely similar to contemporary commercials first appeared. While in the early part of the century quack medicines and addictive substances (often one and the same) predominated advertisements, by 1800, face creams, toothpastes, hair dyes, soaps and even convenience foods (such as soups and sauces) were promoted to a cross section of middle-income consumers using previously unimagined associations and qualities.[48]

These groundbreaking ads were more literal than visual or metaphorical. Eighteenth-century commercials – probably at the insistence of a culture not as far removed from the realities of production as are most Westerners today – generally underlined the purported utilitarian worth of the commodity in question. Nevertheless, deception was commonplace. While the claims made might have been ridiculous (even to some eighteenth-century readers), the supposedly useful qualities of almost every product was routinely addressed. An elixir called *Prince's Cherry Lotion*, for example, claimed that 'A Lady of Distinction has declar'd that most of her teeth became loose and some dropped out ... but after using four bottles of *Cherry Lotion* the remainder of her Teeth became quite firm.'[49]

Note a general trend: in the process of de-personalizing producer–buyer, seller–customer and even seller–seller relationships, the exchange of things and the circulation of commodities became both more complex *and alienating*. The older moral economy of relatively stable, familiar transactions gradually was pushed aside in favour of goods bought and sold among increasingly anonymous interests. While advertising and its power to influence emerged in the context of historical developments involving abstract relationships and unmet existential needs, the success of ads (and, later, national brands) perpetuated one of the most important characteristics of capitalist consumption – commodity fetishism.[50]

Fetishism generally refers to the belief that something has supernatural powers. Unlike reification – a term referring to treating an object (such as a commodity) or an abstract relationship (such as a contract) as a living entity – commodity fetishism constitutes the illusory view that something that has been or can be purchased entails (or can deliver) capacities that have little or nothing to do with the thing itself. Taken from Marx, such fetishes are said to be possible when the biography or history of a commodity has been forgotten or displaced. By distancing humanity from where things come from and how they are made, consumption can proceed with little thought as to something's origins and consequences. As David Harvey summarizes,

> The conditions of labour and life, the sense of joy, anger, or frustration that lie behind ... production ..., the states of mind of the producers, are all hidden ... as we exchange one object (money) for another (the commodity). We can take our daily breakfast without a thought for the myriad of people who engaged in its production. All traces of exploitation are obliterated in the object (there are no finger marks of exploitation in the daily bread) ... [F]etishism explains how it is that under conditions of capitalist modernization we can be so objectively dependent on 'others' whose lives and aspirations remain so totally opaque to us.[51]

It is through this removal or displacement of what lies behind the world of purchasable things, and the occlusion of human relationships with media such as money and advertising, that people prospectively value commodities *not* in terms of the skills, sweat and time employed in their creation but, instead, in terms of the socially constructed meanings associated with them. Again, commodity fetishism (and thus the institution of capitalist consumption) was initially experienced among England's bourgeoisie, not its workers. After all, for most who worked in that country's factories, mills and mines, not only was the process of exploitation directly experienced, most could directly see the benefits accrued by their wealthy employers. But as Thompson demonstrates, nineteenth-century workers were not primarily united in resistance as a result of their mutually inadequate wage. 'The issues which provoked the most intensity of feeling,' he says, 'were very often ones in which such values as traditional customs, "justice", "independence", security or family economy were at stake, rather than straightforward "bread-and-butter" issues.'[52] Money, beyond the need for survival wages, remained secondary until the twentieth century – the century in which the institution of capitalist consumption was consciously expanded to the working class. Until then, workers *primarily* saw themselves *as producers, not consumers*.[53]

In 1852, the world's first department store, *Le Bon Marché*, opened in Paris. Beyond lower prices and an unprecedented selection of goods, *Bon Marché* and later the department stores in London, New York and other cities encouraged customers to wander about, inspect merchandise and, in the absence of personal interactions with salesmen (implying, for the first time, that an imminent purchase was *not* expected), *fantasize about the lifestyles they could acquire*. For the middle class at least, the experience of visiting the department store – with its fixed prices, impersonal transactions and the tangible demonstration that almost anything was (materially) attainable – communicated the idea that people, *as consumers*, now seemingly were free to lead the life (at least the home life) and become the person *of their own choice*.[54]

In his history of late nineteenth/early twentieth-century America and its consumerist cultural transformation, titled *Land of Desire*, William Leach argues that the department store emerged in response to revolutionary developments involving the mass production and distribution of goods. Establishing electricity-powered factories, the building of railways and, later, the consolidation of local retailers into regional and national chains involved unprecedented capital investments and debt. Business leaders and investment bankers, looking to pay for these innovations and generate profits, sought to promote dramatic increases in consumption. After 1880, writes Leach, 'business began to create a new set of commercial enticements – a commercial aesthetic – to move and sell goods in volume'.[55]

Although the importance of electricity was primarily acknowledged as an efficient source of energy – lowering production costs which reduced prices, thus expanding sales prospects – its broader significance went further; electricity also facilitated Taylorist efficiencies[56] by enabling the design of expansive, single-story plants instead of multi-storied factories. Improvements in the lighting and organization of production lines was one result, as was the ability to extend operations well into the night.[57]

From a marketing perspective, electricity, along with the strategic use of glass and colour, enabled retailers to create a kind of 'fairyland environment' for their wares.[58] In the late nineteenth century, these technologies and materials were, for the first time, mobilized to sell both goods and consumerist ideals. Shop windows were illuminated, as were billboards and fashion shows, all with the goal of promoting a '*this*-worldly paradise that was stress-free and "happy"'.[59] Electricity also became the dominant means of lighting not just window displays but also entire urban areas devoted to shopping, making such activities community events, spectacles and, perhaps more importantly, manifestations of what science, capitalist-driven change and consumption itself had to offer society's obedient, hard-working citizens.

Twentieth-century advertising and working class consumption

In early twentieth-century America and elsewhere, experts in the relatively new field of psychology were recruited to 'scientifically' manage middle-class consumption and, more ambitiously, transform the thoughts and behaviours of workers. As workers became objects of rational calculation under the guise of Taylorism, consumers became the targets of prospective manipulation through commodity fetishism and other means. In the words of Boston-based department store magnate and business lobbyist Edward Filene (writing in 1931), the 'time has come when all our educational institutions ... must concentrate on the great social task of teaching the masses not what to think but *how to think*, and thus to find out how to behave like human beings in the machine age'.[60]

Driving this ambition was an unprecedented spike in productivity (as measured in terms of work output per hour),[61] a general growth in incomes and important developments in the realm of consumer credit. By the mid-1920s, the wages paid to American workers were the highest in the world.[62] In part, this was a result of the anti-union strategies of corporate executives like Henry Ford who, responding to his workers' resistance to Taylorist techniques, raised wages to assuage militants and entice his own workforce to purchase what they produced.

In the inter-war years, electricity powered commodities, ranging from refrigerators to toasters, phonographs to fans, gradually became household 'necessities'. Emblematic of both the period's economic boom and increasingly successful efforts to manage consumption, in 1927, the New York department store *Gimbels* installed 27 escalators (then the most ever in one building). Consumers, prompted to visit and browse by advertising, able to buy things with money they didn't have through credit, efficiently moved from one department to the next courtesy of omnipresent escalators (which were able to, according to *Gimbels's* management, 'In one hour ... transport a city'[63]), New Yorkers were enticed, catered to and transported.

While the Taylorist-inspired growth in mass production compelled developments involving mass consumption (tantamount to journalist/philosopher Samuel Strauss's observation at the beginning of this chapter that because 'the windmill goes around ... the wind must blow'), there was no certainty that these and other methods of stoking demand would work – no guarantee that commodities traditionally thought about as superfluities would become desirable conveniences and, later, necessities, particularly if their acquisition meant debt and insecurity for what generally had been a frugal culture. Yet the transformation took place.

French political commentator and educator André Siegfried visited the United States on several occasions from 1901 to 1925. 'A new society has come to life in America,' he wrote, 'the very basis of the American civilisation is no longer the same ... [It was not] clear to me in 1901 or 1904, it was noticeable in 1914, and patent in 1925.' Linking this change to the ascendancy of mass production, Siegfried said that it had become 'obvious that Americans have come to consider their standard of living as a somewhat sacred acquisition, which they will defend at any price ... [T]hey would be ready to make many an intellectual or even moral concession in order to maintain that standard'.[64]

Many Americans saw this change also. For Strauss, Americans were rapidly losing interest in 'wisdom' and 'the continuity of life'; what was fashionable, young and 'new and improved' were becoming priorities. Insightfully, Strauss argued that while capitalists and socialists remained 'at each other's throats, ... the issue between them is, Which can ensure the distribution of the most goods to the people?'.[65] Indeed, with the Great Depression, fears of a domestic rebellion – particularly in light of the then recent revolution in Russia – impelled business leaders to redouble their efforts at promoting capitalist consumption.[66]

Let us be more precise. What, Siegfried, Strauss and others perceived – what we are referring to as the institution of capitalist consumption – first reached 'maturity' in early twentieth-century America. This emerged as a result of three forces that coalesced at this place and time. *First*, as noted above, America's dramatic rise in industrial productivity was accompanied by a widespread recognition that domestic markets also had to be developed. *Second*, the atomization of individuals, the alienation of workers from their labour and the modern development of almost 'free floating' identities – the outcomes of contract-mediated relations, Taylorist production techniques and the more general proliferation of impersonal relationships – constituted social conditions amenable to the rapid cultural shifts described by thoughtful contemporaries. Distanced from traditional meanings and secure identities, the modern urban worker was relatively open to those suggested by predominant vested interests. As both the rise of psychotherapy and the mass public's interest in 'personalities' (such as cinema stars Mary Pickford and Charlie Chaplin) indicated, making sense of one's own identity and purpose had become something of a commonplace concern. Into this vacuum came a *third* crucial development: the technology-facilitated growth of newspapers, magazines and radio as advertising vehicles.[67]

The press, radio and branding

Advertising became the primary source of income for newspaper and magazine owners in the early twentieth century. With innovations such as electrical printing, graphics and the ability to produce sections and inserts appealing to specific audiences (such as a fashion section sponsored by a local department store), publishers re-assessed their means of generating revenues. Rather than selling newspapers or magazines to readers, their primary goal became the selling of consumer 'eyeballs' to advertisers. In this context, the priorities of commercial interests became as important (if not more important) as were the interests of readers. Instead of asking what would the public like to read (hopefully resulting in sales and subscriptions), the more pressing question became how do we deliver a sponsor's prospective consumer to our publication's advertisements?

This reframing of publishing's economic goals generated livelier, more visually pleasing, evermore stimulating publications. In attempts to appeal to as large a consumer base as possible, politically subjective stories and factual articles generally were replaced by sensational reporting and 'balanced' analyses.[68] For example, foreign wars (the Crimean and Boer wars in Britain and the Spanish-American war in the United States) were found to significantly increase audiences and advertising revenues. As publications became delivery platforms for mass market advertisers, 'the working man's perspective' increasingly came to be part of mainstream political discourse. However, in catering to sponsors' needs, papers and magazines did more than just explicitly or implicitly cross class boundaries; they also simplified and sensationalized public sphere interactions. Particularly with the rise of radio as a competitor for advertising, as Innis put it (with some amount of exaggeration), 'a prevailing interest in orgies and excitement' emerged.[69]

Radio came into prominence in the 1920s. Its initial advertisers both produced and sponsored programmes.[70] For the most part, these were isolated broadcasts – usually just one component of a company's promotional endeavours. It was only with the introduction of regularly scheduled programmes and the formation of national networks that radio realized its full potential as a marketing medium. Like the newspaper, radio revenues were based on delivering 'ears' to advertisers and, with the rising number of competing stations, programming gradually became more sensual than intellectual, more entertaining than enlightening. But unlike newspapers, radio became a central means of coordinating truly national marketing campaigns as nationalistic references were used to connect disparate listeners. Business interests used patriotism and personalities to promote their products and further institutionalize capitalist consumption.

More profoundly, efforts to promote or 'manage' consumption through the commercial and largely sensual priorities of mass media outlets compounded cultural orientations towards individual satisfactions and present mindedness. In this process and the extension of consumerist priorities to workers (particularly in the context of an ongoing, mass existential crisis), conceptual systems structured to seek happiness and truth through the acquisition of things contributed to the neutering of American working class militancy, particularly its capacity to organize in pursuit of some kind of post-capitalist political economic order. Unlike the socialist ideal, capitalism offered and delivered tangible commodities; it constituted a mostly enjoyable and sometimes empowering experience whereas alternative societies were 'things of the past' or simply too 'distant' to seriously contemplate.[71] In this cultural environment, abstractions concerning long-term efforts to forge a world without private property and materialist values become increasingly difficult to imagine. Instead, other abstractions – ones mythologizing individualism and the simple (but dubious) relationship between acquisition, freedom and happiness – become normalized, even among the relatively poor.

In the United States, New Dealers such as sociologist Robert Lynd insisted that a consumption-based re-ignition of capitalism, in light of the rise of fascism and communism, constituted 'the only way that democracy can survive ...'.[72] Indeed, for the first time, policymakers and executives came to view rising working class incomes and their expanding participation as consumers to be essential prerequisites for the defence of something more fundamental than the realization of profits – capitalism itself.

The aggregate purchasing power of consumers subsequently became the focus of New Deal reforms while state policies facilitating labour's growing spending power were instituted in relatively 'developed' countries after the War. Such reforms, while designed to fuel capital's survival and growth, also aimed to dampen working class militancy. Industrial labour's agitation for 'a living wage' sufficient to provide workers with an 'American standard of living', for example, had been pursued in the United States since the start of the century, and organized efforts to empower employees in the workplace or, more ambitiously, in line with collectivist ideals, had all but disappeared. Also, in light of management's commitment to the mechanized, Taylorized factory, unions generally turned towards the easier task of bettering members' wages.[73]

Engaging workers in the institution of capitalist consumption also involved the initially difficult task of *not* associating products with where and how they were made. To repeat, rather than a location or activity to be reminded of, work generally had become a place to escape from – both literally and figuratively. By removing, dislocating and re-contextualizing a good through commodity fetishism, the thing being sold could become the object of one's consumerist dreams rather than workplace nightmares. As American copywriter Helen Woodward put it, writing in 1926, 'If you are advertising any product, never see the factory in which it was made.'[74]

But, again, the task of changing how people (in this case, workers) thought and acted was far from automatic. Underlining, again, that capitalist consumption is an institutional construct, previously socialized inter-subjective norms persisted. Long-established ways of thinking and acting could not be transformed overnight, especially in times of economic uncertainty. As Stuart Ewen explains,

> Traditional family structures, agricultural life styles, immigrant values which accounted for a vast percentage of the attitudes of American working classes, and traditional realms of aesthetic expression – all these were historically infused with an agglomeration of self-sufficiency, communitarianism, localized popular culture, thrift and subjective social bonds and experiences that stood ... on the frontiers of industrial-cultural development. *It was these [inter-]subjective experiences of traditional culture that stood between advancing industrial machinery and the synthesis of a new order of industrial culture.*[75]

Alongside advertising, the expansion of credit and, later, a Depression-deepened realization that higher wages among workers could facilitate more consumption, state policies and resources were mobilized to transform public thinking. In the United States, for example, the federal Department of Commerce was established to promote production *and* consumption. In 1926, under the leadership of Herbert Hoover, the Department initiated its Census of Distribution – also called, at the time, the 'Census of Consumption'.[76] More than just mapping how much and where consumption was taking place, it involved research aiming to, among other things, advise business regarding potential demand, fashion trends, display methods, the organization of parking and even how to use colourful lights to stimulate spending.[77] Through public relations campaigns and other methods, the Department of Commerce also promoted home ownership as a means of both 'stabilising' working class communities and stoking consumption by filling homes with goods. Particularly after 1945, the widespread availability of mortgages, automobile loans and, later, credit cards – even to the working class – were encouraged through state policies and government legislation.[78] These facilitating measures, alongside the emerging sophistication of marketing and, more generally, a growing emphasis on individualism in American and other Western cultures, generated the consumers who fuelled the post-War economic boom.

* * *

Two premises borrowed from Freudian psychology informed post-War advertising strategies. *First*, human motivations are largely hidden (buried in the subconscious) and, *second*, these could be elicited through conversations structured around the psychoanalytical strategy called 'free association'. This model, quite unlike mainstream economic theories built around the 'sovereign' consumer, assumed that people rarely made rational choices and that they were influenced by images and sensations more than by reason. From a sociological perspective, insecurities regarding identity and one's relationship with others were played upon as advertisers associated their products with the consumer's sense of himself/herself, as well as his/her desires and fears.[79]

In conjunction with the creativity of advertising and marketing personnel, these strategies were first 'scientifically' applied by corporations selling brands. Brands originated in the nineteenth century as producers 'trade-marked' their goods as a way of undermining the power of wholesalers. Through advertising, consumers learned to ask for a specific company's brand rather than just a quantity of flour or detergent or cloth. But it was only after 1945, with national mass media (especially radio and television) and the mass exodus from cities to suburbs (the latter deepening the individual's sense of displacement and existential uncertainty) that branding became an essential part of capitalist consumption. The 'floating' individual of modern society (living in a 'community' lacking front porches, town centres and even side-walks) turned away from generic products and towards commodities that moored him/her to an ever-acquisitive purpose and identity. With the growth of competition among brands (when film was no longer simply *Kodak*, tissues *Kleenex* and vacuum cleaners *Hoovers*), brands emerged to become vehicles for finding and holding still more 'unique' identities and meanings. In sum, brands became the means to promote nationwide sales and lifetime consumer loyalties through their purported powers to fill social-psychological vacuums. In the context of an endless search for security, *Cheerios* could be associated with a mother's love, *Tide* could be linked to family happiness and *Coca-Cola*, even more abstractly, simply could become 'the real thing'.

Television, suburbia and the commercialization of conceptual systems

Arguably the most powerful medium for elaborating such existential abstractions was – and in much of the world remains – television. While invented before the Second World War, commercial TV did not come to saturate American homes until the 1950s (in effect replacing the hearth as *the* gathering place for families). Driving its development were an array of manufacturers seeking sales through brand-based marketing strategies. Post-World War II workplace innovations generated another spike in productivity and, with the unprecedented clout of organized labour, workers soon had more 'disposable' income than ever before. Credit and the housing boom associated with suburbanization stimulated a mass demand for automobiles that, in turn, facilitated a further expansion of metropolitan areas. The move to the suburbs, especially among relatively skilled workers, also divided work and home communities, limiting the cultural overlaps that had occurred when neighbourhoods were more coherently class based.[80] Americans became evermore mobile and domestically isolated – conditions that, in effect, deepened the public's demand for consumption-associated identities.

Television subsequently became the core medium of American mass culture – a development facilitated by spatially induced divisions associated with suburban living and the related impulsion to 'connect' with larger communities. But, as with commercial radio, the nationwide TV audience itself became a commodity as their viewing time was 'sold' to advertisers. Television programming thus evolved in ways that prioritized entertainment and sensual stimulation. Particularly in response to the advent of more competition and the remote control channel changer, TV deepened many of the conceptual orientations promoted through the press and radio.

On the specific implications of television, we defer to media scholar Neil Postman. In a speech Postman gave to an audience of Austrians on the subject of that country's introduction of commercial TV in the 1980s, he presented 'a series of prophecies ... based on the experiences of my country [the United States]'[81]:

> As audiences come to expect fast-paced, visually exciting programmes, they will begin to find issue-oriented public-affairs and news programmes dull. To compete ... news and public-affairs programmes will become more visual and personality-oriented. As a result, there will be a decline in the public's *capacity to understand and discuss* events and issues in a serious way.[82]

'Of course,' Postman adds, 'newspapers and magazines will go out of business; others will change their format and style to compete with television for audiences ... They will become more picture-oriented and will feature dramatic headlines, celebrities, and sensational stories.'[83] More generally, with commercial television's influence on conceptual systems, Postman believes that 'a general impatience with books will develop', particularly those that communicate complex ideas. The result is a decline in the analytical and critical skills of readers. 'I suspect,' Postman predicted, that a 'concern with history will also decline, to be replaced by a consuming interest in the present.'[84]

The cultural implications, says Postman, 'will be devastating'. Image and style will become the focus of political life; policies will involve public opinion shifts more than long-term efficacy; 'movie stars will be taken seriously as political candidates'. As people become accustomed to spending their evenings at home in front of the TV, Postman predicted a decrease in public gatherings in parks, pubs, union halls and other venues.[85] Particularly as a result of television and advertising's emphasis on fashion (that is, what trends are 'in', what celebrities are 'cool,' and what commodities are 'now'), 'the values of youth, ... the immediate gratification of desires, the love of the new, [and] a contempt for what is old', all will come to the fore.[86]

With these changes in mind, Postman told his Austrian audience to

> ... banish from your mind the naïve but commonplace notion that com-
> mercials are about products. They are about products in the same sense
> that the story of Jonah is about the anatomy of whales. Which is to say,
> they aren't. They are about values and myths and fantasies. One might
> even say they form a body of religious literature, a montage of volumi-
> nous, visualised sacred texts that provide people with images and stories
> around which to organise their lives ... Commercial television adds to the
> Decalogue several impious commandments, among them thou shalt seek
> to amuse thyself continuously, and thou shalt avoid complexity like the
> ten plagues that afflicted Egypt.[87]

Removed from traditional communities, alienated from their own labour,
geographically and culturally isolated from their class identity, television's
saliency in shaping the conceptual systems of most Westerners has been significant indeed. Particularly in the United States, and now increasingly in
the rest of the world, television has emphasized the primacy of consumerist
inclinations and identities. This structuring of consciousness and our now
commonplace use of commodities to shape and affirm the purpose and
meaning of life, once understood as a long-term historical process, clarifies
how and why capitalist consumption has been so influential in relation to
other core institutions. The pernicious character of the capitalist dynamic
involving consumption's ever-widening and deepening influence elucidates
its presence in education, religion, family and other key nodal points of
daily life. Rather than a top-down effort to transform humanity into consumerist 'zombies', a more nuanced, historically accurate assessment recognizes that workers and citizens themselves became capitalist consumption's
unwitting agents.

Once internalized as cultural norms – once structured into the conceptual systems used to process information and experience into reality –
people tend to reproduce and even disseminate the institution of capitalist
consumption through their own mediated relationships. To secure the
student's attention, the teacher replicates the visual and sensual techniques developed by the press, radio, TV and now the Internet. To jibe
with cultural norms, the Church and Synagogue (or, rather, the religious
communities they serve) condone the exchange of commodities to celebrate religious events. To affirm one's care for a child in the context of consumerist norms, the birthday or graduation or even completion of a chore
are routinely associated with money or gifts. When a toddler is given a
Barbie and told by her parent 'I love you', love and commodities are
linked.

Transforming conceptual systems

To summarize this history, the categories time and space constitute helpful heuristic tools. How human beings conceptualize and organize time and space reflects and affects political economic relations involving, of course, power-laden relationships structured through mediating institutions, organizations and technologies. In the history sketched above, such media, including the law, chapmen, fixed prices, states, mechanical clocks, newspapers, religion, department stores, electricity and television, have been portrayed as the constructions of vested interests that, once established, influence the warp and woof of relationships, thoughts and practices.

In every social formation, culture and sub-culture, some ways of organizing and conceptualizing time and space through various media tend to dominate. Certainly, as we re-trace the history of capitalist consumption, we see how consumption – as itself a universally mediating institution – was constructed by various agents, influenced by and influencing other mediators. How then might we assess this history in terms of time and space, and what insights do these categories provide in anticipation of examining consumption in the context of globalization?

Human life involves the construction, maintenance, modification and destruction of spatial-temporal relations. Snapshots of this ongoing process can be taken by asking and answering three inter-related questions: how are space and time *experienced*?; how are space and time *perceived*?; and, how are space and time *imagined*?

For the most part, both indices are experienced, perceived and imagined in terms of enculturated norms and the structuring of everyday relationships. As Table 3.1 below summarizes, most human beings in pre-modern social formations lived an overwhelmingly localized existence. Experientially, in the absence of transportation or communication technologies (often only the feudal lord had a horse), the scope of geographical life was framed by the distance and routes one could safely walk in daylight. Time, similarly, was bound by ecological circumstances and the needs of the agrarian economy. Through private property rights and the compulsion to leave ancestral homes, travelling salesmen, canals and innumerable other mediators were constructed (such as the telegraph, telephone and, much later, the Internet). These media opened up life spatially, leading to activities and relationships taking place with relatively little regard to distance or physical barriers. Temporally, the mechanical clock (itself impelled by relations mediated by the wage labour contract), led to the common experience of time framed by commercial and organizational priorities – a way of living that has decisively abstracted people from nature, the seasons and even (as a result of electrical lighting) the daily movements of the earth in relation to the sun.

Table 3.1 Pre-modern and modern experiences, perceptions and imaginations

	Space		Time	
	Pre-modern	**Modern**	**Pre-modern**	**Modern**
EXPERIENCED	localized, relatively unmediated relationships and geographically delimited activities	additional, relatively mediated relationships and, through technology and other media, geographically extended activities	time is continuous, bound with ecological, agrarian priorities	time is mechanized, bound by largely commercial, organizational priorities
PERCEIVED	intimate knowledge of local surroundings; taken-for-granted relationships predominant	general knowledge of local surroundings; alienated, estranged relationships the norm	life changes slowly, punctuated by anticipated and unanticipated disruptions managed through religion and superstition	life changes quickly, anticipated and unanticipated disruptions commonplace yet managed through mechanized knowledge; present-mindedness and belief in 'progress' predominant
IMAGINED	little interest in conceptualizing other places or non-local geographies except in times of military conflict	conceptualizations of other places normal but framed in mostly acritical and/or commercial ways	existential questions present; religious beliefs and relatively unmediated relationships (incl. with nature) delimit alternative conceptualizations of past and future	existential questions pervasive; mystical beliefs and relatively mediated relationships facilitate seemingly diverse imaginings but framed in mostly ahistorical and commercial ways

As we move from experience to perception (and then to imagination), socialization and media become more influential. Spatial realities in pre-modern society, generally speaking, were intimately understood and, indeed, taken for granted. Relationships of all kinds, usually involving face-to-face interactions, were taken to be unalterable. Through spatial disloca-tion and increasingly mediated relations, perceptions of space were opened up to such an extent that, particularly in cities, alienated and estranged rela-tionships became normal. On the other hand, such 'open' perceptions have deepened the individual's focus on himself/herself and the here-and-now. Time, in pre-modern conditions, was generally perceived as continuous, with change anticipated through gradual processes such as ageing, punctu-ated by the commonplace terror of illness and death. In contrast, modern human beings tend to perceive change as an ongoing condition and death as something distant and surreal. Both present-mindedness and vague notions of long-term 'progress' through economic growth became com-monplace, not just because of pervasive consumerist messages but also through their socialization as commodity consumers whose life experiences are demarcated by evermore elaborate (and expensive) acquisitions. In modernity, conceptual systems, forged through experience and media, evoke perceptions of space and time that focus on the individual mostly in the here-and-now.

As for what is imaginable, the pre-modern human being had little interest in or capacity to conceptualize other places. In modern society, however, imagining other locales has become a daily occurrence. This has been enabled (and even encouraged) through literacy, travel, television, and even the now taken-for-granted availability of foods and goods from all over the world. Yet, despite this geographic stretching of imaginations, these thoughts are mostly acritical or they are framed in largely commercial ways (that is, 'knowing' Thailand as a result of a one-week holiday, Mexico as a result of a favourite local eatery or the Middle East as a result of daily news coverage).

Temporally, the pre-modern imagination was relatively constrained in its conceptualization of the past and future by nature, direct experience and religious faith. Modern humanity, on the other hand, possesses a relatively open-ended imagination facilitated, it should be underlined, not only by liberalism and the tangible individual freedoms associated with it but also by the relatively abstract qualities of modern existence. With power rela-tions mostly occluded and the growing technological capacity to profit from fantasies (in terms of 'dream vacations', pornographic images, celebrity lifestyles or a plethora of gambling opportunities), modern society encour-ages creative and fantastic thought as long as it frames these in the context of commercial realities and their prescribed boundaries vis-à-vis what is politically permissible and economically feasible. One is reminded here of a cartoon portraying two goldfish in a goldfish bowl. The big goldfish (presumably the parent) tells the small goldfish (the child), 'in this world, you can do *anything* you want!'.

The 'freedoms' experienced through consumption frame the boundaries of imaginable resistance. In most Western countries over the course of the twentieth century, capitalist consumption became *the* institution through which happiness and a better life were pursued. Indeed, democracy itself has been transformed through its promulgation and use. Rather than the individual's participation in political and economic life, producing a modicum of civic well-being, the 'freedoms' of the consumer – the 'right' to access and possess things for one's own benefit – has all but taken precedence. Spatially, the individual (and possibly his/her family) has taken the place of community and class as the primary unit of one's political imagination. Temporally, the now, the young and the fashionable have toppled continuity, wisdom and the long term. With a general decline of workplace autonomy and creativity, alongside urbanization and the related impersonalization of relationships, corporations and other vested interests developed capitalist consumption in ways that promoted commodified ways of seeking identity and meaning. Through advertising and marketing, state policies encouraging consumption, and (especially after 1945) the commitment of unions to 'standard of living' improvements, capitalism's (and democracy's) success or failure became increasingly framed in terms of consumption.

Since the 1980s, prospective crises – both economic and political – have been held at bay due largely to the economic capacity to grow consumption through credit and the related enculturation of consumerist lifestyles. Today, instead of concentrating on the workplace or state as core sites where reforms should be pursued, anti-status quo activists now are inclined to 'network' through the Internet, seek reforms by engaging in 'alternative' modes of consumption and rebel using so-called culture jamming strategies. In relatively 'advanced' political economies, consumption has become the primary framework in which consent is pursued and, paradoxically, resistance is mounted. Even Greenpeace now accepts contributions through *Visa* or *Master Card*.[88]

* * *

The power implications of how space and time are organized and conceptualized underline the profound and complex role played by capitalist consumption in our contemporary world (dis)order. The so-called developed world has, over the course of hundreds of years and through a range of influential media, normalized conceptual systems that both liberate *and* constrain questions concerning 'what is possible?'. In some ways, cultures that have not yet attained the disposable incomes nor disassembled certain statist or pre-modern institutions are 'freer' than entirely 'modern' political economies such as the United States. Comparatively unmediated relationships (sometimes out of necessity) here persist and abstractions such as the wage labour contract, the price system and the commodity fetishism, used in the West to alienate human beings and open their conceptual systems up to mystical, ahistorical, acritical norms, remain relatively underdeveloped.

Beyond the realm of the approximately 25 per cent of humanity living in abject poverty and a step away from the wealthiest 28 per cent who have yet to become the world's so-called 'consumer class' (see Chapter 1) lies another 47 per cent undergoing a period of rapid and uncertain 'development'. As we discuss in our next chapter, the future of the globalization project and, indeed, the long term of the human race may well be in the hands of this plurality. In a sense, their acceptance, rejection or reformulation of modernist ways of acting and thinking, and the capacity of capitalist consumption to itself affect a broad range of other mediators, constitute decisive variables determining how current trajectories will unfold.

4
Global Civil Society or Global Consumer Society?

> There are no global citizens, only global consumers; no global states, only global capitalist firms; no commonweal, only an aggregate of what individuals and nations and consumer markets want; no global cultural or national identities which are by definition parochial and local, only the new, hollowed-out identity conferred by brands.
>
> —Benjamin Barber[1]

In recent years, optimistic analyses concerning globalization – specifically those forecasting the decline of state authority and the related rise of a progressive global civil society (GCS) – have been pervasive, especially among left-leaning intellectuals and activists. Such prognostications, involving the strategic use of ICTs and, among post-structuralists, the resistance of the so-called 'networked multitude',[2] have not only dominated critical discourse about post-Cold War international relations, they have, in effect, reified globalization itself – unintentionally emptying it of its history, obfuscating the forces, processes and mediators shaping contemporary developments.[3] In this chapter, we argue that instead of the dawning of some kind of cosmopolitan 'global village', the dynamics behind the globalization project and the institutionalization of capitalist consumption are, for the most part, the same dynamics that drove the history presented in Chapter 3. Instead of the flowering of some kind of global civil society, another kind of GCS may well be emerging: *a global consumer society* (at least among the world's relatively wealthy).

The globalization project will not and indeed *cannot* end nation state power, let alone dilute the structural power of capital. In the early twenty-first century, a third face of power, assembled through both capitalist forces and consumerist mediations, is becoming increasingly influential, affecting even the thoughts and activities of capital's diverse opponents. To take just one example, proponents of an ICT-enabled GCS generally (and unknowingly) buy into the abstraction of the state and civil society as distinct entities. One result is an embrace of civil society as the 'place' of progressive politics.

This analytical move, as we will see, is both empirically shallow and strategically wrong-headed. In what follows we argue that, among other factors, the mediating role of capitalist consumption is poised to expand within the inter-connected realm of a non-dichotomous state-civil society complex, at least among those experiencing economic growth. The cultural and political consequences of this are mostly negative.

These consequences – involving political, economic and cultural tensions and contradictions – are addressed in subsequent chapters. In this, our task is to put history and theory to work; our aim is to assess what kind of world (dis)order is, in fact, emerging – a global civil society or a global consumer society?

GCS and globalization theory

The concept of GCS involves some extraordinary claims; through emerging forms of transnational associational life, a new political, economic and cultural order is said to be under construction. The agents of these developments are a 'medley of boundary-eclipsing actors – social movements, interest groups, indigenous peoples, cultural groups, and global citizens'.[4] Structurally, interactive communications technologies are providing groups and individuals with unprecedented capacities to form transnational networks. These, it is believed, have the potential to circumscribe status quo (state system-based) ways of relating and thinking. The formation of some kind of GCS, most probably modelled after liberal-democratic ideals and neoliberal regulatory regimes, thus appears to be emerging from the ashes of the Cold War era.[5]

For this kind of GCS to emerge, transnational intersections of culture, meaning and identity are required, and these entail the shared development and sustained implementation of a range of technological, organizational and institutional media. A central pillar in this grand conceptualization is the recent growth (if not explosion) of ICTs. Relatively new applications in telecommunications and computers, exemplified by the Internet, are thought to be essential. Together, such developments are lauded as the means through which a prospective revolution in the exchange of information, consciousness and, thus, a new progressive world order is becoming possible.

Before examining such claims directly, it is helpful to note their more general lineage. These prognostications fit into an even larger raft of analyses which Justin Rosenberg calls 'globalization theory'. Rather than an argument presented as an *explanandum* (globalization as the outcome of particular forces and processes) globalization itself has become the *explanans*, somehow explaining the changes it also describes.[6] In his critique of this approach, Rosenberg reveals that contemporary conceptualizations regarding the annihilation or 'emptying' of space and time, when applied to globalization-related developments, have themselves been unwittingly attributed to spatial and temporal changes.[7] The *explanans* has become the *explanandum*.[8]

While a historical and sociologically rigorous analysis of spatial-temporal changes such as those characterizing globalization impels us to avoid reifying the objects of study, globalization theory, says Rosenberg, routinely naturalizes the very phenomena under scrutiny. Rather than a *theory of* globalization, the overwhelming tendency has been to begin with globalization as the starting point – itself *the dynamic* of a new historical trajectory. Explanatory capacities on issues related to globalization have, as a result, been skewed in such a way that globalization's status *as a project* is obscured beyond recognition. One outcome has been that strategic efforts at reform have spiralled into the idealistic dead ends of GCS (mostly among liberals) and the global multitude (among post-structuralists).

Before treading deeper into this morass, let us first reiterate components of the analysis by Pasha and Blaney in their aptly titled evaluation of GCS, 'Elusive Paradise'. In it, they argue that while both GCS developments and the discourse related to it are part and parcel of the globalization of economic and social relations, these relations are rarely conceptualized in the context of 'the unequal and alienated relationships of capitalism'.[9] Proponents of GCS, they contend, tend to see it as an almost autonomous process, somehow removed from and in opposition to the state system.

Martin Shaw, for one, views GCS developments as a response to the failings of states. According to Shaw, a struggle is underway 'between the instincts of statesmen to maintain the principles of sovereignty and non-intervention, and the pressure from global civil society to transcend them'.[10] Richard Falk conceptualizes globalization as taking place in opposition to the state system. 'Territorial sovereignty,' according to Falk, 'is being diminished on a spectrum of issues in such a serious manner as to subvert the capacity of states to control and protect the internal life of society, and non-state actors hold an increasing proportion of power and influence in the shaping of world order.'[11]

Outside the disciplinary purview of international relations, post-structuralists inspired by Hardt and Negri's book, *Empire*, take the GCS argument to another, more obtuse level. For them, the Westphalian inter-state system is collapsing under the weight of both neoliberal reforms and even more weighty (and seemingly uncontrollable) transnational flows of people, information and wealth. For the political left, so-called class-based 'master narratives' are being replaced by less dichotomous struggles. As such, and in light of the assumed ascendancy of intellectual and immaterial workers networking through the Internet and related ICTs, the global has become the new focus of resistance. Empowered through the very technologies developed by capital to widen and deepen its exploitative relationships, this multitude of heterogeneous interests supposedly will become capitalism's antidote. In this regard, a metaphor used by Deleuze and Guattari – the 'rhizome' – has been put to use.[12] As with a plant's subterranean growth and horizontal development, the multitude now is said to be organizing against capitalism in ways that reflect a 'molecular revolution', undermining the hierarchical, the constant and the seemingly eternal as represented by and through the state. Importantly, the 'empire' being resisted is not one led by an overarching hegemon (such as the United States); it is a post-modern world of domination that transcends nation states.

Globalization or developments associated with it, because they undermine the power of states, supposedly reveal sovereignty to be little more than a 'metaphysical' concept. Likewise, national interests and identities – mythological outgrowths of now declining statist arrangements – similarly are doomed. The response from progressives seeking a more just, environmentally sustainable world is thus the multitude's rhizomatic resistance through the auspices of a global justice movement – a movement like no other in terms of its geographic scope and political-cultural diversity.[13]

While the assumption that nation state power, sovereignty and, thus, the international state system are in irretrievable decline is dubious (as explained below and elsewhere), the strategic assumption that the global now constitutes the most important and democratic site of resistance is a notion riddled with ahistorical miscalculations. As Ursula Huws has documented, assumptions as to the growing predominance of intellectual and non-material forms of labour, and thus capitalism's contradictory reliance on prospectively empowering ICTs, is empirically and logically questionable.[14] Moreover, as discussed in Chapter 2, assumptions that information (or, in Hardt and Negri's terms, the networking multitude) is straightforwardly the prerequisite of more accurate and thoughtful modes of knowledge ignores, among other things, the crucial role played by conceptual systems.

Let us dig deeper. Global justice movement activists and theorists, because they understand the Westphalian system to be a social construction (which, of course, it is), assume that its 'reality' is disposable. The reader will note the rather fantastic leap taken from premise to strategic conclusion. Not only does this approach ignore the structured history of states as power-laden institutions (ones still monopolizing, as Weber recognized, the use of violence), terminating this history by simply organizing and acting as if 'its days are numbered' may work if the subject of reform is an individual's mindset (as proselytized by self-empowerment gurus ranging from Oprah Winfrey to Anthony Robbins), but its effect on the structures of capitalism – involving sovereign nation states – surely is limited. Indeed, this 'strategic' perspective has produced poor results. Given years of declining union organization and, tactically, the retreat of domestically focused class-based political activities, the growth of both social-economic disparities and the globalization of environmental neglect constitute empirical outcomes that have been depressingly predictable.

Seeing states as both irrevocably in decline *and*, paradoxically, as the world's primary orchestrators of oppression reveals more than just an absence of sociological precision; it ignores past and contemporary examples of states as nodal points of wealth redistribution, civil rights protections and even, in some cases, concerted efforts to resist injustices and atrocities. Of course state sovereignty is the historical outcome of capitalism's ascent (as explained below) but this in itself does not mean that states are the antithesis of social justice and democracy.

Given such poorly reasoned assumptions, at the very least, this state system–GCS dichotomy needs to be reassessed. For instance, the notion that the political characteristics and capacities of any form of civil society are comprehensible in the absence of a developed notion of historically structured power relations itself gives us reason to pause. This is especially the case given the importance of conceptual systems and, as this book has elaborated, the third face of power. At a minimum, then, we need to address GCS and the claims made by globalization theorists in light of, to quote Susan Strange, 'the power to decide how things shall be done'.[15] To do this, the political economic context of GCS developments needs to be elaborated.

Historically, prior to the ascendancy of capitalist relations in Europe, political sovereignty – the sovereignty of the feudal lord – was directly and explicitly implicated in the process of surplus extraction. Political inequalities thus were formalized as legal and even cultural norms. For economic production and social reproduction to take place in feudal and most other non-capitalist societies, political power was exercised through *relatively unmediated* structures; capitalism, in contrast, is characterized by more complex, *relatively mediated* power relations (see Chapter 3).

Having said this, we would do well to avoid defining sovereignty in terms of the practical ability of the state to command the behaviour of citizens relative to non-state or extraterritorial agents. Nor should state sovereignty be viewed as simply some kind of residual legal authority. Instead, it is far more useful to define sovereignty as the social form of the state in a society where *political power is formally divided between public and private spheres*. Through this definitional clarification we are compelled to recognize the complexity that is the state–civil society dynamic. Crucially, it also provides relief to the shallowness and distorting effects of debates concerning the contemporary state and its 'strengths' and 'weaknesses' in the face of globalization.[16]

In the absence of this historical context and definitional accuracy, it is little wonder that GCS progressives have been free to assume globalization itself to be some kind of new and autonomous phenomenon – one implying the declining authority of states. But more than this, we should recall that the third dimension of power and conceptual systems affect *all* human beings, even critical intellectuals. As discussed below, capitalist consumption's penchant for ahistorical and individualistic thinking surely constitutes an under assessed variable in this myopic chapter of intellectual history. How else to explain why facts such as the actual *growth* in sovereign states (rather than their decline) has taken place despite the state's postulated fall? And how else to explain the selective amnesia concerning historical parallels to contemporary globalization?

In the nineteenth century, for example, a seismic eruption of globalized relations occurred, organized through the economic, cultural and military leadership of the British state. Yet, as Rosenberg points out, 'nobody, apparently, argues that this transnationalisation of British society challenged the sovereignty or territoriality of the Victorian English state. And yet, if it did not, on what precise grounds should the continued expansion of transnational relations today be expected to undermine the sovereign form of the states-system?'.[17] Additionally, we might remind ourselves that the use of technologies and other methods to integrate and speed-up worldwide political, economic and cultural relations is not new either. For Marx, writing about capitalist relations about one-hundred-and-fifty years ago, a universalizing tendency was apparent which, from his perspective, involved both increasing the pace of the production process[18] and de-territorializing nations and cultures through commodification. But unlike contemporary theorists, Marx did not 'explain' this time–space compression as itself the outcome of time–space compression; instead, he traced it to the historical structuring of human relations and the social dynamics these relations generated.[19]

While qualifications that globalization today is different than the globalization of yesterday are debatable, 'What if,' Rosenberg asks, 'the notion of an ultimately contradictory relationship between sovereignty and transnational relations, that *sine qua non* of Globalization Theory, was itself simply wrong?'[20] Perhaps what is generally called globalization isn't really new? Perhaps the nation state isn't in decline. Perhaps the state's role and capabilities are simply changing (possibly back to what they generally were before the Second World War).

In light of these possibilities, an alternative explanation is the one implied throughout this book – that globalization is not itself an *explanans*; instead, the globalization project is the latest juncture in a long history of generally accelerating inter-dependencies and abstract interactions traceable back to sixteenth-century England. In this regard, the assumed 'decline' of the state constitutes not much more than its reorganization *back* to earlier norms of state–civil society relations. Given the shock of the Great Depression and the tangible counterforce to capitalism that was the USSR, Keynesian welfare provisions in retrospect may have been temporary necessities – in effect, dampening prospectively anti-status quo sentiments in 'developed' political economies. Organized labour, for instance, shifted its focus away from having collective power at the point of production and towards the participation of its constituents in the realm consumption. With the collapse of the Soviet Union and, along with it, state socialism itself, classical state–society relations could re-emerge with neoclassical economic theory as its guide.[21]

Under these conditions the globalization project could take flight. This 'back-to-the-future' transformation involved, among other structural reforms, a massive retreat of post-1945 stat*ist* policies but not the state itself.[22] In fact, states have been and continue to be the authors – or, more accurately, the essential mediators – of the globalization project. As Leo

Panitch has documented, even the World Bank does not view itself (nor other international organizations for that matter) as substitutes for the nation state; rather, its officials believe it is their job to push forward the neoliberal restructuring of states in such a way that, according to the Bank, 'a mechanism *for countries* to make ... commitments [is *instituted*], making it more difficult to back-track on reforms'.[23]

Into the vacuum of state socialism's collapse – and, with it, hundreds of millions of people quite suddenly entering the global workforce for relatively low wages – capitalist interests quickly organized. Western governments, still reeling in the aftermath of the post-1973 'stagflation' recession, generally were accommodating. This turn of events bolstered efforts to lower inflation by neutering unions and their ability to earn higher wages and protect jobs. Also, to encourage the development and dissemination of ICTs (technologies seen to be necessary by corporations seeking to exploit communism's collapse, enabling them to increase production process efficiencies and 'flexibilities' both domestically and abroad), technology-related laws and regulations were reformed, bringing unprecedented growth and competition into the fields of telecommunications and informatics. Led by the United States, 'developed' countries impelled 'developing' nations to enter into new trade agreements, culminating in the WTO. Theoretically, these were designed to promote the principle of 'comparative advantage': more substantively, they would, first, lower production costs; second, secure capital's access to raw materials as well as needed workers; and, third, expand consumer markets. Finally, through these state-mediated and state-enforced arrangements, intellectual property rights were won overseas, facilitating the so-called information economy and its rapid development.

In the context of this acceleration of long-standing capitalist dynamics, the post-Cold War vacuum was filled, informed by neoliberal policies whose implementation involved a range of responses from generally weakened, culturally atomized workers. Prognostications that 'the end of history'[24] had arrived and that a new world order was nigh thus were understandable. 'Globalization', as a neat way of summarizing these complex forces and, importantly, as a tidy means of bringing some certainty to a period characterized by much uncertainty,[25] soon was conceptually embraced or grudgingly accepted by left and right, conservatives and radicals. Nevertheless, as Rosenberg demonstrates, 'No new form of society was emerging – rather, *the organic tendencies of the old were now reasserting themselves, in a new situation, and on an historically unprecedented scale.*'[26]

ICTs, identities and the GCS delusion

According to the *Oxford English Dictionary*, to delude is to 'cause to accept foolishly a false or mistaken belief'. Indeed, believing that some kind of progressive GCS is almost naturally unfolding, assuming that states are little more than the disintegrating real or metaphysical tools of capitalist exploiters, concocting metaphors and prioritizing them over empirical evidence and logical argument, all reflect delusions that obfuscate the historical realities at hand. In this section, we move forward by re-focusing our critique, examining the role of ICTs in prospective GCS developments and, more particularly, their assumed implications in the shaping of identity.

Capitalist relations, once structured into society and international relations through a range of media (from the nation state system to corporations, from private property to consumption), compel more than just economic growth; capitalism also generates a dynamic that promotes increasing efficiencies in production, distribution, exchange and consumption. ICTs clearly constitute both tools of this dynamic and, through complex cultural processes, material manifestations of capitalist society's prioritization of spatial expansion and control (as in accessing and managing resources, workers and consumers) as well as temporal immediacy, efficiency and, for the individual consumer, 'freedom' and convenience.[27] From the latter's perspective, few contemporary applications more clearly illustrate this than personal communication devices such as the BlackBerry and iPod.

As its maker's website puts it, 'Every BlackBerry device offers the freedom and connectivity of an all-in-one mobile phone, email device, web browser and organizer.'[28] Advertising and marketing firms now see such devices as perhaps the most important vehicles for the growth of their businesses and as the means through which corporations can establish and maintain potentially lifelong 'relationships' with individuals; marketing practitioners, for instance, now talk about establishing a 'meaningful' and engaging 'dialogue' with customers.[29] Instant and universal personal communications, funnelling individuals into an endless array of commodified activities, is fast becoming the norm of daily life, at least for the relatively wealthy.

Similarly, *Apple's* iPod is chiefly a music device that also can be used to view photographs and play podcasts. The next step for these personal technologies is *Apple's* iPhone (and subsequent devices from other companies), which enables consumers to do virtually any telecommunications task. Beyond their use as devices that keep people electronically inter-linked with others at all hours and in all locations (particularly to and through corporate interests), the proliferation of these technologies underscores the predominance of cultures now made up of supposedly 'unique individuals' whose immediate gratification interests are routinely catered to. *Apple,* marketing the iPod as the ultimate means of expressing one's individuality (presumably as a result of its capacity to store thousands of one's favourite songs), for example, takes the technology's reification one step further: the purchaser can get a personally selected laser-engraved message forged onto his/her iPod, presumably as a means of making the machine a 'one-of-a-kind'.

Note the paradoxes at play here. The iPod (at least in 2007) has become a 'must have' commodity, especially among the relatively young. Its fashionableness – that is, its *mass* appeal – is the outcome of its use as a means of *individualizing* people – a result of a demand both to belong to one's commercial culture *and* to forge and maintain a unique identity within it. Deepening the fact that the individual now finds or reaffirms his/her identity through (and, has become socially and psychologically dependent upon) a mass market commodity is the engraved message component of the purchase. Ask any 18-year-old if it's okay to get one's iPod engraved by a third party – presumably in line with the engraving's purpose to forge the commodity's uniqueness – and the response almost certainly will be 'absolutely not'. For most, only *Apple's* signature font and lasering technique will do. To etch in a personal message using any other means would almost render the iPod in question and, more pointedly, its owner, a laughing stock.[30]

Note also the iPod's status as a 'must have' neo-modernist commodity. Rather than the means of attaining a social or psychological need (as with modern consumption), the iPod and other such devices *themselves* have become social-psychological destinations. Simply owning this mass market, corporate produced commodity tells everyone and oneself both, 'I belong' *and* 'I am unique'.

To reiterate a core point made in previous chapters, capitalist consumption, in the context of modernist and neo-modernist culture, has become the core institutional means through which the universal need for meaning and identity are pursued and 'found'. But as Don Slater observes, 'The danger in consumer culture is its ability to offer false satisfactions to real needs ... These needs themselves become false when they are experienced as needs for more commodities rather than less alienation, unfreedom, injustice.'[31] Personal communication devices, more obviously but altogether in line with the contemporary world of commodities *writ large*, are desired precisely because they serve the social-psychological needs that exist in people (particularly in 'developed' political economies) to feel that they both know themselves and belong in relation to others. Marketers and advertisers have been aware of this for at least half a century and have progressively colonized the spaces and times of our lives with associations that link commodities with existential questions. ICTs generally, and personal communication devices more particularly, are used to pursue this agenda. 'The distance between the aesthetic illusions of the commodity and the needs of people in an alienated society make the thirst for commodities insatiable ... [absorbing] the individual through his or her psychic structure ever deeper into the system.'[32]

*   *   *

To assess the implications of this pernicious cycle in terms of an emerging global civil society or global consumer society, we need to revisit earlier discussions regarding conceptual systems (Chapter 2). In its most tangible form, GCS can be viewed as a transnational community in which legal norms, codes of conduct and even social mores transcend and stand above the sovereign authority of individual states. The idea of a global citizenship based on 'globalization from above' in which elites identify with one another and a theory of 'globalization from below' involving 'a growth of human solidarity arising from an extension of democratic principles' constitute polar extremes of what appears possible (at least among those embracing the delusion).[33] For GCS progressives, however, GCS holds at least the potential to universalize, and make politically accountable, basic standards of human rights, environmental protection and other such demands. Through an emerging consciousness characterized by nascent global communities and, hence, global identities, a more peaceful world is said to be on the horizon.

To repeat, for GCS theorists, information – and the process of its exchange – is thought to be inherently affecting. But implicit in this thinking is the simplistic understanding of the relationship of information to knowledge critiqued earlier – the relationship of what is communicated with what is known. GCS proponents, for the most part, tend to treat information and knowledge as if they are one and the same. Emerging transnational associations, facilitated by eroding technological and cultural barriers, involving a broad range of people exchanging information, are seen to be the bases of nothing short of a transformation of consciousness into 'global' ways of knowing.[34] The Internet, for example, is perhaps the core technology through which information will transform the ways in which people understand both the world and their identities in it. Since the Internet enables people to exchange information instantaneously and at relatively low costs, more people will share and be exposed to more information. More precisely, this belief that significant improvements in electronic communications lead to improvements in the lot of humanity involves the assumption that, according to Nancy Stefanik, 'all the world's residents ... [will] learn from each other'.[35]

A more guarded optimism – avoiding this kind of borderline technological determinism – can be found in the work of other GCS theorists. Richard Falk, for one, understands that the Internet is being used by a range of interests, including actors representing the aspirations of transnational corporations. Rather than endorsing ICTs as tools for democracy, corporations instead generally use them to promote a disciplined and malleable workforce, as well as new and loyal consumers; nevertheless, for Falk, the Internet also constitutes a medium of potential emancipation. In the hands of progressive activists, the 'World Wide Web allows for an empowerment of globalization-from-below in a manner that seems presently difficult to subdue or ignore'.[36]

Falk's *general point* is correct. From the much-cited Zapatista movement in Mexico to the less well-known resistance efforts of the James Bay Cree

Indians in northern Quebec to the networking of a range of interests leading to the anti-WTO protests in Seattle in 1999, many examples can be cited
to illustrate the utilization of new technologies in support of a range of progressive activities.[37] But although the Internet, the BlackBerry and other
such technologies have largely annihilated the spatial and temporal barriers
of electronic forms of communication, the assumption that these break-
throughs also are facilitating a historically significant *qualitative* transformation in *how people think* clearly requires more investigation.

What is missing in many accounts of how technologies are shaping
prospective GCS developments are assessments of precisely *how* information
modifies interpersonal and intercultural understandings, identities and
realities. To take this point one step further, the very logic used to prognos-
ticate a cosmopolitan, and even progressive GCS, is essentially the same as
that used in anticipation of a far more disturbing future. The concept of
cultural imperialism, for example, brought into prominence through the
political activism of mostly Third World governments calling for a 'New
World Information and Communication Order', beginning in the late
1960s, involved similar assumptions.[38] In the literature associated with this
movement, telecommunications satellites and other developments involving information technologies and transnational communications were
directly associated with the interests of giant corporations and their Northern
nation state benefactors.[39] Given the interests and structural conditions shaping the implementation and use of these technologies, critical theorists and
activists assumed that more information crossing borders would produce a
world characterized by ever-growing consumer appetites, pro-free market
ideologies and, ultimately, a consent-based form of American hegemony.[40]

This perspective remains an important framework for many students of
the political economy of communication.[41] For them, the opening up of
national borders for commercial interests is viewed as a contributing factor
in the relative commercialization of the public sphere and the ascendancy
of neoliberal regulatory regimes. Private corporations and states who accommodate or promote their own interests are chiefly responsible for encouraging quite the opposite of the cosmopolitan global citizen envisioned by GCS
progressives; instead, these forces will stimulate the predominance of acritical and perhaps anti-intellectual thinking. Even the Internet, because of the
dominance of private sector interests in its development, is far more likely
to promote a global consumer society than some kind of harmonious global
civil society.[42]

As with the optimism in the writings of many GCS proponents, a central
problem that emerges from this pessimistic perspective stems from the for-
mula that information *is* knowledge. But people are not intellectual sponges.
The information we receive – whether it is an advertisement promising happiness through consumption or an email from an NGO comrade involved in
a human rights campaign – does not always (or straightforwardly) become an

ingrained part of one's own 'reality'. In response, GCS theorists might argue that this comparison is inappropriate. After all, the interactive qualities of new ICTs facilitate a circumvention of status quo mass media and its messages. Unlike, for example, the transnational direct broadcast satellite systems being planned in the 1970s, the Internet-based technologies of the twenty-first century enable people to be directly involved in constructing their global identities. In other words, new technologies facilitate globalization 'from below' because, for the first time, people, rather than states or corporations, control the flow and exchange of information.

Again, this way of looking at things too readily equates information with knowledge, and far more analytical rigour is needed before we can embrace such rosy predictions. Information and experience are mediated into what is known using learned, inter-subjective and implicitly power-laden conceptual systems. These conceptual systems are forged through socialization processes that involve our direct relationships with people and our indirect relationships with media (including technologies). The implications of this are elaborated in the pages that follow. For now, suffice it to say that, *experientially*, the ICTs emerging to mediate daily life for most of the world's well off – technologies such as the BlackBerry, iPod and iPhone (and their descendents) – surely mark the ascent of a more atomized consumerist culture rather than a collectivist global citizen.

GCS's more sophisticated proponents

One GCS theorist who has escaped the limitations of empiricism is Ronnie Lipschutz. In his support of the argument made by James Rosenau – that world populations are becoming more analytically astute and thus politically capable[43] – Lipschutz writes that

> It is not the contact [i.e. the communication of information] itself but the ability to use data as *knowledge* that is the critical element – data are the electronic bits transmitted by communication systems; knowledge involves having the skills to use the data toward specific ends. The relevant skills have been spread, perhaps unwittingly, by the growth of post-secondary educational institutions around the world, as well as by changes in the world economy. Because political systems are so diverse, the particular channels of articulation of this new competence vary from one country to the next. However, the general effect is one of the creation of networks of global political activity in parallel to the state system.[44]

Elsewhere, Lipschutz goes beyond this focus on 'skills' and acknowledges the role of culture and local experience in shaping how people come to understand their world.[45] In his writing on changes in the meaning of nature, for instance, he recognizes that interpretations of what 'whale' or 'forest' mean will usually differ between someone whose livelihood is directly related to them and a person brought up and working in other contexts. However, he goes on to argue that these infrastructures need not necessarily determine how people interpret information.[46] Larger or external cultural forces can intervene 'via various channels of information' and can, he says, modify 'the meaning of *self* in relation to place'.[47] He theorizes the information-to-knowledge process in terms of what he calls 'social learning' and, borrowing from Peter Haas, argues that the processing of information involves socially learned 'understandings about cause-and-effect linkages'.[48]

Beyond this instrumentalism (informed by the assumption that people process information in accordance with their perceived interests), Lipschutz understands human knowledge to be both more complex and varied:

> Every human society has its own system of beliefs (myths, norms, rules), social relations, and production practices that form a single, more-or-less coherent framework ... Within each one's framework, these beliefs, relations, and practices must operate in a regular fashion if the overall fabric of the society is to remain intact and be reproduced over time.[49]

Thus, human beings do not process information into what is known in necessarily 'rational' or instrumental ways; instead, mediating conceptual systems are shaped by family socialization, lifestyle, work experiences, customs and mythologies – *by dynamically structured cultural characteristics that reflect and affect the third face of power*. In the contemporary era of globalization, involving instantaneous transnational communications, Lipschutz believes that such personal and local predilections are being increasingly 'influenced by knowledge and practices originating elsewhere'.[50] A continuous struggle between the global and the local is underway and this, he says, is in part due to the relevance and resilience of local cultures.

In sum, Lipschutz thinks that what we know is ultimately a process of the mind. Thus, what shapes this process is of crucial importance if we are to assess the transformative implications of ICTs. He concludes that, as a result of globalization and related communication (and transportation) developments, new forms of collective identity are emerging.[51] He believes that, ultimately, transnational networks of knowledge and practice will transcend significant aspects of the state system.[52]

Martin Shaw is also optimistic about a prospective GCS. Shaw bases his prognostications on a dialectical approach, as does Lipschutz; yet, perhaps more so than Lipschutz, Shaw bases his optimism on what may be described as a more functionalist argument. While the complex and often contradictory dynamics of globalization will, for Shaw, generate environmental, cultural and economic crises, 'it is through such crises that we can increasingly identify global society and the development of its institutions'[53] – through, for instance, the 'global coordination of communications ... [,] ideas and values ... become increasingly commonly held'.[54] Conflict in this emerging configuration of shared realities is the precondition to an eventual integration of people sharing common global interests. Indeed,

> the conflictual aspects of diversity, where cultural differentiation is linked to political conflict, can be seen under the rubric of global integration. Conflict sharpens awareness of mutual dependence and promotes the development of common responses and institutions for regulation, which in turn involve cultures of cooperation.[55]

Unlike Lipshutz, but like many GCS progressives, Shaw substantiates his optimism by relying on what is essentially an empiricist notion of how information is processed into knowledge. A growing awareness of global injustice and environmental degradation, forged mostly through non-state communication networks, somehow will lead to a shared sense of global responsibility. But again, to assess such claims, we need to examine more than just what information is being exchanged, who is involved and how its communication is taking place. We also must assess those factors conditioning conceptual systems amidst the globalization project and, more precisely, the role of transnational, national and local communication in relation to this conditioning.[56]

Before proceeding, a few words regarding Falk's book, *Predatory Globalization*, are warranted in relation to these conditioning factors.[57] As mentioned above, the optimism expressed by Falk is tempered by his awareness that any progressive transformation will entail a political struggle against vested interests possessing significant resources. Indeed, those seeking a 'people-oriented' form of globalization are largely limited to 'guiding [the] ideas' that underlie how globalization is being structured – a development, for the most part, being driven by corporate-based interests.[58]

Of course, as Falk himself recognizes, there are specific exceptions to this general tendency. Ronald J. Deibert, for one, has investigated the use of the Internet to enable transnational lobbying networks opposing the Multilateral Agreement on Investments.[59] Richard Price, similarly, on the subject of international security norms related to landmines, has documented the process in which Internet-based networks have facilitated the kinds of communities and discourses needed to modify (or, using his term, 're-socialise') state policies.[60] But these examples, praiseworthy as they are, and the many other studies emphasizing the importance of such networks in support of progressive interests, are not our primary concern here. Instead, our argument is that the ahistorical and dichotomous treatment of civil society–state relations, the generalizations made as a result of this conceptual starting point (not to mention defining state sovereignty ahistorically) and the general absence of power concerns related to either historical structures or mediating conceptual systems render the GCS/'globalization theory' perspective something of a delusion.

From delusion to the reality of illusion

In critiquing the notion of a dawning and progressive GCS, we now proceed to explain the prospects of an alternate future – a future dominated by illusory realities mediated by capitalist consumption.

To reiterate, the prognostications of GCS progressives and those who, instead, anticipate some form of globalization 'from above' entail assumptions regarding the annihilation of temporal and spatial barriers. With the removal of these through ICTs, human beings, it is assumed, can develop identities that are as affiliated with 'the global' as with 'the national' or even 'the local'. Shared information and mostly mediated 'virtual' experiences will generate conceptual systems that are relatively inclusive and cosmopolitan. Information involving environmental crises, human rights abuses, economic disparities and other issues will be increasingly interpreted in terms of the global commonweal rather than the problems of distant 'others'.

Arguably, the foundational theorist shaping such perspectives is Anthony Giddens.[61] According to Giddens, globalization is an extension of modernization in that it involves what he refers to as the process of time–space distanciation. Through the use of new technologies, conceptions of time and space are becoming increasingly removed from the here-and-now. It is in this sense that social relations are being established and maintained in ways that are removed from local contexts.[62] As Giddens summarizes,

> we live 'in the world' in a different sense from previous eras of history. Everyone still continues to live a local life, and the constraints of the body ensure that all individuals, at every moment, are contextually situated in time and space. Yet the transformation of place, and the intrusion of distance into local activities, combined with the centrality of mediated experience, radically change what 'the world' actually is.[63]

As with all forms of knowledge, conceptions of time and space, while always related to the here-and-now, are understood through the mediation of conceptual systems. In the absence of the capacity to process information into ways of knowing that accommodate global identities, any form of global citizenship – and its implications – would be *impossible*. How then can we evaluate the probable effects and wide scale use of contemporary time–space annihilating ICTs on conceptual systems? Although there can not be a universally applicable answer to this, we think it is safe to say (especially following Chapter 2) that while the information gathered through various transnational media may have some effect in modifying conceptual systems, the information garnered through early-life socialization and day-to-day experience warrant existential priority.[64]

At one level, this distinction between the effects of here-and-now versus long-distance communication can be simplified in terms of the direct versus indirect (that is, *relatively mediated*) qualities of each. Of course, to repeat points made earlier, there is no such thing as a human relationship that is unmediated. Socialization, cultural context and, of course, conceptual systems are employed in the mediation and construction of reality. Different relationships are *qualitatively* different and a distinction should be made between those involving communications that are *relatively direct* and those that are *relatively indirect*. At the core of this difference lies the relative (but not absolute) importance of face-to-face relationships in the formation and shaping of conceptual systems.

This is not to say that thousands of hours of ICT-mediated activities do not affect conceptual systems. Nor is it to say that Giddens and GCS progressives are entirely wrong in their claims about the transformative implications of time–space distanciation. We are arguing, instead, that *our more mediated relationships have a relatively limited influence*. Transnational communications simply cannot, by themselves, directly stimulate the kind of progressive global community anticipated by most GCS theorists; instead, such relatively mediated forms of communication are more important in that they indirectly affect *lifestyles*.

An awareness of how others live undoubtedly opens conceptual doors and these have facilitated (but have not in themselves determined) the formulation of innumerable cultural hybrids. But there are, of course, material limits to such lifestyle possibilities. As John Tomlinson observes, 'such lifestyle choices are made within an experiential context that remains, in important ways, stubbornly local'.[65] Briefly put, *local relationships tend to prescribe the context through which global influences are potentially adopted and understood, and transnational communications can, over time, modify this context by influencing changes in lifestyle that, in turn, affect conceptual systems.*

The importance of changing lifestyles is not completely ignored in the GCS literature; for example, transnational communications have been associated with a growing awareness of those (mostly indigenous peoples') lifestyles that appear to be in some state of harmony with the natural environment. Lipschutz, for instance, argues that even in a community that depends on the exploitation of the environment for its livelihood, an awareness of other lifestyles can challenge long-standing practices. This, however, involves more than the straightforward reception of information and its adoption into personal knowledge; modifications in 'everyday worldviews and practices' also are involved.[66] This emphasis on awareness facilitating changes in lifestyles that then modify conceptual systems, from an analytical perspective, is far more palatable and useful than the notion of information itself directly reshaping consciousness.[67]

At the risk of our approach being labelled 'essentialist', how we live is *relatively* more affecting than what we read, see or hear in shaping the conceptual systems used to process information and experience into what is known. In relation to this, information from afar can and does affect how people live their lives and, indeed, the gathering of such information and interaction with others around the world through new technologies may constitute a significant aspect of one's life. But having said this, the conceptual systems through which information is processed into knowledge are themselves most directly the expressions of 'ways of life' that are inescapably rooted in personal history and material realities. As such, the act of doing more work, spending more leisure time or engaging in more politics online – in communicating with others across spatial and temporal barriers – is generally most affecting in so far as it involves changing how lives are lived from day-to-day.[68]

As noted previously, many GCS theorists point to the inter-active and potentially universal qualities of ICTs, enabling groups and individuals to form their own meaningful networks, thereby circumscribing status quo (including state system) conceptualizations of reality. At one level, this general perspective underplays the ongoing role of states in setting and regulating the parameters of what communications technologies are made available and to whom.[69] Furthermore, efforts to promote ICTs and information-laden commodities have been led mostly by large-scale commercial interests rather than by NGOs, indigenous peoples, or the working class, and, for the most part, have unfolded in the structural context of marketplace dynamics. The widespread adoption of 'personalised' technologies, for example, arguably constitutes a reflection of historically structured cultural norms (in which we are self-serving, ever-consuming individuals) while perpetuating these characteristics through everyday practices. Rather than being used to liberate individuals from status quo communications, for most – particularly those lacking either the knowledge, time or incomes needed to escape the embrace of large-scale service providers (the dominance of *Google* being only one of the most recent) – such technologies may well deepen existing dependencies and, more essentially, be used in efforts to entrench already pervasive conceptual systems.

The Internet, for example, is fast becoming a transnational inter-active marketplace of mostly sensual come-ons and commercial opportunities – a far cry from its promise to become a truly democratic forum for the exchange of information. Of course this latter use is still with us and is unlikely to vanish. But given the rate of its commercialization and the persistent (if not growing) disparities in world income and technological capacity, the predominance of capitalist political economic structures and dynamics point to the very opposite cultural developments of those anticipated by GCS progressives. Not only is the experience of relating to others in cyberspace qualitatively different from meeting in a coffee shop, pub or union hall, when information is thought of and treated as little more than a commodity, national and international laws and regulations tend to treat publics as consumers rather than citizens.[70]

Politically, in recent decades, the consumer, as an agent conflated with the rights and actions of the citizen, has become the primary instigator of change for many liberals, feminists, social democrats and other progressives.[71] The post-Cold War turn to post-structuralism among critical scholars has reflected and furthered this tendency. For example, previous concerns regarding US/Western cultural imperialism have now been overshadowed by academic arguments vaunting the ability of people to make their own meaningful interpretations of commercial media. Others celebrate how corporate commodities have sometimes been used in ways that reflect, it is assumed, the resilience and even the autonomy of local or indigenous cultures.[72] Consequently, marketers and advertisers, pleading their 'innocence', now have legions of left-leaning allies whose work at least implicitly supports the myth of consumer sovereignty. As cultural studies scholar John Clarke observes, 'The effect, ironically, is to replicate that view of capitalism which capitalism would most like us to see: the richness of the marketplace and freely choosing consumer.'[73]

Of course, as discussed, capitalist consumption does entail genuine choice, freedom and even the exercising of power; in fact, its role as an institutional mediator of hegemonic order involves this directly. But on closer inspection, in light of our understanding of capitalist consumption as a historically structured institution and our awareness of conceptual systems, the parameters of this 'sovereignty' are materially and sociologically limited. More importantly in light of GCS idealists and proponents of the networked multitude, this post-structuralist orientation has tangible implications. 'It both reflects and adds to the shift towards consuming individualism,' writes Clarke, 'and away from the realm of collective, public and political agency ...'[74]

International organizations established or reformed along neoliberal lines have further entrenched the primacy of the consumer. Perhaps not coincidentally, the implicit or explicit treatment of people as individual consumers rather than citizens provides transnational capitalist interests with more clout in the realm of public policy; certainly more that they otherwise would have had had nationally defined priorities emphasizing class organization and civic engagement remained dominant. In political struggles framed in terms of national rather than consumer sovereignty, governments are sometimes mobilized at the expense of corporations. Democratic politics, conducted through the still relatively influential institutional mechanisms of nation states (including elections, referenda and constitutional rights), sometimes make private sector activities more accountable. In effect, the globalization project, GCS strategies and 'globalization theory' more generally have variously undermined post-1945 cultural norms regarding the efficacy of national struggles.[75]

As Barber puts it, 'Nowadays, the idea that only private persons are free, and that only personal choices of the kind consumers make count as autonomous, turns out to be an assault not on tyranny but on democracy. It challenges not the ... power by which tyrants once ruled ... but the legitimate power by which we try to rule ourselves in common.'[76] One reason for this is the fact that asking the question 'what do I want?' as a consumer or as a citizen constitutes two very different things. For the consumer, this question and one's answer to it usually involves relatively selfish, short-term decisions. For the citizen, 'what do I want?' instead entails relatively collective, long-term calculations. As a consumer, I may want to drive a car. As a citizen, I may not want my city to be congested with carbon dioxide emissions. As a consumer, I may welcome *Wal-Mart's* low prices. As a worker, I may recoil at *Wal-Mart's* influence on wages and tendency to seek out extraordinarily exploitative manufacturers. Through the institutionalization of capitalist consumption and its structuring of consciousness through conceptual systems, such citizen or class-based questions are being pushed to the cultural periphery or are themselves increasingly framed within the individualistic and immediate-gratification parameters of a consumerist mindset.[77]

The optimism of most GCS progressives should be tempered for yet another reason. Contemporary developments in transnational communications are being led and increasingly dominated by private sector interests whose profit-making priorities are most influential in determining both who will use new technologies and what they will be used for.[78] As a result, the people most likely to participate in non-commercial transnational communications are the relatively wealthy and educated. Simply put, poverty constitutes the most obvious barrier in efforts to communicate, let alone fundamentally reshape conceptual systems.

Even in the absence of commercial structures and individualistic immediate gratification conceptual systems, generally speaking, the various interests taking advantage of new technologies may be limited in their efforts to involve mass audiences for lengthy periods of time. Such sustained dialogues are probably needed if significant modifications in lifestyles and, subsequently, conceptual systems are to take place. As Robert Fortner writes, 'Discourse is not increased by such a system. It is channeled and is specialised: it is not enabled, but enfeebled. People are empowered to preach, but only to their own choirs ... The excess of information has the effect of reducing social inclusion even as it increases interest-based communion.'[79]

Putting aside the consumption-induced emphasis on ever-changing, fashionable issues, the kinds of information exchanges foreseen by GCS progressives are unlikely to take place on anything approaching the global or temporal scales envisioned. Concerns over the disparate availability of communications technologies (that is, the so-called 'digital divide') as conveyed, for instance, by some international organizations (ranging from the United Nations to the World Bank) are secondary to the actual potentials that these technologies have in influencing how people conceptualize themselves, their realities, and thus what is 'imaginable'. Given both the political economy of their development and relatively *un*mediated forms of communication that more fundamentally affect conceptual systems, the prospects for a progressive GCS forged through some kind of globalization 'from below' appears depressingly remote. Moreover, as Pasha and Blaney see it, if ever realized, the GCS unfolding likely would feature 'relatively shallow, passive, and/or exploitative selves, oblivious to deeper social purposes and relationships and committed to inequality and domination as aspects of their personalities and 'social' commitments'.[80]

Historically, citizens rights and capabilities largely have been determined by struggles concerning the first, second and third faces of power much more than just access to information and communication resources, although the latter undoubtedly has facilitated or retarded the former. Capacities involving wealth, institutional access and socialization surely remain central in the structuring of democracies. In the context of contemporary trajectories and abstractions, a GCS driven forward by a progressive global citizenry thus would clearly involve a revolutionary re-casting of both international and global mediators as well as conceptual systems – conceptual systems now more firmly rooted in the soils of political economic inequality and commodified relationships than progressive transnational interactions.

Towards a different GCS

In anticipation of further assessing the role of consumption in 'developing' countries (Chapter 5), it is helpful to specify two systemic problems facing capitalist political economies. First, capitalists face the problem of generating an endless growth of commodity consumption. Simply put, the drive to improve the efficiencies of production (often involving the lowering of wages, adoption of new technologies and the outsourcing or relocation of jobs to low wage locales) can both lower prices *and* reduce the spending abilities of prospective consumers. Certainly the best-known example of this contradiction and the resulting crisis took place in Western economies in the 1930s. As a result of the general ability of commercial interests to limit rising wages – at the time involving the suppression of organized labour – prospective markets dissipated. Profits made through this widening gulf between productivity and wages inflated stock prices until the 'bubble' burst in 1929–30. Investors subsequently pulled capital out of the system while states, following classical economic theory, did virtually nothing to increase either demand or the money supply. The result was a general collapse of the economy.

In the absence of capital's collective organization through states, capitalism has little capacity to plan ahead and anticipate its own reproductive needs. In other words, capitalism, as a political economic system, cannot *itself* think; it needs people to do that. Left to itself, as Rosa Luxembourg observed, 'Capitalist production is primarily production by innumerable private producers without any planned regulation. The only social link between these producers is the act of exchange ... These experiences remain private, not integrated into a social form.'[81]

Another systemically generated macro-threat to capitalism stems from the compulsion among financial interests and corporations to find new 'investment opportunities' – opportunities needed to grow capital resources (itself a necessary compulsion in competitive market systems). Periodically, these are delimited and the result is another kind of crisis.

Rather than the direct outcome of people's inability to buy the commodities, this potential collapse stems from receding opportunities related to investment. Marxists generally call this a crisis of 'overaccumulation' – a phenomenon which David Harvey defines as 'a condition in which idle capital and idle labour supply ... exist side by side with no apparent way to bring these ... resources together to accomplish ... useful tasks ... [as] indicated by idle productive capacity, a glut in commodities and an excess of inventories ...'[82] To overcome such tendencies several temporary solutions are possible, including the option of devaluing production process inputs; in effect, lowering costs related to raw materials, labour power and other essential components in order to generate more investment and prospective profits. For capitalism to survive, more than just the perpetual growth of consumption is required. The political economy also needs, periodically, variously executed and often violent reorganizations, usually enforced through state-based authorities complicit in the task of lowering costs.

As Harvey elaborates in his book, *A Brief History of Neoliberalism*, the contemporary imposition of neoliberal policies began in earnest in the 1980s. In response to the insistence of US officials that OPEC member states, particularly Saudi Arabia, deposit their oil profits into New York-based financial firms (possibly compelled by threat of military invasion), American banks were awash in money seeking investment (namely, in so-called petrodollars). Through the auspices of the US Treasury and the IMF, outstanding loans originally made to Latin American states at 5 per cent interest rates, by the 1980s, were being paid back at rates often exceeding 16 per cent. Under these crippling conditions, Washington-led efforts to orchestrate domestic reforms in Mexico, Chile and other countries were pursued, setting the stage for the subsequent globalization project. To repeat, this was (and remains) a project driven forward by explicit efforts to significantly lower the costs of doing business and to expand profits – efforts increasingly involving resources and workers in 'developing' economies.[83]

The structuring of global capitalist relations, instigated in places by primitive accumulation and institutionalized through property rights, the wage labour contract and other mediators now are being promoted through the financial offices of the world's wealthiest countries.[84] One neglected component of this process is that the costs of effectively 'writing off' otherwise socially useful assets (including labour) generally transcend those that are measurable in terms of money. For example, in China, through its official promotion of capitalism (referred to by some as 'capitalist Leninism'), thousands of state-, township- and village-controlled enterprises have been privatized or shutdown altogether. In addition to shedding expenditures and welfare obligations associated with public works, vast pools of cheap labour have been made available to profit-seeking interests, lowering costs for domestic capitalists as well as foreign investors.

The vast majority of Chinese live in the countryside, but their numbers are shrinking. From 1995 to 2002, while the country's overall population grew 14 per cent, 9 per cent fewer people lived in rural China. Most left for urban centres in search of work. Reflecting the transformation of agriculture through capitalist enterprise (rather than the retreat of the agrarian economy more generally), the number of citizens labouring in the countryside remained roughly constant over these same years.[85] And while per capita wages have increased dramatically, particularly in cities, according to a study by Azizur Kahn, unemployment rates have risen:

> This was due to a dramatic fall in employment in state and collective enterprises, caused by their restructuring away from the past system of using employment as a concealed method of unemployment insurance. There has been a rapid increase in employment in private, foreign, joint-stock enterprises and self-employment categories; but these have not been fast enough to offset the fall in state and collective enterprises on a *per capita basis.*[86]

The greatest income disparities among workers in China are found between established residents and migrants. Most of the former still tend to be employed by firms directly or indirectly associated with the state while the latter usually work for private interests, often performing casual jobs.[87] Not surprisingly, given these low costs and labour 'flexibilities', China has been flooded with the foreign investment of corporate interests who then sell what their employees produce to foreign markets and relatively well off domestic consumers.[88] As of 2003, China surpassed the United States as the world's biggest recipient of direct foreign investment, receiving $53 billion.[89]

By 2015, it is estimated that half a billion Chinese will have been displaced from public sector and agrarian jobs. Most will relocate to urban centres where, as with people in England dating from the fifteenth century, they will be 'free' to enter into wage labour contracts.[90] Five hundred years ago in England and again today in the 'developing' world, the battering ram of primitive accumulation breaks down traditional ways of living and thinking, laying the groundwork for capitalist relations involving consumption. Through its imposition, what Marx called 'the commodity form' becomes the predominant way of structuring social interactions. In principle, under capitalism, all relations, activities and objects can be exchanged as commodities and, to repeat, this dynamic begins with private property and the commodification of labour. Through these state-mediated reforms, human beings are compelled to sell their labour as a commodity *and* consume commodities to survive.[91] The role of capitalist consumption as an institutionalized way of acting and thinking, and its role in shaping conceptual systems, as we see taking form again in the 'developing' world today (explored further in Chapter 5), begins here.

Let us be clear about the political implications of this process. Before capitalism, power was visibly part of everyday life as experienced through hierarchies, obligations and customs. A core reason for this transparency was the very public nature of surplus extraction. Whether it was the tribute paid by the peasant, the tithe handed over by the serf or the involuntary labour performed by the slave, workers were, formally speaking, explicitly 'unfree'. In such social formations, political inequality, visibly imposed by various authorities (the lord, the priest, the master), was both overt and fundamental to social reproduction.[92] But now, through capitalism – in a society mediated by contractual relations 'freely' entered into among abstractly equal participants – such disparities are occluded and political resistance generally is muted. Rather than the result of tradition, obligation or, more pointedly, the barrel of a gun, in capitalist political economies, surpluses (the bases of potential profits) are extracted through often mysterious 'market forces' backed by 'the rule of law'.

Since, as Rosenberg explains, 'the labour contract' is 'a relation of exchange between legal equals, the process of surplus extraction is reconstituted as a private activity of civil society'.[93] Historically, following initial assaults on traditional relations, rather than resisting capitalism as a political economic order, organized rebellion gradually came to focus on bettering one's workplace conditions or increasing a group's standard of living – the latter typically measured in terms of the quantity and quality of commodities that a union's membership could purchase from one year to the next.[94]

Surely it is no coincidence that the most remarkable examples of organized anti-capitalist resistance today are taking place in 'developing' parts of the world where IMF or World Bank diktats have *compelled* states to sell public assets, slash community services and privatize commonly held enterprises. Both in the past and present, out of the maelstrom that is primitive accumulation, a crucial transformation takes place: the state and state-based policies, to facilitate the power of private capital, are reformed in ways that separate the 'political' public sphere from the seemingly 'apolitical' private. Laws, elections, state sovereignty and a broad range of other institutional developments usually affiliated with the rise of capitalist liberal democracy are concomitantly constructed, insulating the private sector and propertied interests from direct scrutiny despite their disproportionate extraction of surpluses.

Through the long-term normalization of capitalist relations, power inequalities are shrouded in a fog of 'rights', contracts and, in the realm of consumption, the common sense supremacy of 'consumer sovereignty'. To reiterate a point made in Chapter 2, the consumer – as long as he/she has some disposable income or anticipates securing it – is, under these political economic conditions, free to buy the commodities of his/her choice. Moreover, such commodity choices are seemingly apolitical private decisions made by apparently 'rational' individuals. Over time and in light of systemic pressures to increase production efficiencies, the loss of autonomy and the rise of alienation in the workplace are roughly counter-balanced by the independence and sense of achievement (not to mention the material comforts) attainable through consumption.

Mediated by the institution of capitalist consumption, individual freedom itself functions as a tool enabling the imposition and reproduction of otherwise jarring inequalities. Accommodated by globalization and enabling this project to establish itself through consent (at least among those prospectively able to participate as consumers), another kind of GCS may be under construction – a disparately emerging global consumer society.

* * *

GCS progressives and related 'globalization theory' idealists have shelved historical, macro-level conceptualizations of power in favour of the microphysics of interest group struggles, an almost fetishistic treatment of ICTs and a politics dominated by pluralist interests and identities. In their analysis of transnational networks, Keck and Sikkink, for example, counter the focus on inter-state relations in mainstream International Relations by, instead, examining 'dense webs of interactions and interrelations among citizens of different states which both reflect and help sustain shared values, beliefs, and projects'. As such, power in this world (dis)order is viewed as 'the composite of thousands of decisions which could have been decided otherwise'.[95] Beyond the general absence of historical structures and affecting mediators, among other things this and related approaches simplify complexities related to identity, meaning and society. Because conceptual systems are used to process information and experience into knowledge, human beings are not simply 'free' to pick and choose their preferred versions of reality.[96]

Assumptions that 'the self' is essentially the outcome of rational or autonomous selections made by individuals from an expanding menu of border-crossing information sources are more than just dubious, they are predicated on unfounded assumptions about the implications of ICTs. For one thing, this menu, including everything from virtual shopping malls to political blogs, from pornography websites to academic articles, is not experientially or intellectually neutral. The ways in which media are structured affects both the information that is available and how that information is used. What has been called the emerging 'hypermedia environment',[97] for instance, involves the absolute and relative growth of 'personalised' interactive information portals, the rapid growth of transnational communication networks and a deepening awareness of 'the global' as a shared spatial reality. But then to go on to argue that such developments will likely facilitate a progressive GCS – involving the re-construction of conceptual systems through virtual rather than material realities, the assumption that influential structures associated with capitalism will become less influential and the assertion that human identities and meanings are ripe for some kind of progressive transformation – is dubious indeed.

Following the logic and evidence laid out in this chapter, such a transformation instead will require, *first*, a change in practice or, in more everyday parlance, lifestyles. Day-to-day life (most essentially at the local level) will have to be re-structured in ways that will encourage socialization processes quite different from those largely focused on facilitating capital accumulation and representative or consumerist (rather than direct) forms of democracy. Through globalization, what has been called the global–local dialectic[98] no doubt will continue to unfold. Locally, this likely will involve degrees of indigenization in which different cultures creatively incorporate various elements of foreign cultures. However, given the nature of all three dimensions of power, the affecting role of media such as capitalist consumption, and the ever-present importance of structured conceptual systems, it appears unlikely that most of these interactions will take place under conditions that in any way involve some sort of 'equal' or 'reciprocal' exchange. Not only has the menu of prospective realities been whittled down, the disparities that such interactions reveal could well generate conflict rather than co-operation. As Arjun Appadurai writes,

> Globalization involves the use of a variety of instruments of homogenization (armaments, advertising techniques, language hegemonies, clothing styles and the like), which are absorbed into local political and cultural economies, only to be repatriated as heterogeneous dialogues of national sovereignty, free enterprise, fundamentalism, etc., in which the state plays an increasingly delicate role: too much openness to global flows and the nation state is threatened with revolt – the China syndrome; too little, and the state exits the international stage, as Burma, Albania, and North Korea, in various ways, have done.[99]

Similarly, Harvey has argued that the globalization project's accompanying annihilation of spatial and temporal barriers is more likely to generate competitive and perhaps even reactionary forms of localism and nationalism rather than some kind of McLuhanesque 'global village'. The reason, again, involves pervasive, historically entrenched structures and affecting mediators. In a world characterized by rapid change, free-flowing capital and falling spatial-temporal barriers, concerted efforts to make 'the local' comparatively attractive for investors, or portraying its culture as relatively (and chauvinistically) ideal, tends to become *more* rather than less likely.[100] In an increasingly interconnected world – one in which rapid change and instability have become cultural norms – and given the place-based conditions of day-to-day human existence, one's identification with a particular locale most probably will remain an important psychological mooring.

In this clinging to some kind of place-bound identity, to quote Harvey, 'oppositional movements become a part of the very fragmentation which mobile capitalism and flexible accumulation' feed upon.[101] Not only do commercial interests play on these insecurities – offering relief and social-psychological security in the form of commodities – they routinely fan the flames of local chauvinisms and national patriotism. Surely the largest American or Greek or Korean flags are proudly flown not in front of important national ministries but, more usually, over and above one's local used-car dealership(!).

We close this chapter with some thoughts in response to how GCS progressives tend to assess the implications of instantaneous communications. Generally speaking, they emphasize the advantages of spatial reach but, in so doing, neglect questions concerning duration. ICTs associated with globalization are structurally oriented to shrink the time frames of decision-making. Whether such decisions involve the bombing of an enemy, the security of one's investments or the messages one wants to send to a friend, the Internet, the general commodification of culture and related values placed on speed and efficiency arguably have set the stage for volatility and deepening insecurities. As transnational investors respond to market 'signals' with spasmodic acts of panic selling, as consumers fail to keep up with the demands of producers to buy more commodities more often, as the environmental crisis reaches a point of no return and as people around the world become increasingly concerned with the here-and-now ('why hasn't he text-messaged me yet?'), our cultural capacity to appraise problems in terms of a relatively balanced consideration of both space and time appears to be in decline.[102]

The time needed to individually and collectively reflect and critically assess the undesirable implications of the globalization project generally is being reduced, not enhanced. While a progressive global civil society is delusional, a global consumer society – at least one involving those with the capacity to take part – is demonstrably under way. In our next chapter, we examine how this is taking shape using India and China as case studies.

5
'Developing' Political Economies and Global Consumer Society

> High thinking is inconsistent with a complicated material
> life based on high speed and imposed on us by mammon
> worship.
>
> —Mahatma Gandhi

In Chapter 2 we argued that a segment of people living in 'developing' political economies now seem relatively well positioned to critically assess the globalization project. Unlike those living in abject poverty or those enculturated in the day-to-day norms of capitalist consumption (the world's so-called consumer class), people situated between these extremes appear to have greater potential to respond reflexively, creatively and, in some cases, progressively. More specifically, those now experiencing previously unknown affluence, yet possessing living memories of pre-modern consumption, now occupy a prospectively pivotal historical position.

For those whose conceptual systems were forged in societies valuing collective and qualitative aspects of development, rather than individualist and quantitative, neither the 'naturalness' nor the 'inevitability' of globalization and its related neoliberal policies are taken for granted. To some extent, these cultures are works in progress – *relatively* open to renewing traditional ways of living while forging new political trajectories.

For hundreds of millions in China, India, areas in Eastern Europe, parts of Central and South America and other 'developing' parts of the world, the ways in which most Westerners have, over the course of many generations, organized and conceptualized time and space have not (yet) become 'just the way it is'. For some, capitalist relations are being structured into daily life (primarily through media such as private property and contracts) while pre-modern, collectivist and statist institutions, organizations and technologies persist. These include, among others, universal or quasi-socialist state-based services, communal religious activities, entrenched community or class-based organizations and informal (sometimes non-monetary) institutions of exchange.

In this chapter, we address the development of capitalist consumption in India, China and other rapidly growing economies. Through these case studies, we demonstrate that capitalist consumption, while adopted and practiced in culturally specific ways, promotes the universalization of individualistic, short-term, immediate-gratification modes of thinking and living. The globalization project generally (and capitalist consumption specifically) 'frees' modernizing cultures by elaborating more mediated, commodified and abstracted norms into daily life. Here, as we will see, existential questions emerge alongside prosperity while fetishistic associations blossom. Yet, given the unprecedented pace of these changes, 'traditional' values and relatively non-abstract realities linger. For some, a window of opportunity subsequently has opened – one in which segments of workers and emerging bourgeoisies recognize that the globalization project is neither inevitable nor necessarily desirable. In these places and times, characterized by great uncertainty, the nation state, in particular, is viewed more positively than it is in the West. Here the neoliberal 'end of history' remains open for debate and the neo-modern common sense that 'geography is history' has not yet been concretized. The implications of this delimited juncture are clear – the globalization project's future is up for grabs.

Global consumer society? The case of India

Next to China, India often is cited as the world's most rapidly developing large-scale economy. Until 1991, India's post independence economic system was directly administered through statist institutions. Following a budgetary crisis that year, its government, prompted by policy commitments related to IMF loans, accelerated the process of liberalizing domestic activities, trade and capital flows. By the time India became a member of the WTO in 1995, the average tariff had been reduced from 130 to 30 per cent.[1]

With a population of more than one billion people (700 million of whom live in the countryside), 40 per cent live on less than the equivalent of one US dollar a day.[2] Wages in India (in 2002) averaged 43 cents an hour – lower than China's 59 cents and much lower than the $20.32 average in the US.[3] However, India is the world's most rapidly urbanizing country with a workforce that is younger and growing faster than China's.[4]

With 70 per cent of the all Indians living in poverty, the vast majority are not routinely engaged in capitalist consumption. In the words of Indian marketer Kishore Biyani,

We divide India into three sets – India One, India Two and India Three. These groups can be understood as the consuming class, the serving class and the struggling class. The studies show that India One (14% of India's population) uses modern retail formats like *Big Bazaar*. India Two (drivers, maids, etc., who serve India One) are 55% of our population but have little income to spend on aspirational buying. The needs of India Three or the struggling class, which lives hand-to-mouth, cannot be addressed by the existing business models.[5]

When taking into account the country's (conservatively) predicted economic growth rate of 6.2 per cent, by 2030 the average annual income should reach $14,000 – a level high enough to enable most to engage in the discretionary spending of Biyani's 'India One' consuming class (those able to spend significant portions of their incomes on commodities other than necessities such as shelter, food and apparel).[6]

In recent years, a large urban middle class has emerged – mostly service sector workers and entrepreneurs whose incomes and spending capabilities are similar to those found in relatively 'developed' political economies. Since the cost of living for many Indians is relatively low, some argue that this Indian consumer class already has 350 million participants. Others, calculating its size in terms of Western averages, estimate that the number now stands at just 5 million.[7]

As the history of England and the United States demonstrate (Chapter 3), the emergence of capitalist consumption involves often problematic changes in both thought and behaviour. In India and elsewhere, developments surrounding this institution entail forces and processes that go well beyond just the economic ability to buy things. For example, the specific ramifications of an emerging middle class and the availability of more domestic and imported products cannot be understood in the absence of core political and cultural dynamics. From national independence well into the 1980s, for example, the Gandhian principle of national self-sufficiency pervaded development policy and discourse. The concept of *swadeshi* – literally meaning 'of one's own country' – was not only dominant, but what has been termed the new swadeshi movement has informed debates and activities related to the contemporary globalization project.

Beginning in 1919, Gandhi mobilized India through both nationalism and staple product consumption. Through his symbolic use of the *charkha* (the typical Indian hand-operated spinning wheel), nationwide agitations against the British involved boycotts of cloth woven in Manchester. In conjunction with the swadeshi movement's emphasis on self-sufficiency and self-reliance, Gandhi promoted *swaraj* (self-rule) through the analogy of mastering one's own desires for the common good. For independence from the British to succeed, Indians would have to sublimate their consumer desires. By striving for simplicity, they could attain both political and economic sovereignty. It is in this context that the history of India was directly influenced by a struggle over the institution of consumption – how Indians (particularly those with higher than subsistence incomes) thought about and practised consumption.

Since Gandhi, consumption has profoundly shaped culture and identity in India, particularly among the relatively wealthy middle class and its understanding of India as a nation.[8] It is not terribly surprizing then that in the wake of liberalization policies beginning in the mid-1980s and, later, in response to the globalization project, swadeshi became a central concept through which debate and legislation ensued. Now, rather than self-sufficiency and community, development was to proceed through an externally fuelled consumption and, in the realm of production, more international competition. While mainstream neoclassical theory assumes that consumers have naturally insatiable and individualistic appetites for commodities, it is precisely the institutional nature of consumption that has been (and remains) central in efforts to comprehend India's responses to globalization, not to mention its potential to change course in the near future.

Through the new swadeshi movement, the Indian response to globalization and its institutional, organizational and technological mediators has done little to support the assumptions of GCS progressives discussed in Chapter 4. Indeed, in India, the globalization project generally has heightened rather than effaced the importance of national and local ways of thinking and acting.[9]

In 1997, the opposition Bharatiya Janata party (BJP) questioned the Indian government for its promotion of what it termed consumerist globalization. One of the most vocal critics was Swaminathan Gurumurthy. He argued that a Westernized Indian elite were behind policies that were unsuited to India's culture and harmful to native entrepreneurs. 'The new model of capitalism,' said Gurumurthy, 'is the American variety – fabricated in USA, a state devoid of wholesome traditions and community life and has opted for atomized individualism.'[10] Beyond even this, domestic proponents of free trade and globalization were said to be suffering from a post-colonial inferiority complex, unable to recognize the value of conserving their own heritage. As Gurumurthy put it, '[t]he nation needs psychotherapy'.[11]

In response, supporters of neoliberal reforms argued that Gurumurthy and others were being reactionary. Amit Jatia, the managing director of an Indian corporation that held the domestic franchise rights to *McDonald's*, saw the new swadeshi movement as 'an outdated mind-set which wants to take India backward'; worse still, their arguments 'send the wrong signals to foreign investors'.[12] Rather than surrendering or selling out to imperialist forces, pro-globalization interests argued that free trade and regulatory reforms reflected India's emerging self-confidence. Like George W. Bush's equivocation of a private sector-driven economy and private property rights with 'genuine freedom', publicist and marketer Pritish Nandy (representing the Hindu nationalist Shiv Sena party) went so far as to argue that the Indian state had a moral responsibility to provide Indians with access to 'the best products in the world at the best possible price'.[13]

Between the two poles of the new swadeshi movement and the pro-free marketers stood influential domestic industrialists collectively known as the Bombay Club. From their perspective, economic reforms opening the Indian market up to foreign competitors had gone too far. Agreeing with moderate advocates of a new swadeshi, they called for some extension of domestic protectionism as a means of compensating for the inefficiencies in place as a result of long-standing statist policies. In other words, these vested interests recognized the vulnerability of domestic firms in light of emerging competition with foreign and transnational corporations; nevertheless, they understood globalization to have economic benefits and coveted free trade's promise of accessing overseas markets and investors.

Here, again, the institution of consumption both mediated the debate and was itself modified by related policy applications. By the end of the 1990s, the BJP adopted the Bombay Club's position by cloaking it in new swadeshi rhetoric. Atal Behari Vajpayee, on the eve of becoming Prime Minister in 1999, explained his party's position as follows:

> What I and my party are opposed to is allowing the Indian market to be swamped by products that offer an illusion of prosperity but in reality meet the demands of a very narrow band of people. Putting it simply, we are against unlimited consumerism, which may appeal to cosmopolitan upwardly mobile Indians, but ignores the needs of 75 percent of the country's population that lives in our villages.[14]

In keeping with its Bombay Club orientation and concerned with unrestricted foreign investment, once in power the BJP argued that the new swadeshi was, in fact, a unique kind of pro-globalization policy. As Finance Minister Yashwant Sinha put it, 'it's pro-Indian without being anti-foreign ... Having recognized globalization as a fact of life we are merely saying that a calibrated approach is needed ...'[15]

In contrast to GCS progressives and their tendency to see such pro-globalization outcomes as a result of declining state powers in the face of transnational forces and connexions, what India and other nation states have experienced stems out of the tensions and contradictions generated by both the project's universalization of capitalist structures *and* local/national responses to these dynamics. In the context of the globalization project and the mediating implications of endogenous and exogenous institutions (including consumption), state and government officials have been compelled to defend some domestic interests (including organized workers and peasants) while, at the same time, accommodating the demands of transnational capital.

Previously, consumption norms involved political and moral questions asked not only by individuals but among Gandhian nationalists as well. As William Mazzarella documents, the traditional or pre-modern Indian consumerist ontology made explicit distinctions between true and false needs, between necessities and luxuries. Out of the new swadeshi movement and debates concerning neoliberal development strategies and, more abstractly, India's participation in globalization, a modified way of thinking about and participating in consumption unfolded. An 'alternative populism,' says Mazzarella, emerged 'based on the figure of the sovereign consumer as the final arbiter of ... normative questions'.[16] Through this institution's indirect influence on assumptions shaping swaraj and thus the Nehruvian planned economy, the introduction of Western consumption norms among the country's emerging middle class facilitated at least some domestic consent for the globalization project. Let us be more specific through the use of recent examples.

Generating a demand for carbonated drinks in this traditionally frugal and utilitarian-focused consumer market involved cultural challenges. How, for instance, might a vendor link the intrinsic qualities of a beverage (whatever it may be) to the long-established tastes and dispositions of potential consumers? Instead of selling their drink by relating it to desirable psychological and sociological associations – the now commonplace method of selling commodities in the West – most Indians had to be told about the drink's 'useful' characteristics relative to water, tea and other established beverages. In the 1990s, among even the relatively affluent, India's consumer culture had 'evolved' little in relation to how Vergil Reed found it when he reported on its unlikely potentials in 1949 (see Chapter 1).

To put it bluntly, India (and other 'traditional' societies) constituted a problem for multinational producers hoping to 'cash in' on its rapidly opening marketplace. Because *Pepsi*, for example, has few obvious utilitarian qualities, whatever intrinsic characteristics it had would need to be presented as tangible reasons to buy it. For *Pepsi* and innumerable others, their products had little to offer consumers who had limited experience with – and even less reason to buy into – the abstract assumptions that predominated consumption in the West. For example, in the 1990s, *Sparka*, a soft drink owned by *Coca-Cola*, was successfully marketed to Indians as a result of its 'superior orange taste'.[17] But, clearly, as with the history of North American, Western European and Japanese consumption, the ability to expand markets in step with India's economic growth would entail a rapid and radical modification of how consumption itself was thought about and practiced. Commodities had to become desirable for more than just what they do; they also needed to be sellable as a result of evermore abstract social-psychological associations.

In the case of *Sparka*, Indian marketers sought to re-brand the drink for adolescent consumers based on some assumed universal characteristics of being a teenager. The most important of these was the need to find one's own identity – an age old and worldwide task involving the adolescent's relationships with others. Thus, in the 1990s, *Sparka* executives ambitiously sought to 're-socialise' the beverage in terms of peer-group interactions and acceptance in situations in which teens were demonstrably enjoying themselves. In this effort, the Bombay-based marketing firm, hired to coordinate the campaign, conducted a comparative study of how teens around the world – in India, China, Thailand, Brazil, Germany, Italy and Mexico – have fun. Their goal was to identify which values and emotions are associated with this state of happiness. Among other conclusions, the resulting report found that teen peer relationships that were fun involved inclusivity (rather than loneliness), optimism, curiosity (while remaining safe), and being 'mainstream' instead of 'edgy'.[18]

An important point to make about this and other efforts to change Indian consumers is that the executives trying to negotiate established cultural norms with a more commodified future are not neutral agents. As Mazzarella discovered in his fieldwork study of the Indian advertising industry, the structural circumstances of their employment compelled marketers to conceptualize people as existing or emerging 'modern' consumers, even when interviewees and focus groups clearly rejected this 'inevitability'. For example, on one occasion, Mazzarella reports that a research coordinator, when confronted with a teen respondent's essay stating that 'I don't like to watch TV', shook his head in amazement and discarded the article with the statement, 'What a loser!'[19] Moreover, the assumption that teens universally or naturally relate to one another in their search for an identity and sense of belonging *in opposition* to traditions and established authority figures (such as parents) also reflects a professional bias. After all, by universalizing youth rebellion, particularly rebellion against established cultural mores and authority figures, marketers in 'developing' countries such as India could tell corporate clients that there was, indeed, a way forward – a 'natural' way to institutionalize capitalist consumption. Capitalists seeking Indian consumers thus could rest easy and Reed's earlier pessimism could be shelved.[20]

Despite these problems, this research and its assumptions were applied by *Sparka's* parent company to sell *Coca-Cola* to Indian teens in the early 1990s. After an absence of almost 15 years (*Coca-Cola* and other transnationals left India in response to state regulations implemented in the 1970s), the *Coca-Cola* campaign targeted teens centring on a 'one-world' (pro-globalization) concept referred to as 'Share my *Coke.*' The outcome was not good. Despite a relatively small promotional budget, a domestic cola called *Thums* [sic] *Up* (ironically sold to *Coca-Cola* by its Indian owners in fear of *Coke's* return and subsequent dominance) out sold *Coke* itself. The lesson that Bombay executives drew from *Coca-Cola's* failed return was that 'soft drink markets like India would have to be convinced to buy soft drink brands on the basis of solid "reason why" appeals rather than ... stylistically sophisticated campaigns'.[21]

Subsequent studies conducted to evaluate the likelihood that consumers would switch brands revealed that Indians overwhelmingly made such decisions based on the intrinsic characteristics of the product at hand. Among beverages, the drink's taste and its ability to refresh dominated such decisions.[22] Even more remarkable was another 'discovery' that followed *Coca-Cola's* initial failure: the world's teenagers are not all the same. In a marketing study conducted in the late 1990s, middle-class Indian adolescents were found to desire a materialist lifestyle involving the typical Western quest for independence *but*, importantly, India's teens differed in that they viewed the needs of their families to be *more* important than their own. Like the concept of swadeshi, traditional values and their personification through parents and elders were not scorned, but generally respected and listened to; for most, even arranged marriages were still acceptable.[23]

Despite their unprecedented access to commodities, transnational media, their use of ICTs and exposure to commercial messages, even India's middle-class adolescents – or, more precisely, their conceptual systems – were as tuned in to the local and national as they were to the global. And as the early twenty-first century unfolds, the Indian city dweller with growing discretionary spending capabilities either is becoming a uniquely Indian consumer (a cultural 'hybrid') or is going through, as most Indian marketers believe, a transition phase *en route* to adopting the consumption norms of most Westerners. Either way, it appears as if the prospects of most Indians becoming active proponents of a progressive GCS are remote; the new swadeshi movement, for example, points to a largely nationalistic response to globalization *or* its use as stepping stone towards the Indian middle class' participation in some kind of global consumer society.

Indian 'middle class' consumption

Another example of this trajectory is discernable in ethnographic research on how middle-class Indians conceptualize their class position and the role of consumption in it. Herein lies a paradox: middle-class Indians consistently use commodities as markers of status, yet simultaneously consciously reject the materialist components of consumer culture. 'Materialism' is commonly held to be 'a condition in which people seek self-realisation or self-expression through goods rather than ... spiritual or social pursuits'.[24] According to one researcher, India's contemporary middle-class generally holds an ambivalent attitude when it comes to acquiring commodities; however, at the same time *it recognizes them to have a utilitarian social function*. '[M]any,' for instance, 'articulate the sense that they have entered a new era, with a way of life thoroughly different from that of some 20 or 30 years ago. They are not speaking simply of the experience of prosperity alone, rather consumption is also understood to have social and moral implications.'[25]

Unlike Western consumers – most of whom have no living memory of alternate ways of organizing and thinking about consumption – the Indian middle class is generally conscious of their relative affluence. Making do with what one has rather than aspiring to accumulate new things, for them, is seen to be either an old way of thinking or a way of life associated with lower classes. In this respect, the typical middle-class person uses commodities to maintain his/her social position – a position that requires one to 'keep up with the times'. Rather than a status generated through traditional caste distinctions or patron–client relationships, this position is assessed in relation to other members of India's urban/professional middle-class, involving the question 'am I at least equal to my friends and neighbours?' In other words, material commodities, for these relatively well off Indians, are not the direct means to an end (as in what we have called the neo-modern mythology that goods entail magical properties – that they, in themselves, embody identity and meaning). Instead, in India (for this group at least) commodities constitute *a means to* belonging *vis-à-vis* one's perceived peers. Unlike in North America, Western Europe or Japan, where purchased goods and services themselves purportedly make the consumer happier, attractive or more powerful, the function of India's emerging form of capitalist consumption is to connect people to one another and, in so doing, communicate one's status to oneself and others.

Underlining this difference is a conscious indictment, expressed by many interviewees, of letting consumerism distance people from their families and larger trans-class communities. Middle-class Indians often call the upper class morally depraved by citing their use of commodities to display their wealth. An 'artificial' life is said to be one that is dominated by things, whereas a more meaningful existence is based on relationships and a simple (dare we say 'neo-Gandhian') lifestyle.[26] To some degree, these sentiments may be seen as either an effort to resist modern Western versions of capitalist consumption (informed, no doubt, by swadeshi and swaraj) or just a temporary, changing perspective. Certainly the contradictions implied by the middle-class' disdain for materialism yet its explicit use of commodities to communicate and make social connections point more to the latter. As our history of Western consumption indicates, urbanization, social atomization, the ascendancy of contractual relations and other developments associated with 'modernisation' suggest that, as Indians become wealthier, the country's version of capitalist consumption eventually will mediate ways of thinking and acting now commonplace in the 'developed' world.

Like the marketers and advertisers who first realized that commodities could be sold by relating them to the social and psychological needs being neglected in urban industrialized America, Mumbai-based executives now recognize that the moral, social and nationalistic values still held by the new Indian middle-class can be used to sell goods and, less directly, develop the institution of consumption. As consumer culture itself is viewed as a threat to social bonds and Indian traditions, marketers and advertisers now commonly relate the latter ideals to the products they want to sell.

For example, in a 1990s advertisement for a popular toothpaste, marketers fused Ayurveda – India's ancient system of medicine – to an obviously modern/global image (Illustration 5.1 below). In this and innumerable other advertisements, products (and capitalist consumption) were sold in terms of Indian tradition and self-sufficiency in the context of globalization.[27]

Source: The VICCO group.

Illustration 5.1   VICCO toothpaste advertisement

If successful, over time (particularly once those with living memories of other ways of conceptualizing and practising consumption have passed away), rather than using commodities as signifiers in the process of connecting with others, commodities themselves may become the abstract manifestations of these very values and ideals. Once this cultural hurdle is cleared, consumption *itself* prospectively becomes a staple component of hegemonic politics. The search for meaning and identity – the quest for stability and power in the midst of the globalization project's instabilities and accelerating pace of change – *then* can be attained (temporarily, of course) not through relationships and introspection but, rather, through the check-out line.

Ashis Nandy, among others, has argued that Hindu nationalism constitutes, for some, an answer to the insecurities associated with gobalization and modernization. For example, he writes that it frames a moral discourse against unbridled materialism and, indirectly, the West.[28] Once the institution of consumption becomes as abstracted as established institutions such as religion and the nation, it also can serve as a response to the uncertainties now being compounded through the globalization project. By buying goods that purportedly embody the importance of community, tradition and even 'Indianess', the modern consumer tangibly can express his/her values and needs while materially getting something out of taking part. Adapting what Nandy says in relation to Hindu nationalism, for the middle-class Indian, capitalist consumption prospectively enables the individual to be psychically '*in* the world but not *of* it'.[29] Through his/her participation as a consumer, the individual is seemingly sovereign and autonomous and, as such, the neoliberal ideal behind the globalization project becomes part and parcel of not only personal identity but also, prospectively, India's national *zeitgeist*.

* * *

In the age of globalization, India has emerged as one of the most important and economically powerful countries in the 'developing' world. As discussed above, this recent history has involved a sea change in public policy. Statist activities have been radically reformed. Yet, as with all political, economic and cultural formations, India retains core elements of its past – particularly its nationalism as expressed through swadeshi. Out of the neoliberal maelstrom, the Indian middle-class (thus far) has retained its nationalist identity and traditional values *but* in new and commercialized forms. Here, the development of capitalist consumption is taking place with Indian responses to, or interpretations of, globalization being used to sell things and, as a by-product, further commodify relationships.

India's historical trajectory – at least among its middle- and upper-class minorities – is similar to the one experienced in Western political economies. As with China (addressed below), in its own complex way, India is becoming part of an emerging global consumer society. But having recognized this, given that the institution of consumption is a work in progress *and* in light of the ongoing saliency of (neo-)Gandhian principles, nationalism and ongoing economic disparities, Indians could well revise their participation in globalization through more progressive policies – prospectively counter-balancing the reactionary tendencies characterizing politics in many 'developed' countries.

Beyond the streets of India's cities and villages or the corridors of official power in New Delhi, the meanings and implications of the globalization project are being negotiated and, for the most part, accommodated through the institution of consumption. But, to repeat, Indian conceptual systems – forged through both experience and mediations – are far from sanguine. Global and national political economic conditions change and, when they do, the capacity of Indians to limit capitalist consumption's influence arguably provides the nation with the intellectual pluralism needed to respond through creative and prospectively progressive forms of political engagement.

Global consumer society? The case of China

The People's Republic of China (PRC) has a population of about 1.3 billion people. Through economic liberalization – including entry into the WTO in 2001 – accompanied by massive (mostly state-financed) infrastructure investments, the PRC's economy is growing rapidly. Foreign and domestic capital inputs are financing its development much more than spending by domestic consumers.[30] As in India, most Chinese live subsistence lifestyles. However, due to its rapid economic growth, increasing numbers are earning the discretionary incomes needed to participate in capitalist consumption. Approximately a hundred million Chinese earn at least $5000 a year,[31] enough, given the relatively low cost of living in most parts of the country, to enable this minority to buy more than just necessities.

Assuming that the PRC's economy will grow at a rate of *at least* 5 per cent per annum (from 1980 to 2000 it grew 10 per cent each year), by 2030, the average person likely will have the wealth needed to consume as much as the average Greek, Portuguese or New Zealander does today.[32] Indeed, given that China's growing balance-of-trade surplus is worrisome due to the upwards pressure it puts on the country's currency (the renminbi) and, related to this, the PRC's dependency on export markets (especially the United States), the Chinese state has been encouraging citizens to spend more money, even if it means going into personal debt – a practice that generally goes against the grain of cultural norms (as it did for most Westerners born before the 1930s). State officials now, for example, encourage banks to increase their lending to consumers directly or through the proliferation of credit cards.[33] In the words of one Chinese marketer, 'We have to increase the number of people with a microwave ... from 200 million to 1.2 billion. That's where our future lies.'[34]

Consumption in China also has an influential history – a history whose complex dynamics and structural implications are shaping contemporary trajectories. This past, as with India's, features foreign domination. Until the Communist Revolution of 1949, the Chinese political leadership and, thus, its domestic affairs had been variously influenced by overseas interests. While in the early twentieth century, China began to manufacture and import consumer goods – mostly to sell to its urban elites – the cultural implications of this early influx of commodities and, with them, commodified social relations (exemplified, at their extreme, by the scourge of opium addiction) became a central concern for anti-imperialists, nationalists and domestic manufacturers fearing competition. Indeed, over the past century, what commodities people consumed and how consumption has been carried out became focal points for how many Chinese conceptualized themselves in relation to the modern (and now 'globalizing') world.[35]

Out of imperialism, Japan and Western states imposed 'unequal treaties' restricting, among other things, China's tariff-setting autonomy. Inundated by imports, vested interests sought to limit foreign dominance and cultural influence by promoting 'nationalistic consumption' through what was called the national products movement. This heterogeneous alliance of domestic manufacturers, radical student groups, state officials and others organized protests and campaigns aimed at compelling merchants and consumers to sell and buy only Chinese-made goods.[36] The scale and ideological saliency of this movement was extraordinary. Its cultural impact was important not only in anticipation of the 1949 Revolution, but also, as we will see, contemporary China's economic liberalization dating from 1979.

By the 1930s, a broad number of 'authentic' or 'patriotic' Chinese products were sanctioned by the national products movement; for instance, women who wore imported fabrics were either betraying the nation or were metaphorically labelled as prostitutes and manufacturers using non-Chinese raw materials were said to be not 'authentically' Chinese. Various systems of certification emerged, initially through the efforts of organizations claiming to oppose imperialism and, later, by the national government.[37] As early as 1928, a National Products Exhibition was held to demonstrate, through the display of an array of everyday goods (including, it was boasted, the authentically Chinese towels in the men's room), how one could and should live a 'pure' Chinese life through the consumption of domestically made commodities.[38]

Financed primarily by domestic capitalists, the movement represented a cross-section of Chinese who, together, forged a nationalist identity mediated by consumption. Unlike the history of the West, where the institutional development of consumption centred on the inter-related rise of the atomized individual and the forging of his/her 'sovereign' identity through meaningful commodities, the Chinese forged an explicitly nationalist form of consumption – a consumption that materially communicated one's membership and loyalty to the abstract nation. The national products movement, writes historian Karl Gerth, 'denied the consumer a place outside the nation as economy and nation became coterminous'.[39] In this sense, the institution of consumption in early twentieth-century China was similar to India's in that they were both irrevocably intertwined with the nation; however, while the Indian swadeshi movement sought independence through simplicity and self-reliance, the Chinese had no qualms about spending and consuming, as long as the commodities were irrefutably indigenous.[40]

As illustrated below (Illustration 5.2), citizenship, nationality and consumption were inter-connected. In an advertisement run several times in the national newspaper *Shenbao* in the early 1930s, proponents of the national products movement equated the world of nations (as well as China's domestic regions) with the world of commodities. According to Gerth, the advertisement also portrays the movement's fear of imperialism

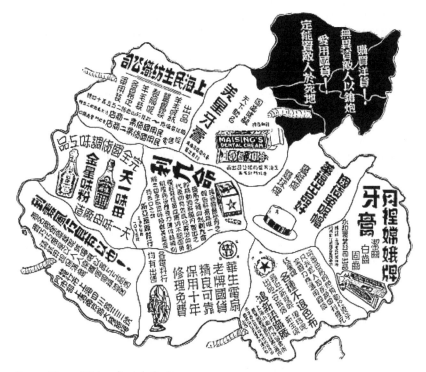

Source: Harvard University Asia Center.

Illustration 5.2   A nation of products (1931/32?)

Source: Harvard University Asia Center.

Illustration 5.3   Sincere toothpaste advertisement (1935)

and/or foreign competition. The silkworms, for example, are used to liken China to a mulberry leaf – a nation ravaged through the voracious appetite of foreign exploiters (Manchuria, shown in black, had been annexed by Japan in 1931). 'The implication,' writes Gerth, 'was that the production, circulation, and consumption of national products acted as a figurative insecticide that ensured national salvation by preventing foreign products (silk worms) from gradually conquering the Chinese market (mulberry leaf).'[41]

In Illustration 5.3 above, we see a slightly later advertisement, this one promoting a specific product – *Sincere* toothpaste. The banner running over the top of the advertisement reads 'National Product Sincere Toothpaste'. The words on the lower left tell consumers 'Let's collectively strive to promote national products to recover economic rights.' Beyond the obvious connotation of the toothpaste's portrayal as a canon repelling invaders, it is interesting to note that *Sincere* (as discussed below) was one of the country's largest department stores – a store that relied on the sale of foreign goods to attract its more cosmopolitan customers (the English translation on the toothpaste's label reflects this contradiction).[42]

Despite the movement's patriotic appeals, its success was limited by two factors. First, the concept of China as a nation was new or alien to many. As such, the movement relied on more than jingoistic references; it also involved protests, intimidation and, later, legal restrictions. Second, the appeal experienced by many emerging middle-class city dwellers (as in eighteenth-century London or twenty-first-century Mumbai) to be 'cosmopolitan' prompted non-Chinese consumption choices, particularly among those influenced directly by fashion.

As in late nineteenth-century Western Europe and North America, the early twentieth-century Chinese department store constituted one of the first and most influential places through which capitalist consumption was directly experienced. China's largest city, Shanghai, in which the country's most modern and 'international' middle-class resided, had several.

Sincere and *Wing On* were two of the largest and most influential. As Kerrie MacPherson explains, these retailing centres mediated the historical and traditional with the modern and, indeed, the 'global':

> They reflected variations in management or in the organization of distribution and supply, as custom and history dictated, that left them their discrete identities ... Yet, they all shared defining features that shaped new shopping behavior and experiences that departed from ... merchandising practices of the past. First, the organization of a broad spectrum of goods in departmentalized sections under one roof; second, the visible display of goods available ...; [and] third, fixed and marked prices (often touted as 'fair') that favored high turnover by shortening the selling process ... [E]ntrance to the department store, unlike traditional shops, entailed no obligation to buy thereby facilitating a new kind of shopping behavior.[43]

As in the West, the telegraph, the railroad and the steamship played crucial roles in enabling Shanghai department stores to reform urban middle-class consumption. However, given the logistical complexity of the department store, the fact that only a small minority of Shanghai's residents could afford most of the products sold, and the conservative slow-to-change characteristics of consumption (as with most institutions), local markets, whose medium of exchange was haggling rather than fixed pricing, remained dominant. Nevertheless, in the early years of the national products movement, Chinese entrepreneurs, such as the founder of *Sincere*, Ma Yingbiao, were seen by some as patriotic heroes – particularly due to their retailing of domestically produced commodities. From 1919, however, *Sincere* and other department stores also faced boycotts and even protests by their own employees as a result of selling Western and Japanese products.

Yet the fashionable demand for foreign imports and, thus, the popularity of department stores among China's wealthier, more cosmopolitan shoppers, was essential for the department stores' success. Whether the products being sold were domestic or foreign, these retailing giants introduced important cultural changes. *Wing On*, for example, adopted the Western norm of being courteous to customers (even to those just browsing). Innovations in credit also were advanced and, in the 1920s, mail order, telephone and home delivery services were introduced.[44] More generally, the scale and complexity of the department stores' marketing and advertising activities were, in China at least, unprecedented. In sum, Chinese department stores, based on Western models, elaborated the modern mythology or norm that the consumer was the central and supposedly sovereign fulcrum around which commercial and even social life revolved. At least for China's well off urban population, individual immediate-gratification priorities were ascendant.

Post-revolution consumption

With the Revolution of 1949, *Wing On, Sincere* and other department stores were either closed or taken over by the state.[45] More generally, with the elimination of private property and the economic onus turning to collective needs, the emergence of China's version of capitalist consumption was interrupted by a political-cultural emphasis on production. The new, less dynamic and domestically focused 'socialist department store' was established and, with it, remnants of China's early consumerism paradoxically survived.

Confusion over consumption norms deepened with the Cultural Revolution of the 1960s. Traditional Chinese products – once reified as the embodiments of patriotism and the nation – were banned while, simultaneously, foreign commodities (from whiskey to clothing) were removed from shelves, as were 'high class' goods such as cosmetics, jewellery and even mechanical toys. At what was then the largest department store in the country – the *Wangfujing Emporium* in Beijing – 6583 items were banned, constituting 21 per cent of the store's inventory.[46]

To repeat, from 1949 through to the economic liberalization policies that began in 1979, consumption – with the ironic exception of the 'cultural purge' of the 1960s – was officially de-emphasized ('ironic' in that by purging the country of thousands of supposedly harmful goods, they were, as under capitalism, once again being reified). With the exception of informal activities such as the local distribution of fresh produce, the infrastructure and expertise needed to disseminate a large number of goods – a capability pioneered by department stores at the turn of the century – had been neglected for three decades. In the wake of liberalization, the need to modernize these distribution networks became apparent. This led China to open its market further to private-state partnerships, private sector interests and foreign investors. Since joining the WTO, China even has encouraged foreign retailing chains (including the world's largest retailer and second largest company, *Wal-Mart*) to establish themselves domestically in part to help the country modernize its distribution infrastructure.[47]

While some proponents of an emerging GCS see such reforms as the beginning of the end of nationalistic identities and eventually even the Chinese state, few officials and Chinese intellectuals share this view. The core reason lies in their understanding that the nation state constitutes an essential mediator of the globalization project itself and, with this in mind, state policies should be crafted to counter-balance prospectively deleterious outcomes. Moreover, state–civil society relations are not seen to be oppositional but, rather, they are historically, culturally and structurally interdependent. In this context, progressive GCS perspectives that view civil society as the foil to state-based incompetence or oppression make little logical or empirical sense.

Apart from the state's capacity to counter-balance the homogenizing tendencies that some assume are coterminous with globalization (including, for example, some kind of American or capitalist cultural imperialism), a more difficult challenge involves the potential for localisms to flourish amidst the fragmenting and individualizing dynamics of structured capitalist relations. Both the competitive and the atomizing implications of the globalization project – from technologies such as the Internet to the pervasiveness of institutions such as the price system – concern PRC officials and intellectuals more than nonsensical assumptions about the nation state's decline.

According to a survey of such perspectives published by Nick Knight, members of the Chinese status quo find comfort in the conservative nature of most cultural formations. For example, values and patriotic emotions stemming from the revolutionary period still resonate with people as evidenced by the ongoing popularity of state-produced television programmes emphasizing such themes among both the elderly and rural residents.[48] Still, China's rapidly growing urban population, experiencing the dislocation, cultural segmentation and psychological anomie that characterized the European and North American experience with modernity, appears to be similarly vulnerable in the face of some rather 'un-Chinese'/'non-socialist' influences. China's youth, in particular, now are more open to a rejection of idealism in favour of pragmatism, turning away from collectivist interdependencies and towards personal independence.[49] Clearly no institution is more influential in mediating and promoting these changes than capitalist consumption. According to Knight, '[e]veryday life ... is ... increasingly infused with manifestations of Western ...values ... [T]he lifestyle of Western materialism, and in particular American excessive consumerism, is becoming fashionable ...'[50]

To their credit, most Chinese intellectuals reject some sort of defensive response, based on some kind of ideal or 'essential' Chinese culture. Instead of being reactionary (as are most fundamentalist religions), the state is seen as a crucial agent in facilitating the ongoing development of a more cosmopolitan Chinese culture – a culture structured to buffer consumption's less appealing dynamics.[51] Some Party theorists have even advocated the positive implications of global influences and the prospective elaboration of global socialist principles. The mainstream view, however, is less ambitious. Cao Tianyu, commonly associated with the country's New Left, suggests that the challenge for China is to develop an 'alternative modernity', one reaching 'beyond the logic of capitalist expansion'. More specifically, Cao stresses the role of the nation state and patriotism in response to the seemingly overwhelming long-term influences of market relations and capitalist consumption.[52]

In China, as in India, state policy and the nation are both complementary and oppositional to capitalist consumption. For the Chinese, public education is mandated to redress 'money worship, hedonism, ultra-egoism and other decadent ideas'[53] while, in India, marketers themselves mobilize the nationalist new swadeshi as a means of selling goods and services. Moreover, Chinese officials view the introduction of commercial agents in its mass media as a means of developing the country's own pro-socialist culture products for domestic *and* international consumption.[54] In contrast to this effort to 'go global', China (using technologies purchased from Western corporations) also plans to continue its efforts to censor politically undesirable Internet communications while using ICTs to monitor potential dissidents.[55]

Like India, not only is the developing institution of capitalist consumption mediating China's economic and cultural 'modernisation', the role played by consumption in the ongoing elaboration of conceptual systems – characterized as they are by ongoing nationalist orientations – again demonstrates the inadequacy of GCS prognostications. Remnants of the national products movement, through its implicit embrace of commodified social relations, paradoxically has enabled the socialist state to become perhaps the key agent (at least domestically) of the globalization project. The patriotism that dominated the pre-1949 movement now plays a central role in counter-balancing capitalist consumption's institutional development. Nationalism was the antidote to imperialism before 1949; after 1979, it again has become pivotal in both facilitating *and* redressing 'free market' forces.

The 'developing' world and abstract universalisms

As in the third face of power, capitalist consumption in relatively 'developed' political economies has become a taken-for-granted common sense – an institution so influential that its effects generally are not consciously noticed. The institution's influence on the conceptual systems used to process information and experience into 'reality' has facilitated the dominance of here-and-now thinking and a prioritization of individual short-term needs and desires over community, class and their long-term interests. The very fact that today's Indian and Chinese middle classes (and similarly situated consumers around the world) are still aware of the institution while the relatively wealthy of the world generally are not underlines both its predominance in already 'developed' countries and the potential for alternatives in others. We can briefly summarize this point by comparing Chinese with American norms over the day-to-day necessity of food.

In a marketing study conducted in Nanjing (population 2.8 million), middle-class shoppers – the targeted demographic of foreign and domestic grocery stores – were interviewed with the goal of understanding why many were reluctant to buy processed (canned, frozen, dried, chilled, semi-prepared and prepared) foods.[56] From 1993 to 1998, over 30 supermarket companies established approximately 700 branches in the city. They assumed that the growing disposable incomes of Nanjing's middle class, coupled with its hectic lifestyle, would generate a demand for their stores and processed foods. In practice, however, long-established conventions concerning what most Chinese eat constituted an unexpectedly pernicious barrier to sales. In China, access to fresh produce and 'still alive' meats (and the time-consuming norm of selecting and preparing these foods) turned out to be both culturally engrained and bad for the supermarket business.[57]

While younger, wealthier Chinese are more open to change (as, for example, the success of *McDonald's* and other Western fast food franchises demonstrates), those who are older or lacking the incomes needed to buy relatively expensive foods are less adaptable.[58] But, again, the most important factor keeping these stores on the cultural periphery is China's domestic obsession with fresh ingredients. Veeck and Burns report that

> Shoppers observed buying fish would reach into the tub and pick up a number of fish with their bare hands to choose the more lively (and presumably more tasty and nutritious) ... Consumers also manually inspect live chickens and ducks ... One shopper ... felt the abdomens of 12 different live chickens 'to check for insect bites and feel how fat they are.'[59]

Even what Westerners consider to be 'clean' or 'dirty' is different. For example, many food shoppers in Nanjing avoid vegetables that have their soils washed off; in this cultural context, dirt indicates less time and distance from the farm. In China and other parts of the world, the notion that the food one buys and eats should be abstracted from its place of origin and the conditions of its production makes little sense. Soil, for many, thus is a sign of safety and cleanliness[60] while, in the West, preservatives, artificial colouring and an emphasis on marketing and packaging are more than just acceptable – they are normal.

Importantly, more than just 'cultural tradition' is responsible for slowing the growth of supermarkets and processed foods in China. Food itself, for most Chinese, constitutes a core means of reaffirming relationships and identities. Spending limited time in traditional markets and preparing meals 'from scratch' remains, for many, a familial responsibility. Based, arguably, on the long-standing inter-dependence of extended families and the need to consume nutritious foods amidst supply shortages, eating in China is not primarily an individual activity (as it is in America) – more fundamentally it is a familial and social obligation in which the needs of children are primary.[61]

Of course the popularity of fast food restaurants, especially among the young, signals a different future unfolding. Through urbanization, the wage labour contract, increasing competition and the inter-generational articulation of capitalist consumption, individualized eating practices involving

more processed foods can be anticipated. Children already are the most pervasive consumers of these in China. Almost every school in Nanjing, for
example, has kiosks located near entrances, selling ice cream bars, candy
and other snacks to young customers. Domestic and foreign corporations,
seeking to modify eating habits, also supply processed foods to schools
directly. In a country of predominantly one-child families, as one Nanjing
mother commented, '[a]dvertisers know that it's easy to get money from
parents ...'[62] In China, as children's conceptual systems are being forged, the
young, in effect, are being employed to re-socialize their parents.

* * *

In Chapter 2, we argued that capitalist consumption has become a core
mediator of the globalization project. Among those with the wealth needed
to take part, the buying and possession of commodities tangibly demonstrates the power and autonomy of individuals – giving people, in effect, a
substantive reason to go along with globalization. Also, by normalizing
change itself, consumption constitutes a kind of institutional mooring. In
light of the dubious claims made by GCS progressives, and taking into
account the evidence marshalled here and in other chapters, we are now in
a position to make another important point: beyond its role as a hegemonic
medium, capitalist consumption also constitutes something of a Trojan
horse for capital – it opens doors and, once 'inside', problematically but
effectively modifies cultures in ways that facilitate a slew of structural and
conceptual changes.

Capitalist consumption is not just being exported or universalized.
Indeed, components of it are, but others are infused with local and national
dimensions. More to the point, the globalization of capitalist consumption
itself entails, to use the words of Mazzarella, 'the assembly – in a piecemeal,
contested, and multi-local manner – [of] an entire social ontology'.[63] In
'developing' political economies, traditional, 'pre-modern' dichotomies
involving true or false needs reflecting moral and social dimensions of the
institution gradually are erased. Rather than the long-term needs of others –
as reflected in the European feudal 'just price' or the Gandhian swaraj or the
Chinese association of consumption with struggles against imperialism and
the importance of family – the modern institution of consumption offers 'an
alternative populism based on the figure of the sovereign consumer as the
final arbiter of all normative questions ...'[64]

It is through this abstraction – through the use of media that associate
commodities with identity, meaning and happiness – that an ensemble of
capitalist institutions and neoliberal reforms are exogenously imposed and
endogenously accommodated. In this process, states play perhaps *the* crucial
role through their powers relating to tariffs, credit, education, mass media
regulations and other structural conditions, as well as their monopolization
of both what is legally binding and, of course, the use of coercion. In this

complex, the strategic position of marketing and advertising firms cannot be overstated as these are the primary agents negotiating the cultural transition from norms characterizing pre-modern consumption to those associated with the modern and, prospectively, the neo-modern.

As Mazzarella points out (conveying the work of Dipesh Chakrabarty), histories of capitalism are usually written in terms of an imagined dualism: 'either the agents of globalising capital are seen to dismiss/destroy difference entirely (the cultural imperialism thesis ...) or they seize upon cultural difference for their own purposes, domesticating it by means of commodification and offering it up for consumption'.[65] In this latter, relatively post-structuralist, interpretation difference primarily becomes a matter of individual preference and the marketplace becomes little more than the structure in which one's freedom to choose among a dozen brands of peanut butter is idealized. But both the history of the West and the contemporary experience of 'developing' political economies suggest that something more complex is going on. Just as capital rarely obliterates existing norms and local or national particularisms, at least not entirely (due, in part at least, to the relative importance of direct relationships and experiences in shaping conceptual systems), 'the process of commodification requires a suppression of embodied idiosyncrasies and local conjunctures – the particularity of use-value is in this sense subordinated to the generality of exchange value ...'[66]

Through the use of local or national history and tradition, advertisers and marketers introduce or re-introduce capitalist consumption into the 'modernising' culture. Once established, it is elaborated, usually through younger consumers. Indeed, the post-structuralist tendency to dismiss Marxist concerns over commodification, and sometimes even celebrate the consumer as a sovereign arbiter of identity and lifestyle, often involves the assumption that local or national 'hybrids' reflect the triumph of individual choice over the homogenizing inclinations of capital. But it is at a more profound level – that of conceptual systems – that we find consumption's role as capital's Trojan horse. It is through the institution's mediation of the past with the future and the particular with the universal that we find capitalist consumption's most profound historical implications.

The global commodification of human relations

As in the pre-capitalist West and, more recently, in much of India and China prior to globalization, goods and services, for the most part, served mostly utilitarian purposes. To use Marxist parlance, the 'use value' of an object (the power of something through its use) was closely associated with its 'exchange value' (the value of something in relation to other things). In pre-modern societies, commodities are generally acquired and used to satisfy needs that are not primarily social or psychological. A bar of soap, for example, is used to clean one's skin and little more. With capitalism and modernity, historical forces and processes abstracted this norm. Commodities became vehicles to satisfy the many sociological and psychological needs that private property, urban living, the wage labour contract, the price system and other dominant mediators of daily life generally neglected. For the emerging bourgeoisie of London in the eighteenth century and the middle classes of Mumbai and Beijing more recently, the relationship between use and exchange values became more obtuse. The bar of soap that once just cleaned skin now had a connotative use also, usually one constructed through the guise of a much deliberated and promoted brand identity. Through its purchase and use, magical benefits are said to follow. A simple bar of soap now becomes the key to being more successful at work, finding romance and love or feeling younger and more energetic. With neo-modern society, such abstractions have become even more fantastic as the commodity itself embodies a social or psychological need or desire. As a recent advertisement for *BMW* puts it, 'Happiness is not around the corner. Happiness is the corner' (Illustration 5.4). Here, the treacherous conditions of one's (life) journey are not just surmountable through the use of a commodity; the commodity *itself* empowers.

Source: BMW.

Illustration 5.4 BMW advertisement

While exceptions exist (and in some places persist), the historical shift in how consumption is conceptualized and practised reflects and effects even more affecting developments. Among those who are successful at making the money needed to buy the commodities used to communicate identity and meaning, the power of the 'sovereign' individual/consumer (whether or not he/she has power in the role of citizen) is tangibly affirmed. For those able to participate in the globalization project as consumers, the abstractions this entails are largely *in sinc* with capitalism's systemic tendencies to fetishise commodities and alienate human relationships. With these conceptual systems structured into everyday realities, it's little wonder that market relations are routinely reified – unsurprizing that the biases and actions of individuals and corporations validate one another through a common sense tautology of circular reasoning.

In this chapter, the historicist approach used previously has been applied to get 'into the heads' of those whose political economies are being 'modernised' as a result of the globalization project. As the examples of India and China illustrate, the project's success involves at least two seemingly oppositional dynamics. On the one hand, the nation, with its localisms and traditions – structurally mediating conceptual systems through daily life in a particular place and time – compel varying degrees of heterogeneity. At one level, then, capitalist consumption is structured and practised differently, in different locations and at different historical junctures. This again is what some analysts are looking at when assessing globalization as a process that consists of (or itself generates) a proliferation of global-local ('glocal') hybrids. On the other hand, the commodificaton of human relations involves a more affecting homogenization of conceptual systems. In China, for instance, commonalities are emerging amidst the fragmentation of contemporary consumer culture; here and elsewhere, the anomic, acquisitive and individualized are being universalized.[67]

As explained in Chapter 3, such conditions are ideal for the marketer whose direct goal is the selling of a commodity and whose indirect long-term effect is the institutionalization of particular ways of thinking about and acting in relation to consumption. The biggest challenge facing *Cadbury's* chocolate in many 'developing' countries, for example, has been the reluctance of domestic consumers to buy things for themselves impulsively.[68] Other corporations seeking to forge new markets elsewhere (in Russia, for example) have been hindered by the socialized norm of repairing things rather than buying something new; of acquiring what is needed through barter or reciprocal exchange rather than purchase; and a long-established reliance on family and inter-personal networks to get something done as opposed to a private sector service provider.[69] As a kind of Trojan horse for the globalization project, capitalist consumption, through practice, normalizes social relations that are relatively impersonal and, through the anonymity of prices, malleable. In effect, the emerging norms of consumption marginalize familial and social obligations, facilitating two even more fundamentally influential mediators: private property and contracts. The historical dynamic, initiated over five hundred years ago, continues.

* * *

To more fully explain the changes taking place in many 'developing' countries, we again apply the concept commodity fetishism. In those premodern societies where the exchange of goods and services is coordinated through gift-giving rituals, individuals give others what they know they need in anticipation that the outcome will be the reciprocal receipt of something useful. In this type of political economy, both parties would need to know one another well enough to facilitate this kind of useful exchange. They also would need to anticipate that those who have been given gifts will be around long enough for this reciprocity to take place. Quite unlike contemporary capitalism, in which exchange often takes place anonymously through the price system, the gift economy relies on relatively unmediated forms of exchange. Also unlike capitalism, with its labour mobility and the predominance of relatively 'private' lifestyles, traditional gift economies rely on a lack of mobility and the general absence of privacy.

In pre-capitalist societies, the fact that people generally stayed put and knew one another enabled gift giving and, later, in light of greater mobility and autonomy, the development of the barter system. Only capitalism, with its vast production of wealth, enabling a massive growth of population facilitated by related technological and administrative innovations, bases exchange on the price system and its related abstractions.

Capitalism's success has very much relied on its capacity to 'free' people from such intimate relationships as required by gift exchange systems. In terms of its systemic drive to accumulate capital through the realization of surplus values by selling commodities for a profit, capitalist political economies have developed new means of selling goods and services by infusing them with *meaning* – meaning, it must be emphasized, sought by people as an indirect result of this same freeing-up process.

As addressed in Chapter 3, the contemporary history of capitalist consumption has been dominated by marketers and advertisers and their application of ever more complex methods of promoting their brands in response to the need to sell things *and* a general cultural decline of intimacy, identity and apparent meaning. As advertising executive Douglas Atkin argues, 'established institutions are proving to be increasingly inadequate sources of meaning and community. On the other hand, there has been a growth of a very sophisticated kind of consumerism ... Alongside alternative religions, brands are now serious contenders for belief and community'.[70]

Commodity fetishism is more than just the incidental outcome of historical developments, namely the wealth, mobility and cosmopolitan freedoms that have emerged in conjunction with capitalist modernity; it has also been directly promoted by an increasingly transnational multi-billion dollar marketing and advertising industry. The core point we are making here is that *the power of the marketing and advertising firm depends on the paradoxical gutting of intimate community relationships and the emptying out of traditionally meaningful lifestyles.* Modern commerce, it can even been argued, has made a science of fetishisation. The age-old and essential exchange of goods and services now, in the words of Don Slater, 'breaks down social experience into minute and discrete calculations and into calculating (and competing) individuals; it abstracts all social phenomena from their substantive context, transforming them into movable, transformable, alienable objects; the imperatives of the cash nexus dissolve all social ties ...'[71]

How consumption is organized and thought about – how it is institutionalized in various political, economic and cultural formations – thus constitutes a rather central struggle – one through which old relations can be replaced by new, and traditional social relations may be transformed into modern. Most importantly, from the perspective of capitalism's vested interests, unprofitable lifestyles need to be modified in line with 'the good life' of consumerism. The methodology of this dynamic involves the creativity of marketers and advertisers taking advantage of and promoting commodity fetishism.

The historic decline of relatively unmediated relationships, and the vacuum of meaning that has emerged in its wake, has opened the door to a potentially radical restructuring of conceptual systems. Commodities, under capitalism, now are routinely distanced from the social relations and ecological conditions of their production, while the functional utility of goods are obscured or lost altogether in the context of marketing and advertising. As Martyn Lee points out, 'the success of today's consumer economy actually depends upon the regulation of the symbolic and cultural dimensions of commodities; that is, the exercise of control over the *economy of symbolic or cultural goods*'.[72] More profoundly still, the way in which consumption is institutionalized, and the political, economic and cultural struggles surrounding this process, is central in the hegemonic framing or counter-hegemonic disruption of the world's emerging market civilisation.

Emptied of their history, commodities are filled with fantastic qualities. They are increasingly sold and valued for their symbolic worth rather than their utility. But to assume that people simply accept any meaning associated with a good or service as a result of the wizardry of marketers and advertisers is quite wrong; more product promotions fail than succeed. People are not intellectual sponges, absorbing the messages and meanings imposed on them by others. Instead, *we participate in the construction of this fantasy world and this precisely is the basis of consumption's power in contemporary life.* The meaning of a commodity and, more generally, the meaningfulness of consumption, are *negotiated* realities. The sexual energy that a particular automobile can bring to us or the self-confidence that our membership at a gym delivers or the sense of intimacy that friends provide when we consume a particular brand of beer are all constructions, of course, but they are constructions that people often embrace *within the parametres of existing conceptual systems.*[73]

This is not to say that such needs are natural or innate, although a strong case can be made supporting this from a sociological perspective.[74] Capitalism itself is not *the* barrier to a utopian return to an intimate and meaningful life; instead, what we are arguing is that capitalism has systemically generated the tendency for people to organize their lives and relationships through relatively mediated abstractions involving, among others, private property, contracts, prices and the moment-to-moment distortions of commodity fetishism.

While some make their living promoting commodity fetishism and stoking the dream world of consumerism, most of us simply take part in this complex through our participation as the buyers of commodities and through our fantasies related to these purchases. The 'self-evident' qualities of the car or gym membership or beer are generally accepted and not collectively dismissed in large part because not only do we want to believe but we also actively participate in consumption as an aspiration (if not *the* aspiration) of our lives.

Here, we must recall the *negotiated* rather than asymmetrically coerced or imposed nature of common sense. Today, in increasingly diverse and distant cultures, the act of consumption and its idealization through advertising, social interactions and significant lifetime events (such as weddings, birthdays and the like) itself conveys a 'normal' and 'desirable' way of life. This, in turn, marginalizes traditional relationships and ways of seeing. The contemporary institution of consumption, in effect, communicates new or 'modern' identities and ideals. The woman or the child, for example, is no longer merely an appendage of a patriarchal structure. Wives and children are also consumers and, progressively, may be individualized as such. Indeed, one of the reasons that capitalist consumption ideals are usually embraced involves the institution's liberating features: the individual is emancipated from being, practically and conceptually, little more than a subordinate part of a whole. Yet on this point we are reminded of the fable of the python and the hare. The 'reciprocity' of capitalist consumption's institutional development in 'traditional' cultures is like the python's consumption of the rabbit: it may seem as if the hare now is inside the snake *and* that the snake has been altered by its presence. But, over time, the hare's body is digested and the python is free to pursue its next meal.[75]

Common sense and resistance

While consensual forms of hegemony involve a shared and negotiated common sense, consumption – with its active promotion of the family or individual as primary consumers – not only diminishes the needs of society as a whole and the long-term interests of the collective, the institution also tends to promote consumer (rather than citizen or worker) identities and the immediate satisfactions of the seemingly autonomous person. Emancipation from stifling traditions and daily want understandably seduces people in a diverse range of cultures into the open arms of capitalist consumption *but*, in leaving one form of oppression behind, another kind is enthusiastically pursued. The primary agents of capitalist consumption – marketers and advertisers – then inform us of our real or imagined insecurities, desires and shortcomings. Commodities are offered up as kind of aspirin to relieve the pain. But, of course, the headaches come back, then 'new', 'improved' and ever-more individualized aspirins are offered up again and again and again.

The role of consumption as an institutional medium is thus paradoxically dependent on perpetuating discontent by individualizing problems, promoting consumer identities and offering up answers to life's maladies in the guise of carefully framed, commodity-based 'solutions'. If we learn to see ourselves as consumers, rather than as producers or citizens, we are more likely to frame our concerns and aspirations in terms of 'working harder to get my share' instead of 'working with others to change collective conditions'. Moreover, controlling one's own destiny through consumption, particularly in the context of a political economic system in which the wage labour contract implies seemingly countless possibilities to make money, constitutes a more immediate and apparently feasible option for those seeking to improve their lives in relation to revolutionary or collective alternatives. The hegemonic power of consumption directly involves the fact that people *choose* to take part. But while we choose to see ourselves as either producers or consumers, the role of marketers and advertisers in promoting what Raymond Williams called a 'system of organised magic' obscures this choice.[76]

Rather than the result of declining state powers in the face of a globalization – either a globalization from 'above' or 'below' – our focus on capitalist consumption's development in India and China more accurately can be described as the outcome of local/national responses (both conscious and sub-conscious) to domestic and foreign efforts to commodify social relationships and reform conceptual systems. In this sense, the histories addressed in this chapter reflect a contradictory challenge that might be framed in terms of a question: how can national/local citizens and workers respond effectively to the dynamics structuring capitalist relations if, over time, the commodification of their cultures and conceptual systems atomizes and temporally delimits the parameters of prospective resistance? Again, a social-psychological form of divide and rule rather than an imperialist tidal wave or the flowering of autonomous responses appears to be the essential process at work. It is in this sense that capitalist consumption constitutes something of a Trojan horse for the globalization project; by modifying conceptual systems, it forges both divisions in the political culture and, more generally, stimulates the same kind of social-psychological vacuums experienced during the modernization of the West. Of course the short-term response may not be to embrace commercially defined means of finding identity and meaning. These vacuums, under certain conditions, instead may trigger responses at odds with both globalization and capitalist consumption.

While the prognostications of GCS progressives are, at best, simplistic and, at worst, delusional, the fortunes of another GCS – a global consumer society – remains (at least in India and China) tied to another institution: the nation state. Beyond the importance of state policies shaping the parameters within which capitalist consumption unfolds, many consumers in these 'developing' countries recall or utilize pre-modern ways of thinking and acting. These cultures thus possess conceptual systems that have not yet been fully enculturated in terms of the 'me-first', immediate-gratification norms of most Westerners. Here, meaning and identity have not yet been chained to the acquisition of things.

Although the commercial abstractions now pervasive in the West are the subjects of some amount of (conscious and sub-conscious) scrutiny in much of the South, they may well become predominant in this region, first with India and China's young professional middle class and, later, with workers also. But having recognized this long-term trajectory, we hypothesize that a window of opportunity is upon us. For those who have escaped the abject poverty of the past without yet entering the invisible cage of the modern/neo-modernist pursuit of evermore commodities, the intellectual capacities suited to respond to the globalization project critically, creatively and progressively (involving the nation state) now appear to be in place.

In Chapter 6, we return to the 'developed' world – particularly the world as it is conceptualized by the US foreign policy status quo in Washington, DC. As we will see, capitalist consumption has also had an effect on the thoughts and activities of government officials. Our core argument in what follows is this: capitalist consumption has contributed to the relatively ahistorical and reactionary policies of both the Bush administration and, more poignantly, many Western opponents to the globalization project. A cause and consequence of this state of affairs is a general consumption-mediated neglect of our modern/neo-modern culture's appreciation of time that, we argue, likely will culminate in its violent annihilation.

6
Neo-Imperialism, Consumption and the Crisis of Time

> The United States, with systems of mechanized communication and organized force, has sponsored a new type of imperialism imposed on common law in which sovereignty is preserved *de jure* and used to expand imperialism *de facto*.
>
> —Harold Innis[1]

The power of the American state in international affairs has been subjected to countless strategic studies, critical assessments and resistance projects. In the midst of what may become a seemingly endless 'war on terror', debates concerning the policies informing the use of America's military resources now are congealing around the problematic process of occupying and eventually 'democratising' Iraq and, with it, the rest of the Middle East. In the following pages we take a step beyond and back from such analyses by relating the rationale behind these policies to what Innis many years ago referred to as a civilizational crisis involving *time*. While much attention has been paid to the spatial conquest, occupation and reorganization of the world through trade agreements, neoliberal policy impositions and ICTs, using our understanding of conceptual systems and the institution of capitalist consumption, herein we address still more profound questions concerning time – how it is being organized and conceptualized, as well as the tragic implications of consumption-mediated temporal norms.

The policies promoted by the Bush White House, particularly since 9/11, should be understood in terms of something more disconcerting than the preferences of an extraordinarily hawkish administration. These policy choices – reflected in what has become a characteristically unilateralist and militaristic foreign policy – are, in fact, rooted in the soils of two mutually supportive historical developments: America's military, political and economic dominance *and* what can be described as a generally arrogant and, from a Gramscian perspective, reactionary common sense. But more to the point, our contemporary juncture in history is pervaded by a temporally

135

delimited understanding of the dynamics and structures shaping contemporary society. As we explain below, even the globalization project's most vociferous opponents – from reactionary terrorists to progressive anti-globalization activists – share the globalization status quo's ahistorical and unreflexive biases. The consequences of this general neglect of time now are upon us: already, early in the twenty-first century, injustice, violence and ecological collapse appear to be mounting and radiating world-wide while both America's foreign policy leaders and the chattering class's most fashionable agents – post-structuralist theorists – advise people to do little more than get in their cars and go shopping.

American policies, we argue, in part constitute the violent fruit of a capitalist consumption-mediated neglect of humanity's collective memory, reflexive engagement and long-term needs. Such tendencies have been ingrained in structures, practices and thinking processes – in, as we have argued, the conceptual systems used to process information and experience into reality. Rather than taking seriously the possibility that the problems facing US and transnational corporate ambitions stem from a spiralling neglect of long-term considerations and, indeed, *reflexive thought itself*, short-term, quick-fix, spatially focused ways of thinking now are embedded into the very marrow of our modern/neo-modern culture.

America's neo-imperialist turn

As discussed previously, the United States has become extraordinarily important in the complex drive to expand and speed-up global capitalism – what we have called the globalization project. While the expansionist tendencies of the United States have been well documented by historians,[2] only in recent years has the notion of a grand neo-imperialist project been the subject of open debate in Washington. Following the Cold War, in the context of emerging problems facing the project, and in response to the terrorist attacks of 9/11, the concept of empire has become an increasingly in-vogue part of think tank and academic hallway discourse. Echoing the self-assumed benevolence of the British in the nineteenth century, and Rome after Augustus, proponents of a neo-imperialist American-centred world order now emphasize the virtues of liberal democracy and the material benefits of the market system.

To clarify the chronology of this neo-imperialist turn, it emerged in the wake of upheavals related to the globalization project. Writing a year before the 2001 attacks, Richard Haas (special assistant and member of the National Security Council under the first President Bush, and the Director of Policy Planning in the State Department under the second Bush), argued in a paper titled 'Imperial America' that the United States should embrace its role as an imperial power. America, Haas argued, not only has before it the strategic opportunity to 'extend its control' over world affairs, but also has a moral responsibility to 'grace' the globe with its model of 'free markets, human rights and democracy, enforced by the most awesome military power the world has ever known'.[3]

Picking up on this point, Stephen Peter Rosen of the Olin Institute opined that a 'political unit that has overwhelming superiority in military power, and uses that power to influence the internal behavior of other states, is called an empire. Because the United States does not seek to control territory or govern the overseas citizens of the empire, we are an indirect empire, to be sure, but an empire nonetheless. If this is correct, our goal is not combating a rival, but maintaining our imperial position, and maintaining imperial order'.[4]

Underlining that an empire is not necessarily a bad thing, *Wall Street Journal* editor Max Boot writes that 'Many have suggested that the September 11 attack on America was payback for US imperialism ... [and that the] United States must become a kinder, gentler nation ... [,] must become ... a republic, not an empire.' Wrong, says Boot:

> this analysis is exactly backward: The September 11 attack was a result of insufficient American involvement and ambition; the solution is to be more expansive in our goals and more assertive in their implementation ... America now faces the prospect of military action in many of the same lands where generations of British colonial soldiers went on campaigns ... Afghanistan and other troubled foreign lands cry out for the sort of enlightened foreign administration once provided by self-confident Englishmen ... Killing bin Laden is important and necessary; but it is not enough. New bin Ladens could rise up to take his place. We must not only wipe out the vipers but also destroy their nest and do our best to prevent new nests from being built there again.[5]

What is extraordinary about these and other proclamations regarding America's 'responsibility' to take on the imperialist mantle is that such proclamations are being made so *publicly*.[6] Until recently, sentences linking the United States with empire were not to be uttered in the polite company of Georgetown and Capitol Hill cocktail parties. Regardless of well-documented indices suggesting a long-established imperialist orientation, to associate America with Rome or the British was out of bounds.

Not long after the Second World War, however, the United States had over a thousand military bases around the world – an overseas presence far exceeding that of any power in history. By the 1990s, this number had been roughly halved (understandable in light of the end of Cold War hostilities), but the trend was counter-balanced by the rising number of US military personnel deployed overseas in temporary operations. In 1999, American forces were present in about one hundred countries.[7] This transition from permanent bases to flexible deployments was not simply a cost-saving measure, but a conscious strategic shift – away from the containment of communism and towards mobility, speed, and overwhelming technological superiority. Today, American military expenditures are greater than those of the world's next seven largest powers *combined*.[8]

While this overwhelming might has become a core doctrine of US defence policy, a question rarely addressed is: what and who is this defence policy *defending*?

Since the early 1990s, a number of the current Bush administration's most influential officials actively promoted the notion that America's unparalleled capabilities constituted a window of opportunity – an opportunity to re-cast global structures in accordance with US strategic interests. A document that concretized this perspective is the Bush administration's *NSS* of 2002. In it, three principles for US foreign policy in the twenty-first century are made explicit: *First*, the existing global dominance of the American military must be perpetuated in order to prevent any prospective rival from aspiring to challenge its position; *Second*, America has the right to take exception to international norms and engage in pre-emptive military strikes; And *third*, US citizens should be immune from prospective prosecutions by the International Criminal Court.[9]

As mentioned previously, the *NSS* also directly associates the capitalist economic system and neoliberal policies with 'development' and political 'freedom'. *NSS* 2006 reiterates this commitment:

> Promoting free and fair trade has long been a bedrock tenet of American foreign policy. Greater economic freedom is ultimately inseparable from political liberty. Economic freedom empowers individuals, and empowered individuals increasingly demand greater political freedom. Greater economic freedom also leads to greater economic opportunity and prosperity for everyone.[10]

Among the Bush administration's achievements in relation to this agenda, *NSS* 2006 lists its efforts to eliminate all tariffs on consumer and industrial goods, including the further opening up of trade in services through the WTO, its negotiation or completion of additional trade agreements with 25 countries, and its initiation of a separate Middle East Free Trade Area (MEFTA) agreement. Of the foreign policy 'challenges' it intends to address, the administration commits itself to oppose those 'nations [that] frustrate the economic aspirations of their people by failing to promote entrepreneurship, protect intellectual property, or allow their citizens access to vital investment capital'.[11]

Not surprisingly, to promote this goal, the White House pledges to strengthen and use the WTO and other international organizations for the purpose of promoting 'growth-oriented economic policies'. The World Bank, for example, will be encouraged to create conditions within nation states that favour 'investments in the private sector' as well as 'economic freedom, governance, and measurable results ...'[12]

To better understand this focus, we first need to clarify the role of the nation state (and, indeed, the American state) in the context of the globalization project. Building on the position presented in Chapter 4, transnational corporations and investors have become more than just integrated into the decision-making processes of domestic states; in recent years, these interests have become increasingly focused on external opportunities. Rather than an either/or argument in which these developments reflect the absolute decline of state power (in which global forces compel states to respond) *or* the ascendancy of transnational structures and networks that somehow determine the thought processes of those implementing domestic and international policies (as in the GCS/'globalization theory' approach), a more logically and empirically sustainable analysis recognizes that most states now are attempting to mediate or manage a complex of vested interests – some seeking to defend their domestic positions (such as nationally or locally focused corporations), some seeking access to foreign markets (such as domestically based transnational firms and those with international aspirations) and, more generally, some seeking raw materials, commodities and labour from other countries.[13]

From this vantage point, the United States stands in a unique position. Like other countries, the American state is engaged in a kind of juggling act: accommodating transnational corporations and investors within its borders *while* assisting domestic interests (sometimes including organized labour) in light of overseas pressures *while also* enabling some to take advantage of opportunities overseas. But the American state additionally stands as the core mediator of an even more ambitious task – it is the only state possessing the power resources needed to unilaterally pursue the more universal globalization project. Not surprisingly then, American officials are perhaps the world's most consistent public sector proponents of the project. In the words of *NSS* 2006,

> Globalization presents many opportunities. Much of the world's prosperity and improved living standards in recent years derive from the expansion of global trade, investment, information, and technology. The United States has been a leader in promoting these developments, and we believe they have improved significantly the quality of life of the American people and people the world over.[14]

Before proceeding, a response to those who view the globalization project as the progenitor of global justice and prosperity is in order.[15] Notwithstanding the ideals conveyed in market fundamentalist discourse, not only does the United States and other 'developed' political economies practice free trade selectively, Western and Japanese officials also consistently 'prevent poor countries from exploiting their few advantages on the world market'.[16] Through the international organizations that the United States dominates – particularly the World Bank and the IMF – neo-classical economic development policies have been imposed on countries with little regard for the preferences of domestic populations or the mandates of elected governments. Historically, such policies were not applied to the world's relatively developed nations and the United States, even today, rarely follows the prescriptions it imposes on others. Highly selective free trade practices, the strategic use of deficit spending, the government's subsidization of domestic corporations (particularly through the Pentagon's ballooning budget), tax policies and other means – all commonplace inside Washington's beltway – are unacceptable options for the world's relatively vulnerable. Some of the more deleterious implications of this foreign policy – infamously referred to by mainstream economists as 'externalities' (such as environmental degradation, cultural upheaval and, of course, the direct or indirect deaths of countless people as a result of military force and the social-economic violence stemming from primitive accumulation) are routinely dismissed under an 'if-you-want-to-make-an-omelet-you've-got-to-break-some-eggs' approach to 'development'.

Far from a moral mission to promote prosperity and freedom around the world, the globalization project constitutes a concerted effort to re-make the world in accordance with the perceived interests of US-based corporations and investors and, more abstractly, global capitalism *writ large*.

Just as those who enjoyed the benefits of Roman Citizenship under the Empire before AD 212 were outnumbered by those who did not, those benefiting from the world order being forged through the American state are in the minority. US foreign policy – involving the distribution of 'goodies' to the compliant and punishments levied against the uncooperative – constitutes a political-economic toolbox drawn upon in the task of prying-open and re-structuring foreign markets in ways that serve the perceived interests of the capitalist status quo.[17]

Rather than simply acting in its 'national interest' (an interest usually dominated by large-scale corporate interests), US policy is fundamentally about supporting the structural needs of transnational capitalism almost everywhere. As President Bill Clinton told the United Nations upon the conclusion of the Cold War, 'Our overriding purpose is to expand and strengthen the world's community of market-based democracies.'[18] This objective and its implementation through the globalization project does more than just funnel wealth out of the 'developing' world into the hands of the already wealthy; it also reforms the global political economy in ways that entrench disparities, further transnational capital's control over space while perpetuating a general political, economic and cultural neglect of time.

Why, specifically, should we call this American-led effort and, indeed, the globalization project more generally 'neo-imperialism'? Beyond references among Washington policy elites concerning the necessity of forging a post-9/11 American empire, following Rosenberg, we recognize that the structural conditions through which capitalist relations unfold entail an elaboration of what occurred in England and other Western countries over the course of centuries. Producers (workers) in capitalist society, unlike feudalism's serfs or other 'unfree' labourers, have no direct access to their means of subsistence. Under capitalism, state-sanctioned property rights and state-enforced contract relations constitute the means through which private entities secure surpluses at the point of production. With mediated capitalist relationships coming to the fore, seemingly non-political relations ironically become the bases of social power. In order to survive, 'free' people are compelled to sell their labour (just like any other commodity) to earn the monies needed to purchase what's needed to survive.

Mainstream analysts and, indeed, Bush administration officials are referring to this form of social power when they pontificate about 'market forces' and 'free markets'. The inequalities formerly transparent in the feudal–serf relationship now are obscured, particularly as a result of the state's unique position as society's 'political' authority while, even more abstractly, private relations mediated by contracts take place in the 'apolitical' realm of civil society. As Marx put it, this new order is characterized by the rise of 'personal independence *based on dependence mediated by things*' (especially commodities, property rights and contracts).[19]

Today we see this transformation taking place at an accelerated pace in countries around the world. As explained in Chapter 4, the collapse of state socialism in the early 1990s, the establishment of new international trade arrangements, the ascendancy of ICTs and the orchestrated reform of domestic economies along neoliberal lines, all coalesced to make 'globalization' appear to be something new, natural and even inevitable. However, as we have argued throughout, the rapid annihilation of space and time that is now such a routine part of contemporary life (and, in the process, the amalgamation of the world's nations and cultures into one disparate, complex marketplace) in fact constitutes a *project* – a political effort led by powerful vested interests, mediated through states, particularly the United States.

All this has involved the internationalization of capitalist society, itself entailing inter-related public and private reforms. The public component concerns the reform and management of the states-system, impelling or compelling countries to play along with a US-centred, capitalist-dominated neoliberal economic order. The private aspect has involved domestic reforms crafted to facilitate the extraction and relaying of surpluses. 'It means,' writes Rosenberg, 'the rise of a new kind of empire: the empire of civil society.'[20]

In past empires, military force was used to discipline or occupy colonies – geographic entities structured to enable imperialist powers to directly manage the extraction of resources and surpluses. In our neo-imperialist era, such incursions are meant to be temporary, designed to establish state–civil society formations favourable to particular private sector interests. Indeed, the capitalist ideal, observed Marx, is the *absence* of a 'conscious, social regulation of production'.[21] The contemporary globalization project thus constitutes a shift away from explicitly public forms of domination and towards seemingly impersonal and private varieties. Capitalist consumption both reflects and deepens this transformation. Everyday life becomes more 'about' the individual and his/her acquisition of commodities involving, of course, the sale of one's own time and skills as commodities. In this neo-imperialist (dis)order, writes Rosenberg, personal independence paradoxically 'is based on relations of dependence (individuals depend on mutual exchange) mediated through things (the exchange relations established between their commodities)'.[22]

The globalization project challenged

The globalization project has owed much of its success to the fact that it constitutes a kind of mythological construction[23] enabling people to get on with their lives through the use of a broadly sketched-out intellectual roadmap – a roadmap involving contradictions but nevertheless constituting a compass amidst the insecurities characterizing the emerging political economic (dis)order.[24] Once the globalization myth ascribes a degree of desirability or inevitability, a sub-set of common sense assumptions such as the idealization of marketplace mechanisms to provide for people's needs, liberal democracy as a universal ideal (as well as the notion that capitalism is the only realistic path to it) and, of course, the view that the days of democratic power through the nation state are numbered, a certain hegemonic framework defining the boundaries of what is imaginable, acceptable and rational comes to the fore.

In recent years, the tapestry representing this myth has been fraying. In the United States, this began in the wake of the anti-globalization protests in Seattle. A number of remarkable people – the former Chief Economist of the World Bank, Joseph Stiglitz, among them – subsequently raised critical questions concerning the project and its corporate rather than human priorities.[25] With empirical evidence coming to light that the poor of the world have been getting poorer (see Chapter 1), it became apparent to many that the recipe for 'development' promoted by Washington was producing a way of life quite indigestible for hundreds of millions, if not billions.

Even before 9/11, a shadow thus had been cast over globalization as a reliable roadmap. Viewing these developments from downtown Washington, the challenge to the project's status as a consensual project compelled relatively few to reassess neoliberal policies and the unilateralist course of US foreign policy (although some occupying DC's political margins – Ralph Nader and Pat Buchanan, for example – certainly did). Instead, resistance to globalization generally did little more than reaffirm the apparent relevancy of military power.

One of the more influential organizations shaping this view and the unilateralist response to foreign opposition is the Project for the New American Century (PNAC). Established in 1997 by William Kristol and others, its active members prior to the Presidential election of 2000 constituted something of a *Who's Who* of the second Bush administration, including Dick Cheney, Donald Rumsfeld and Paul Wolfowitz. The organization's principles are based on what it calls a 'Reaganite approach' to the world. America's 'military strength and moral clarity' inform the need to significantly increase defence and security expenditures, directly challenge hostile regimes and pursue 'economic freedom' abroad. Additionally, the PNAC emphasizes the need to 'accept responsibility for ... preserving and extending an international order friendly to our security, our prosperity, and our principles'.[26]

Such views also were taking root in the late-1990s among others not usually associated with neo-conservative America. Anticipating the need to keep dissenting states and movements in line was Zbigniew Brzezinski, President Jimmy Carter's National Security Advisor, who wrote that the main task at hand is 'to prevent collusion and maintain dependence among the vassals, keep tributaries pliant and protected, and to keep the barbarians from coming together'.[27] For Brzezinski, the barbarians are those who violently resist the globalization project. Now in the context of America's war on terror, they include anyone not sharing Washington's idealization of a capitalist-friendly world order. But as American diplomat John Brady Kiesling, in his 2003 resignation letter to Secretary of State Colin Powell, pointed out, *oderint dum metuant* (Caligula's favourite quotation from the pre-Republic poet Lucius Accius meaning 'let them hate so that they fear') as a motto for handling international affairs is inherently contradictory.[28]

One useful attribute of being aware of the third face of power, conceptual systems and the implications of capitalist consumption and other media vis-à-vis the structuring of consciousness is that they help us avoid evaluating illogical or irrational ways of thinking as 'projections', 'distortions' or even some sort of 'false consciousness'. Throughout much of this book, we have escaped the need to use such problematic descriptors; instead, historicist tools that emphasize the complexity of knowledge and its construction have been applied. In the context of life amidst capitalist structures and commodified relationships, those who possess extraordinary amounts of wealth tend to, directly or indirectly, exercise extraordinary influence in the shaping of reality. Herein we have assessed media (broadly defined to include institutions, organizations and technologies) and the social environments through which human interactions take place, arguing that conceptual systems – the means through which information and experience are processed into knowledge – are directly influenced by such structured environments.

But how, precisely, do media influence these conceptual systems? Simply put, how a medium is structured usually shapes what the people using it come to believe is normal and abnormal. Conceptual systems *then* mediate what ways of thinking and acting are 'reasonable' and 'sensible' versus 'unreasonable' and 'nonsensical'.

This approach, recognizing the affecting potentials of media (broadly defined), is sometimes referred to as 'medium theory'. Its foundational theorist was the early twentieth-century political economist Harold Innis. His main goal was to use media as focal points through which *longue durée* developments could be better understood, particularly in terms of how historical (as well as contemporary) actors *thought/think* and the implications of these orientations. Alongside general political economic structures – the macro-historical structuring of human relationships that usually follow (or coincide with) identifiable dynamics – vested interests reform, maintain or develop the institutions, organizations and technologies used to mediate social-economic relations. As Innis discovered through his analysis of over four thousand years of Western history, the ways in which these media are structured tend to reflect and deepen certain discernable ways of organizing and conceptualizing time and space, usually to the detriment of other methods.

Periods of uncertainty or crisis, for Innis, constitute historical moments in which the ability of dominant interests to directly shape reality (or, in his words, 'monopolise knowledge') – to control how time and space are organized and conceptualized – is challenged as a result of deepening contradictions. Arguably, today, in light of anti-globalization activities generally and Islamic extremism specifically, this sort of crisis is upon us.

Overt challenges to the globalization project reflect what Innis would call the imperial core's flagging ability to control the markets, resources and cultures on its peripheries. Through various means, vested interests, including the American military, have been compelled to help or directly destroy, re-structure or construct institutions, organizations and technologies (strategic media) that they believe will enable them to re-assert or extend their waning control. To use Rosenberg again, opposition to the empire of civil society, pursued through anti-globalization activities, has compelled American state officials to act in ways that lift the veil off some of the 'end-of-history' abstractions they relied upon through much of the 1990s. As Brzezinski writes (probably with the US occupation of Iraq in mind), 'Nothing could be worse for America, and eventually the world, than if American policy were universally viewed as arrogantly imperial ..., selfishly indifferent in the face of unprecedented global interdependence, and culturally self-righteous in a religiously diverse world.'[29]

'Each civilization,' Innis warned, 'has its own methods of suicide.'[30] Indeed, in the context of today's US neo-imperialism (not to mention the abject hopelessness festering in some of the world's political economic peripheries), one should anticipate that temporary solutions, including the 'neutralization' of Saddam Hussein and other such 'barbarians', likely will result in still more entrenched, less resolvable crises in the future.

Time, space and the ascent of the sensual

In the short term, the intensity of globalization's encroachment on various 'traditional' economies and cultures involves stark disparities and conflicts among people possessing different conceptual systems. In the long term, the perpetuation of space-controlling and time-annihilating media (such as the price system, trade agreements, military technologies and a range of electronic entertainments) likely will sharpen already conflicting and contradictory ways of processing information and experience into reality.

Historically structured media, crafted primarily to enhance spatial control, have hastened capital's systemic drive for geographic expansion (that is, its access to markets, labour and raw materials) in conjunction with its interrelated neglect of time. To illustrate this point we return to a central institution facilitating such orientations – capitalist consumption.

Consumption, as elaborated in previous chapters, affects and is affected by the political, economic and environmental circumstances in which it is practised *as well as* by other institutional, organizational and technological media. In relatively 'developed' economies, consumption has played a central role in the struggle to entrench or resist an existing or prospective hegemonic order. Beginning in the 1920s, advertisers and marketers responded to urbanization, industrialization and Taylorist methods of organizing production by associating commodities with the desire for cultural security, love and community. The advertising and marketing industries thus emerged as core agents of capitalist consumption – an institution primarily structured for capital's survival rather than the survival of the species. Resistance to an emerging consumer society in the name of frugality was countered as the institution was reformed through corporate strategies and the growth of disposable incomes and credit. In this process, traditionally conservationist and communally aware ways of living and thinking have been marginalized. Through consumption and its deepening impact on family relations, child-rearing, sexuality, recreational norms, religion and other social institutions, immediate gratification and individualist satisfactions have been promoted to the extent that short term, 'me-first' orientations now play a significant role in the common sense of most Western cultures.

Through its complex promotion of these and the daily experiences of human beings *as consumers*, capitalist consumption has become a crucial medium affecting more general ways of organizing and conceptualizing time and space. This is not to say that the ideals promoted by advertisers are passively embraced. One of the reasons for the ongoing growth of advertising and marketing expenditures, as well as consumption's penetration into traditionally less commodified institutions, is that people often resist. From the vantage point of medium theory, however, our point is straightforward: consumption and other nodes of human relations have influenced not only the consciousnesses of those promoting the globalization project *but also the consciousnesses of those resisting it.*

As in our critique of GCS, we must not romanticize resistance as being voluntaristically 'progressive'. Indeed, in recent years, resistance to the globalization project has been fragmented and temporally limited. As terrorist attacks perpetrated by both Islamic extremists and by white, male 'home grown' terrorists indicate,[31] resistance itself may be becoming more reactionary (as opposed to creative or progressive).

Consumption's contemporary emphasis on individual satisfaction and immediate gratification has exploited *and* deepened the human inclination for social connection and meaning. Television, whose core economic mandate in the United States is to deliver eyeballs to advertisers, links people to their broader (but commercially mediated) communities while simultaneously isolating them in their homes. Personal communication technologies fulfil the desire of many to escape from the here-and-now, distancing human beings from one another while, at the same time, connecting them to others.[32]

Complementing this mediated isolation and perpetuating the immediacy of things is the price system. So long as the individual – through the similarly individualizing wage labour contract – has money, he/she can buy virtually anything, anytime. Unlike the gift economy (in which one had to be an intimate member of a community to receive the goods and services needed to survive), or the barter system (in which some direct relationship with another human being was required for an exchange to take place), money, credit cards and technologies such as the Internet no longer require human beings to know or, indeed, even care about one another.

* * *

According to a study conducted in the year 2000, three-quarters of Americans under the age of 30, and 54 per cent over 50, watch television news with a remote control in hand.[33] This should not be surprising in a culture whose predominant media are structurally oriented to promote immediacy, individualism and sensation to the detriment of thought and duration. American television news (and, indeed, the news presented in other countries) has changed over the decades from a stoic and stationary presentation into an increasingly image-based, sensational experience. Like advertising and marketing, news tends to promote sensual rather than thoughtful desires and responses – an orientation that helps explain Innis's observation that American imperialism relies on its paradoxical *attractions*. Broadcasters explain this sensual orientation and speed-up to be an ongoing response to the remote control, shortening attention spans and their need to generate revenue through advertising. The upshot is the gradual and deliberate proliferation of what are called 'electronic moments': cuts, movements, captions – almost anything to keep the viewer's senses engaged.

Now that the Internet and personal communication devices (involving the unprecedented immediacy experienced by clicking from one image, one idea and one sensation to countless others) are taking viewers away from commercial television,[34] these sensual, visual and experiential priorities are intensifying. News, public affairs and the norms of political discourse are compelled to follow suit as debates are dominated by patriotic sound-bites, black-and-white confrontations and pomposity disguised as expertise. As Todd Gitlin observes – writing about American mass media (but certainly applicable to developments worldwide) – 'broadcasting ... gains our attention by virtue of being kinetic, episodic, personalized, and conflictual, because it systematically breaks large subjects into small chunks ... [I]t leads to simplification ... [and] hollows out public life altogether'.[35]

The use of violence and sensation to capture audiences in an increasingly commercial culture has distanced many from the complex histories underlying conflicts, not to mention their tangible human and environmental implications. In the United States, President Bush thus can issue 'Wanted Dead or Alive' proclamations against America's enemies and few, domestically, think twice about it. Like Charles Bronson's character in the popular 1970s film *Death Wish*, whose law-abiding daily life is shattered when his wife and daughter are brutally attacked, 9/11 was the day on which innocent Americans were victimized. With the United Nations (or, in Bronson's case, the New York Police Department) unable or unwilling to respond in kind, Bush/Bronson believe they have no choice but to take the law into their own hands. America must act decisively to restore order. In this context, vengeance is justice.[36]

To take liberties with Marx, people construct their material and psychic realities, but not necessarily through the conceptual systems of their own choosing. Human beings, structuring or re-structuring media in the context of their perceived political economic interests using existing conceptual systems, are not inherently critical or reflexive. Particular orientations or cultural biases are perpetuated as reforms and inventions take on the priorities, qualities and inter-subjective mandates of already predominant media. As such, the culture – including its ruling class, elites and even many of its opponents – tends to respond to crises in ways that re-instil and sometimes magnify existing biases. Neither the neo-imperialist response to anti-globalization activities nor the reactionary militarism of post-9/11 US foreign policy thus should surprise us.

Temporal neglect-*cum*-imperial policy

Q: Are the American people themselves convinced by all this? Are they convinced, indeed, given the fact that the American government sold these weapons to Saddam Hussein in the first place?

A: Oh, we're not very big on history and right now, today, it's the Superbowl that matters to most Americans ... As a people, we live very much in the present.

—Hume Horan, former US Ambassador in the Middle East, interviewed on BBC World News, 26 January 2003.

US-based responses to anti-American terrorism and, more generally, to those resisting the globalization project, have involved efforts to reinforce or re-structure how time and space are organized and conceptualized. Free trade agreements, for example, are not just opening up markets, they also consti-tute media crafted to recast international relations spatially and temporally. Space has been opened up by delimiting statist norms and, through neolib-eral policies, the buffering capabilities of other governments. Time has been challenged through the speed-up of capital turnover and more general acceleration of everyday life in the name of efficiency. In the words of US Trade Representative Official Emory Simon, the American state is using such international agreements to re-structure 'the overall environment that cre-ates our competitiveness'.[37]

US military applications constitute coercive extensions of these re-struc-turing efforts as disruptions to needed temporal-spatial reforms cannot be tolerated. Terrorist attacks and uncertain energy costs, for example, are dis-ruptive to global corporate planners and to America's consumer-fuelled political economy. Rather than repairing the historical-material roots of ter-rorism and reforming an oil-dependent economic system, policies forged in response to such attacks and crafted to stabilize energy prices may them-selves enrich the soils in which these destabilizing forces are rooted. Since they involve the structuring and re-structuring of media in accordance with pre-existing biases and conceptual systems, such solutions, over time, will tend to exacerbate existing problems, making crises less rather than more correctable.

While many foreign policy hawks called for regime change in Iraq soon after the first Gulf War, the explicit formulation of such a policy emerged in the mid-1990s. Richard Perle (George W. Bush's first Chairman of the Defense Policy Board), for example, co-authored a report for the Washington-based Institute for Advanced Strategic and Political Studies called *A Clean Break: A New Strategy for Securing the Realm*.[38] Perle makes the argument that the best way to secure American interests in the Middle East is for the United States to overthrow those governments pursuing anti-Israeli policies. Iraq was on the top of the report's hit list. Ridding Iraq (possessing the world's second largest proven oil reserves) and the Middle East of Hussein also was viewed as the first domino *en route* to an externally imposed reform of OPEC.

Rather than just access to oil, the use of military power to establish a regime friendly to US interests was meant to send an explicit message to Saudi Arabia (the world's largest oil producer) and others (including Hugo Chavez and his government in Venezuela) that oil must be priced and sup-plied in accordance with the needs of global capital, as defined by Washington. Moreover, the threat of lower oil prices, made possible through Iraq's potential withdrawal from OPEC, would, it was assumed, compel the Saudi royal family to reverse its long-standing tolerance (and purported financing) of al-Qaeda and other radical groups.[39]

The 2002 *NSS*, discussed above, was released not long after 9/11. Beyond its call to develop military capabilities and legal principles to combat terrorism, it asserts America's permanent military dominance in the world: 'our forces', it assures its readers, 'will be strong enough to dissuade potential adversaries'.[40] Since at least 1945, the resources of the American state have been mobilized to maintain the status quo of domestic and/or transnational capital in periods of relative economic stability. In times of recession or depression, when a consensual *Pax Americana* is challenged, American power is usually reasserted through the use of force. In the words of Michael Ledeen of the American Enterprise Institute, 'Every ten years or so, the United States needs to pick up some crappy little country and throw it against the wall, just to show the world we mean business.'[41]

Domestic and international media (institutions, organizations and technologies) are formed or reformed in response to such crises facilitating the search for and maintenance of markets, labour, resources and new efficiencies forged to extend accumulation opportunities. As historian William A. Williams writes, as this history has unfolded, there has, however, been *a traceable 'loss of the capacity to think critically about reality'*.[42]

In assessing US foreign policy and its twenty-first-century neo-imperialist incarnation, we have argued that ahistorical and unreflexive ways of thinking have become entrenched in the minds of key American decision-makers and many of its citizens. One could also argue that this policy turn reflects the dominance of positivist social science in the field of international relations. Usually referred to as neo-realism, it is the dominant approach and epistemology used by US foreign policy experts. For them, *the* unit of analysis is the nation state engaged in a largely one-dimensional contest for power in which the primary resource is military might. From our perspective, neo-realism constitutes yet another structured, power-laden medium – an institution reflecting historical forces and processes, supported but rarely challenged through its use and applications in foreign policy circles. Through neo-realism, US strategic policy represents an ongoing calculation of 'rational' state interests and time is delineated by the number of moves that can be anticipated on the flat surface of a cause-and-effect Machiavellian chessboard.

Of course the very starting point of this institutionalized way of thinking is itself problematic. To reiterate a point made in Chapter 4, the analytical unit of neo-realist foreign policy – the sovereign nation state – is itself an ahistorical abstraction. As is the norm in modern or neo-modern cultures, both states and commodities are routinely reified. As Rosenberg ponders,

> When do the interests of a rising imperial power promote not political subjection but political independence? They do so when the political independence in question is not substantive political possession of resources by an autocratic state ... but rather the consolidation of sovereignty. This breaks the political link with the ... imperial power, while

opening the newly demarcated sphere of 'the economy' to the private power of foreign capital, that is, to the social form of dependence mediated by things. Historically, the US fought communism and anti-Western radical nationalism and supported the emergence of sovereign independence, irrespective of whether it took a democratic political form. In other words, it promoted the separating out of private and public spheres at the international level.[43]

Sovereignty's *faux* division of the public and private, the state and civil society, has long facilitated imperial control over vast territories without the costs and explicit conflicts that almost always accompany direct autocratic forms of dominance (techniques associated with classical imperialism and the first dimension of power). Demonstrating Britain's maturity as an empire, Lord Palmerston wrote in 1857, 'we don't want to have Egypt ... We want to trade with Egypt and to travel through Egypt but we do not want the burden of governing Egypt ...'[44] And as Gallagher and Robinson have so aptly summarized this very modern approach, 'By informal means where possible, by formal means where necessary'.[45]

This mastery of spatial control entails a heavy but often invisible price. It comes with a set of cultural implications that suit an empire's short-term aspirations while undermining its long-term capabilities. As in the contemporary American empire (or, as Rosenberg prefers, the empire of civil society), practices and thoughts of more people in more parts of the world become focused on immediate concerns and here-and-now needs rather than the long term and collective. Instead of the outcome of capitalism levelling world cultures like some kind of sociological tsunami, this tendency may be more accurately assessed as the by-product of two inter-related developments.

First, in light of a world mediated, regulated and governed through abstractions – particularly those that de-politicize social interactions and intimately associate realities with things rather than relationships – conceptual systems that rely on little or no historical context have become norms. Thoughts, let alone actionable concerns, about society's long-term duration thus have become altogether secondary for most people most of the time.

Second, the success of capitalism and its control over space has involved the general speed-up of international economic activities, decision-making time frames and, more generally, daily life itself. This neglect of the long term and acceleration of activities has been structured through a range of media that, in turn, are perpetuated by people using their conceptual systems to reform or create new mediators. As a result of these dynamics and processes, opposition to the globalization project and the neo-imperialist turn in US foreign policy is splintering on the rocks of shrinking attention spans and immediate gratification modes of dissent.

From an Innisian perspective, both capitalist consumption and the neo-realist paradigm share and reinforce one another's obsession with space over time. Both entail powerful vested interests that have little concern for alternative realities, not to mention the reflexive conceptual systems needed for these to be imagined. The closure of such intellectual capacities itself increases efficiencies, as little time and energy is spent asking critical questions. University departments, marketing networks, foreign policy institutions, daily lives, all are structured to think and act as if status quo conceptual systems are simply 'just the way it is'.

Even the future has become the domain of spatial metaphors. For corporations, the present is to be colonized through marketing in order to forge the brand loyalties needed to conquer tomorrow's consumers. For mainstream international relations analysts, current strategies are crafted to carve out territories, resources and military capabilities for nation states. For anti-globalization activists, states are to be circumvented (for the post-structuralist) or conquered (the Marxist) as a better world is seen to be the result of the organization of networks or classes within and across borders. For both the globalization project's status quo and its opponents, the overriding and deepening goal is generally the same: control over and dominance through place and space.

This spiral of self-perpetuating, mediated biases is hindering the capacity of the world's political, economic and cultural peripheries to counter conceptual systems oriented towards timely results. To resist within the geographic or cultural core entails the adoption of conceptual systems oriented towards sound-bite debating points and public relations sensations – arguably a strategy that furthers the very biases that progressives might want to counter. But to resist from outside the core leaves a movement's proponents vulnerable to being labelled 'naïve', 'unrealistic' or, worse still, as 'barbarians' and thus ignored by publics or targeted by American forces and the security services of other 'sovereign' countries.

Suicidal implications

Since the invention of the printing press in the fifteenth century, communicating across geographic spaces has become faster and, at least once the relevant infrastructure has been established, easier. While this capability has accelerated in recent decades (particularly with the rise of digitalized, satellite-mediated communications), it has unfolded alongside a general neglect of collective memory, tradition and even dialogue.

That the ascent of one capability diffuses another is explainable on at least two counts. *First*, the subsequent increase in the amount of information being communicated and the speed of its distribution renders those who pause to reflect, defend past norms and converse in depth and detail both cultural anachronisms and, in marketplace terms at least, competitive failures. A *second* reason why emerging media facilitating more information being communicated faster over greater areas tends to undermine historical, reflexive and long-term thinking stems from the fact that conceptual systems usually perpetuate themselves through new and reformed media. For example, the Internet's origins – a US Department of Defense construction forged to enable the American state to communicate electronically in the context of a nuclear holocaust – reflected a bias towards spatial control. Subsequent applications by commercial interests further reflect these priorities, only now primarily expressed as the need to orchestrate production process activities across various distances and to establish 'relationships' with millions of individualized consumers.

The Internet's reach and speed – hailed by both the globalization project's proponents as well as many of its detractors – also constitutes its greatest weakness. While its infrastructure is predictably robust, the messages transmitted are extraordinarily perishable and overwhelmingly visual. Website content is especially transient and sensational. The lifespan of what is found on most websites ranges from hours to months.[46] Moreover, the predominance of its point and click icon content, along with its ever-growing volume of information (much of it instantaneously available in the form of images or presented through visual cues), together reflect and perpetuate the more general ahistorical, immediate gratification, sensual-over-intellectual predilections related to capitalist consumption.

As for post-structuralist anti-globalization movement claims that ICTs are 'rhizomatically' challenging status quo power structures by democratizing transnational social relations, attention to the qualitative dimensions of thought, particularly with conceptual systems in mind, enables us to pause and reassess this enthusiasm. Kamilla Pietrzyk, for one, has assessed the online activities of the self-proclaimed global justice movement and reports that their primary weakness lies in their limited 'intellectual and creative capacity to engage in reflexive, sustainable forms of oppositional politics'.[47] Among other strategic problems, Pietrzyk demonstrates that movement participants tend to lack institutional memories resulting in repeated mistakes as well as a limited collective ability to plan for the future.

Hartmut Rosa takes this observation one step further, arguing that the speed of socio-economic relations and communications is inversely related to the ability of polities to act (and think) democratically. Among other implications, Rosa underlines the effects on individual and collective autonomy – arguably the pre-conditions of any truly democratic mode of participation. He writes that 'politics today no longer seems to be the actor and pace-maker of social change; quite to the contrary, political agendas have become situationalist attempts at "muddling through", at (often anachronistically) re-acting to ... pressing demands arising elsewhere'. As a result, 'the direction of social development is increasingly determined in other, more fast-paced social arenas. Decisional powers are given back to the economy in the case of economic deregulation, to law in the case of juridification, or to civil society in the case of ethical privatisation. Within the realm of politics, executive decision-making is gaining disproportional predominance over politics by proper democratic legislation ...' In sum, says Rosa, 'democracy is in danger of falling victim to the powers of speed. Its temporal patterns appear to be irreconcilably out of step with the time structures of the global age'.[48]

As for the traditional left – led by organized labour – we can extend our earlier critique of its waning political capabilities (in Chapter 3) by extending Rosa's arguments concerning the decline of autonomy.

Out of the working class's long struggle against capital, workers – at least in most 'developed' countries – now have taken on the very identities that capitalists have long promoted. One of these is that of the consumer – the ever-desirous, selfish and materialistic individual working to buy the things he/she wants both to survive and socially/psychologically get by. But more profoundly, as André Gorz argues, much of the contemporary working class has internalized its dispossession. Stripped of virtually every means of reproducing themselves, 'objective' class-based demands have been abstracted into 'subjective' consumerist desires. Through earlier mobilizations aimed at electing representatives mandated to enhance pay packages and statist benefits (rather than workplace control), traditional aspirations for self-autonomy have been replaced through (and by) the myth of consumer sovereignty.[49]

In this society, virtually '[n]o one produces what they consume or consumes what they produce'.[50] Amidst the globalization project's universalization of mediated contract-based relations, not even cities (let alone individuals or an entire class), whose inhabitants may prospectively organize themselves into some kind of commune, remain materially autonomous. 'The division of labour now exists at transnational levels,' says Gorz, and what is produced, where it is produced and who has access to these products has become almost entirely the domain of private interests making decisions in terms of efficiency and profitability calculations rather than the social needs of the collective. According to Gorz,

> The height of alienation is reached when it becomes impossible to conceive that an activity should have a goal other than its wage or be grounded upon other than market relations. A section of the European feminist movement has taken this course by demanding a social wage for household labour. Following the ... logic of the capitalist market such women thereby call for their *proletarianisation* as an advance over *slavery* ... The logical conclusion of this argument is that professional prostitution is an advance over the traditional couple ... This ... obviously conflicts with the struggle to redefine relations within the couple [or the culture]

and to achieve a balanced, freely chosen distributon of household [and social] tasks between equal male and female partners [and, by extension, among autonomous, thinking, capable citizens].[51]

The dynamics driving this (il)logic forward also accelerates mass commodification, the amount of information being generated and circulated, and the ascendancy of media developed to manage and further these developments. Under such circumstances, as Innis put it more than fifty years ago, 'mechanical devices' facilitate the promulgation of 'useless knowledge' about 'useful facts'.[52] Ahistorical, sensually oriented abstractions consequently mushroom.

Given the ease through which the weapons of mass destruction now at humanity's disposal (especially those controlled by the American empire) can be used to annihilate life, and the globalization of the production/consumption lifestyles now accelerating our planet's ecological death, this historical dynamic and its promotion of reactionary thought over reflexive analyses is nothing short of suicidal.

Contradiction, resistance and a plea for time

The state of Washington's temporal mindset can be further articulated through the typology laid out in George Gurvitch's *The Spectrum of Social Time*.[53] In this book, Gurvitch associates a particular sense of time with various social formations – a general but useful framework in the context of our book and the conceptual systems facilitated through capitalist consumption. Perhaps the most apparent temporal bias shaping our contemporary world (dis)order is what Gurvitch terms *erratic time*. This is a way of organizing and conceptualizing time whereby the present prevails over either the past or the future. It is a temporal bias that, predictably, involves great uncertainty and relatively apolitical collectivities. Media – particularly capitalist consumption – promote such here-and-now sensibilities. Also promulgating *erratic time* are organizations such as the WTO (not to mention the American state) that compel an ever-growing number of people to focus on their immediate survival in the context of 'normal' marketplace insecurities.

Another way in which time is being practised and conceptualized is *time in advance of itself*. This involves the future's 'inevitably' innovative qualities. Certainly, the Internet, the digitalization of television and the emerging predominance of personal communication devices – with the immediacy of their endless and interactive consumerist choices – constitute the most compelling of contemporary technologies mediating this way of organizing and conceptualizing time. The built-in obsolescence of commodities and their purported satisfactions also perpetuate *time in advance of itself*.

A third aspect of now predominant temporal biases is *deceptive time*. This is a rather modernist way of structuring temporal relations involving a largely mechanized and ordered sense of time. *Deceptive time*, says Gurvitch, is experienced through the routines of daily existence, occasionally disrupted by crisis. Again, a broad range of media are involved in its promotion – from the institution of the 40-hour work week, to organizations such as educational systems that structure activity and thought from an early age, to technologies such as mechanical clocks. All serve to schedule and discipline lives and thinking.

In 'A Plea for Time', a paper delivered in 1950, with the power and dynamics behind Cold War US foreign policy in mind, Innis warned his audience that civilizations driven to expand and control space tend to become debilitated by their subsequent neglect of time – a neglect, it should be underlined, that is reproduced through media that affect and are affected by conceptual systems.[54] For some who have lived and worked in Washington, the not altogether original realization occasionally crops up that while America's immediate enemy may well be those who refer to Westerners as 'the infidels', the structurally ignored and more dangerous threat lies from within. It is, among other things, America's general neglect of time, overwhelmed as it is by capital's quest for spatial expansion and control, that ultimately may undermine the country's neo-imperialist aspirations – an orientation succinctly represented by its troops' post-invasion defence of the Iraqi oil fields and Oil Ministry but their neglect of the Iraqi National Museum, its National Library and their holdings representing 12,000 years of history.

Ultimately, coercion is too expensive and unwieldy for a twenty-first-century capitalist world order to function efficiently. While an empire's own death can take place through some kind of suicide by a thousand cuts (witness, for instance, the implications of US military expenditures on federal government spending and the American national debt), we may want to revise this to suicide through a thousand biased mediators.

Paradoxically, with the globalization project and related media problematically but effectively transforming the civil societies of sovereign nations in line with modernist or neo-modernist norms (at least among the world's relatively affluent), this sweeping spatial strategy has produced contradictory results. Ahistorical and materialistic conceptual systems, dominated by fetishistic associations, have emerged hand in hand with mounting existential questions *and* stark disparities in wealth and social opportunity. In 2001, for example, a staggering 78 per cent of the urban residents in 'developing' countries lived in slums.[55]

For those experiencing an alienation and anomie similar to the workers and emerging middle classes in the West a century or more ago, existential questions concerning identity and meaning surely are on the rise. Capitalist consumption, at least among those able to make enough money to overcome subsistence levels of poverty, appears to be mediating some of the 'answers'. However, as noted in Chapter 5, the extraordinary speed in which economic development and social-economic change is taking place arguably makes the contemporary transition from the pre-modern to the modern far more volatile and traumatic than it was for the West. As Brzezinski observes, 'What once took centuries now takes a decade; what took a decade happens in a single year.'[56] In these time-space annihilating circumstances, disjunctures between conceptual systems and shifting experiences may, given the particulars of a culture and people, provoke reactionary responses.

Everywhere, writes Mike Davis, 'the continuous accumulation of poverty undermines existential security and poses even more extraordinary challenges to the economic ingenuity of the poor'.[57] With reactionary rather than progressive responses coming to the fore, unlike the industrial revolution's concurrent rise of a militant proletariat, in the contemporary world populist Islam and Pentecostal Christianity are ascendant.[58] According to Davis,

> In contrast to populist Islam, which emphasizes civilizational continuity and the trans-class solidarity of faith, Pentecostalism, in the tradition of its African-American origins, retains a fundamentally exilic identity. Although, like Islam in the slums, it efficiently correlates itself to the survival needs of the informal working class (organizing self-help networks for poor women; offering faith healing as para-medicine; providing recovery from alcoholism and addiction; insulating children from the temptations of the street; and so on), its ultimate premise is that the urban world is corrupt, injust and unreformable.[59]

Clearly, this implies mixed outcomes for both American neo-imperialism and the globalization project. Into the social-psychological vacuum of identity and meaning the institution of capitalist consumption emerges in different ways amidst various cultures experiencing economic crises. Among those able and willing to internalize its norms, spatially individualistic, temporally ahistorical and intellectually abstract conceptual systems become dominant. Arguably, these are the primary prisms through which today and tomorrow's global consumer society – itself an abstraction made up of a broad range of people, from Washington's foreign policy intelligentsia to post-structuralist online 'hactivists' – understand the world's problems and prospective solutions. For these status quo and anti-status quo moderns/neo-moderns, conformity or divide-and-rule strategies serve the globalization project, at least for the short term; however, among this relatively affluent and powerful minority, Gurvitch's categories *erratic time, time in advance of itself* and *deceptive time* are more than just pervasive, they are profoundly contradictory.

To repeat, in the long term, these constitute conceptualizations ill suited to the challenge of other reactionary opponents (such as al-Qaeda) or still weightier problems such as our dying ecosystem. For the American state – particularly in the face of 'peak oil' – the national debt, Chinese (as well as

Iranian, Venezuelan, Russian and many other) geopolitical tensions and, of course, Islamic extremist disruptions will all, almost certainly, compel militarist responses. As Brzezinski (again) insightfully recognizes, America's future 'leadership ... must be accompanied by a social consciousness, a readiness to compromise ..., [and] a cultural appeal with more than just hedonistic content ...'

To sustain the globalization project, nothing less than 'a national epiphany' is needed among both America's leaders and its polity.[60] For the complex reasons mapped out in this book, this is a tall order indeed. It is especially hard to fathom given the conceptual systems structuring the thoughts and mediations of elites, the traditional left and, of course, the post-structuralist intelligentsia.

In the long-run, a successful globalization project would involve the defence and re-structuring of core media – those constituting key nodal points in forging conceptual systems – conceptual systems both fundamental to the task of establishing rule through consent and essential in shaping how information and experience are understood. But the contradictions facing both the project and prospective responses to it are profound. The orientations and biases that underlie the globalization project – including the systemic drive to control space (that is, to control organizational and conceptual aspects of production, distribution, exchange, and consumption) – tend to involve an accompanying annihilation of time.

Alternative futures

From a political economy and medium theory perspective, an alternative response might involve two broadly defined initiatives. First, key technological, organizational and institutional media need to be identified and re-structured in ways that can help us pursue a more social and reflexive sense of time. Innis, for one, emphasized the strategic need to counterbalance the predominance of linear time (to repeat, an ordered, chronological, progress-focused sense of time) with social time (a relatively organic, reflexive and historical appreciation of time).

Again, to borrow from Gurvitch, three precise ways of organizing and conceptualizing time also can be emphasized in response to the globalization project and conceptual systems influenced by capitalist consumption: *enduring time* is an ecological sense of time – historically associated with peasant or hunter-gatherer social formations; *cyclical time* is a sense of continuous time in which change is understood through continuity – usually associated with mystical/archaic collectivities; and *explosive time* is a sense of the present and past dissolved into a transcendent future – a way of organizing and conceptualizing time in keeping with revolutionary or transformational movements.[61]

The second plank of an alternative to status quo trajectories involves what Ian Parker calls the *re*-mythologizing of globalization. Rather than just de-mythologizing the project – underlining its predominant simplifications, such as the decline of the nation state – instead we might recognize, first of all, that the future is not cast in stone (thus redressing *time in advance of itself*). Using the already dominant discourse of neoliberalism and turning it on itself, rather than a globalization that is largely about the global driving the local (and the absolutes of the marketplace), a re-mythologized global-ization could be about the local or national driving the global.[62] Indeed, this re-mythologized globalization, as it is structured through media, could well emphasize enduring, cyclical or explosive time.

While the systemic drive associated with capitalism generally promotes some amount of cultural homogenization and the conceptual systems needed to survive in a competitive, calculating culture, a strategic effort that might be pursued could stress the politics of global diversity and the demo-cratic choice of nations to interact (or not interact) with others. In fact, some of the ideals being propagated by America's neo-imperialists to justify the globalization project – especially their purported idealization of liberal democracy – can be used as the standards upon which mediated structures associated with the project might be judged as acceptable or unacceptable. Instead of a globalization project dominated by corporate needs and American-based ambitions, globalization instead might be re-mythologized to be more about the flowering of human and cultural rights through insti-tutions, organizations and technologies, and the political-economic empowerment of local and national citizens and workers.[63]

Today's neo-imperialist thinking in Washington, and the fragmented, temporally limited and too often reactionary modes of resistance we are wit-nessing in response to the globalization project underline a point made in Chapter 4 – assumptions that a somehow progressive GCS is 'on its way' are profoundly off the mark. The sobering reality is that the conceptual orien-tations and cultural biases outlined herein reaffirm the need to address third face of power developments directly. The long-standing, and now pervasive, neglect of time – itself a historically structured and mediated development (one we have directly associated with capitalist consumption) – has gener-ated Washington's political culture of arguably unprecedented indifference to the historical-systemic conditions underlying capital's dynamic and destructive tendencies. It has also reinforced the perpetuation of America's short-sighted support of repressive regimes as long as they comply with cap-ital's material and organizational needs. Finally, and perhaps most discon-certingly, consumption-mediated ways of conceptualizing time have contributed to the American and other publics' general inability to think about the long-term implications of their government's reactionary responses to the world's reactionary 'barbarians'.

* * *

The (il)logic of our twenty-first-century world (dis)order, involving never-ending growth as well as expansion through and control over space, constitutes the basis of much of the violence all around us – the violence humanity perpetrates on itself and against its shared ecosystem. This dynamic marches on with little time to reflect, reconsider and reorganize in a sustained, reflexive fashion. These are the historical conditions in which the administration of George W. Bush has forged its neo-imperialist agenda. And while these conditions do not in themselves directly determine the unilateralist, militaristic and reactionary events unfolding around us, they do, we believe, constitute the political-economic conditions through which such neo-imperialist policies will continue.

The ascendancy of a reactionary US foreign policy itself says something important about a more general historical trend: the mediated, spiralling neglect of time. The underlying strength of Innis's political economic approach involving medium theory is that it brings together, historically and holistically (or, more accurately, it specifies the mediation of) agency and structure. Beyond a moment in history in which neo-conservative hawks have seized the reigns of power, historical and cumulative tendencies are discernable involving how what is known is known *and* how the political economic structures and dynamics underlying particular ways of thinking are generating potentially fatal policies among both the globalization project's status quo and its various opponents.

7
Conclusion

Man has lost the capacity to foresee and to forestall. He
will end by destroying the earth.

—Albert Schweitzer

Consumption has become a core mediator of the international political
economy – structuring domestic and international relations, shaping conceptual systems used to process information and experience into reality.

In contrast to GCS progressives and globalization theory analysts, the preceding chapters have situated both globalization and resistance to it in
terms of a state–civil society complex. Indeed, the globalization project, we
have argued, entails more than just increasing inter-state interdependencies,
it also involves sovereign states as its primary means of furthering a particular policy agenda and, more abstractly, de-politicizing private sphere/civil
society responses. Left to itself, notably in the context of predominant capitalist relations, ideals of legal equality often stand alongside economic
asymmetries. While states generally enforce these injustices, state structures
may also be modified or mobilized (usually as a result of sustained, organized pressures) to implement policies leading to change.

As the history of the West and its often problematic reiteration in 'developing' countries demonstrates, the institutionalization of capitalist consumption entails the clearing of a number of hurdles.

First, capitalist consumption is born out of a usually painful – if not
bloody – series of events, involving the removal of people from their
means of physical and psychological autonomy. By stripping populations
of their pre- or non-capitalist modes of subsistence and hollowing out
traditional ways of finding identity and meaning, individuals and
collectivities are compelled to change. Whether the particular circum-
stance of this involves the 'enclosure of the commons', the 'privatisation
of collective assets' or the transformation of norms through the barrel of
a gun, the birth of capitalist consumption invariably entails some sort of
violent 'push'.

160

The *second* step involves dominant interests – whether a domestic ruling class or a foreign imperialist presence or a hegemonic bloc – providing displaced people with alternatives. For instance, instead of growing food for oneself and exchanging one's own products through gift or barter, the peasant, removed from his/her land, may find some sort of waged employment – a contracted task through which money is paid in exchange for his/her labour power. In this way, people are given alternate means of surviving, and human labour becomes the primary commodity sold in exchange for the monies needed to buy other commodities. The birth of the modern worker also constitutes the basis of capitalist consumption.

A *third* step – another 'pull' factor – completes the construction of capitalist consumption. With extended families and age-old communities disrupted, existential questions emerge. Things – commodities – become a means of communicating identity, belonging and purpose. Advertisers and marketers recognize this propensity and consciously use the alienation and anxiety of modern life to forge 'relationships' with consumers. Through historically unparalleled efforts to modify cultural norms, modern consumption emerges and mass commodities, paradoxically, become primary means through which people 'individualise' themselves. Workers and the economy both become dependent on extraordinary, historically structured abstractions – commodified relationships and commodity fetishism linking happiness, autonomy and even freedom to purchasable things.

Of course, in addition to cultural barriers (from traditional frugality to, in the specific case of India, nationalist values tied to an austere lifestyle), economic problems have diverted the institution's ascent. In forging the mediators needed to structure various methods of surplus extraction – whether these constitute the direct extraction of raw materials or the more complex extraction of surplus value through wage labour contracts – the development of markets entailing more than subsistence consumption is, at best, an uneven process. We know this both from our overview of the institution's development in the West as well as our examination of consumption in 'developing' countries today.

For the pre-modern person, daily life involved relatively few abstractions. Spatially, one's world, including a person's imagination, was framed by how far he/she could walk in daylight. Temporally, daily life was dominated by seasonal conditions, the light of the sun and, of course, a sense of continuity in which birth and death were experientially commonplace. In pre-modern society, the individual was part of the whole and his/her 'rights' were inextricably linked to the commonweal. Everyone knew their place, knew their identity, knew how they would occupy their (probably limited) time on earth. In these social formations, there was no systemic dynamic in place compelling people to outdo one another or produce more in less time. Modern cultural norms, such as individualism, competitiveness and insatiable wants were extraordinary. In fact, pre-modern, non-capitalist cultures depended on the suppression of such modern (and for many mainstream theorists, 'natural') traits in that their political economies relied on ecological and social harmony (that is, not over-hunting, not upsetting the social order, not depleting nutrients in the soil) in order to survive.

In the modern world, however, dominated as it is by private property, contracts and a money-mediated political economic system of unparalleled complexity and dynamism, the compulsion to generate new needs and wants grows alongside insecurities and uncertainties. As Harvey writes,

> The struggle to maintain profitability sends capitalists racing off to explore all kinds of ... possibilities. New product lines are opened up ... [and c]apitalists are forced to redouble their efforts to create new needs in others, thus emphasizing the cultivation of imaginary appetites and the role of fantasy, caprice and whim. The result is to exacerbate insecurity and instability, as masses of workers and capital shift from one line of production to another, leaving whole sectors devastated, while the perpetual flux of consumer wants, tastes and needs becomes a permanent locus of uncertainty and struggle ... The resultant transformation in the experience of space and place is matched by revolutions in the time dimension, as capitalists strive to reduce the turnover time to 'the twinkling of an eye'.[1]

As John Kenneth Galbraith documents, the rise of large-scale national and international industries entailed the conscious promotion of an increasingly manageable (or at least predictable) consumer.[2] Spearheaded in 1920s America, this entailed two prerequisite developments: the economic ability of prospective consumers to buy things involving the redistribution and/or substantive rise of wealth *and* the calculated generation, perpetuation and utilization of the relational abstractions and social-psychological insecurities needed to make capitalist consumption attractive.

In some 'developing' countries today, in the absence of the economic means to institutionalize capitalist consumption, traditional or pre-modern means of finding identity and meaning may remain or re-emerge in more reactionary guises. 'Nature abhors a vacuum' and political economies can't tolerate them either. The globalization project's dissemination and acceleration of atomizing capitalist relations, to use another cliché, has been a double-edged sword. The rising tide of religious fundamentalisms, particularly in what Barnett refers to as the non-integrating gap, involves prospectively anti-globalization responses to complex existential questions.

* * *

As a medium through which the old or what is out of style is constantly replaced by what's new and fashionable, capitalist consumption normalizes change itself. This, we have argued, is one of contemporary consumption's most important functions in the international political economy. In a systemically uncertain and ever-changing world (dis)order, this hegemonic role cannot be overstated, especially in light of humanity's proclivity to 'make sense' of things. Capitalist consumption also has mediated the common sense shift from 'we' to 'me'. Through the institution's affect on conceptual systems, the market, in effect, now dominates thought itself – a domination that, over the course of generations, has taken shape largely out of sight. Since capitalist consumption directly involves the activities of many individuals – people engaged as both labour-selling workers and commodity-buying consumers – this process appears to be apolitical. As such, consumption developments seem to be more a matter of free choice than class domination.[3]

Beyond the need to realize profits through sales, consumption is perpetuated by the institution's own inherent falsities. Modern or neo-modern cultures have come to rely on capitalist consumption to mediate inter-subjective identities. The world of commodities also stands as a tangible and, for many, accessible 'carrot' rewarding the socially compliant. 'Work hard and play by the rules' clearly produces more substantive results in the 'developed' world than spiritual promises concerning the after-life or socialist exhortations about human potentials (the latter now an especially 'hard sell' in light of the general failure of twentieth-century state socialism). Yet because the acquisition of things does not and, indeed, cannot provide people with stable identities, lasting happiness and anything more than a surface-level 'meaningful' existence, the practice of consumption leaves most unsatisfied. This failure, however, is accompanied by the truthfulness of the existential needs it purportedly redresses. Despite or, more accurately, because of this contradiction, people return to consumption again and again. For most living in relatively 'developed' parts of the world, the saliency of the needs being pursued coupled with the fact that consumption can never really satisfy them casts the cultures in question into a pernicious cycle – *a cycle involving the perpetuation of conceptual systems generally ill-equipped to imagine 'realistic' alternatives.*

Modern or neo-modern humanity now has so internalized capitalist consumption – internalized its norms and claims through a complex of mediating institutions, organizations and technologies – that other ways of organizing and conceptualizing the world either have disappeared or have been radically marginalized. Enduring time, cyclical time and explosive time have been jettisoned from our conceptual vocabulary. Instead, thoughts are dominated by ahistorical, visual and commercially framed orientations. The predominance of this kind of thinking – particularly its acritical, sensual, immediate-gratification qualities – reveals and compounds a globalization project obsessed with spatial reach and control to the neglect of history, duration and reflexive thought.

One conclusion to be drawn from this is that only a minority of humanity now has the capacity to reflect, act and prospectively transform contemporary trajectories. The structured non-consciousness of most of the world's modern/neo-modern 'core' reflects an ironically 'imagination challenged' society amidst a wealth of information and communication resources. Capitalist consumption and ICTs have, together, generally replaced the thoughtful work of 'perception' with the relatively thought-less experience of 'sensation'. As Wyndham Lewis observed in the late 1920s, this sensory imbalance and the rise of reactionary politics are two sides of the same phenomenon.[4]

Decades of wealth, easy credit and consumption-mediated abstractions socialized over the course of several generations have forged what is, in effect, an invisible cage of non-consciousness. In this context, capitalist con-sumption frames and contains resistance among the relatively well off and enculturated; thus, in much of the West, anti-status quo responses to the globalization project continue to be narrowly conceptualized. Fragmented social movements, identity politics, discourse-focused academics, online activists networking to 'rhizomatically' subvert capitalism, Oprah Winfrey*esque* obsessions with individual empowerment, spectacular television- and Internet-mediated global concerts staged to raise awareness (sponsored by *Microsoft* or *Time Warner*) and other such 'resistance' activities reflect and reinforce consumption-mediated conceptual systems. Space, the individual and sensation are perpetually emphasized over time, the collective and the intellectual.

* * *

The early twenty-first century arguably constitutes a turning point in world history. Beyond the threat of economic recession (precipitated in part by the inability of Western, particularly American, consumers to accumulate more debt – debt needed to keep spending), a mass rebellion among those not yet enculturated or too impoverished to participate (funnelled through religious extremism or tribal, ethnic or nationalist chauvinisms), and the suicidal tendencies of an American neo-imperialism unable to comprehend history and the complexities of duration, the globalization project appears to be on the verge of crisis.

Before elaborating this crisis, let us briefly consider another example of America's pervasive ahistoricism: a subset of US foreign policy referred to as 'public diplomacy'.[5]

Following 9/11, the Bush administration and Congress collectively asked the question 'why do foreigners hate us?'[6] Their answer was that American foreign policy and the US domestic culture had been 'misunderstood' – the outcome of 'biased' foreign media and pervasive distortions on the streets of some cities overseas, especially those of Islamic countries. The 'solution', thus, has been a multi-billion dollar commitment to 'get America's message out' through a new White House Office of Global Communications and other agencies.

Beyond the apparent inability to recognize that America's unpopularity more likely is the result of its international policies – policies that convey

the hypocrisy of US activities vis-à-vis its official rhetoric and, more problematically, its unapologetic imperialist agenda – the methods pursued to
change foreign impressions underline a general inability to understand
other cultures and, more disconcertingly, its own.

Not only has Washington's public diplomacy exercise insulted the lived
realities and cultural intelligence of its target audience (simplistically equating America with democracy, prosperity and individual empowerment
through satellite television, advertising campaigns and 'educational'
programmes), in the context of the globalization project and capitalist consumption, the policy fails to comprehend its own fundamental contradiction –
public diplomacy implicitly admits that neoliberal globalization's promotion
of private sector information and communication activities has generated
distorted realities. At the same time, the policy sends a blunt message to its
audience: in a sea of commercialized information and communication, supposedly 'sovereign consumers' now are unable to see 'the truth', at least not
without the help of state-funded propagandists.

Through all of this, the US occupation of Iraq, its treatment of prisoners in
Abu Ghraib, its interrogations of 'enemy combatants' at Guantanamo Bay –
not to mention decades of imperialist policies – somehow will be forgotten.
Through the magic of Madison Avenue marketing techniques associating
Brand USA with Mom, apple pie and, of course, 'freedom', America's post-9/11
public diplomacy campaign assumes that the rest of the world is as amnesic,
acritical and open to manipulation as is the domestic US population.

In this and other foreign policy examples, it appears as if the empire's
'brainwashers' have themselves been 'brainwashed'.[7] Corporate and political status quos (including neo-realists) simply do not recognize their own
biases.[8]

Responses to such policies, particularly in the West, have become similarly
emotional and mechanized. Contemplation, reflection, conservation and
respect for cultural heritage generally are marginalized. Capitalist consumption, as a historically structured mediator of social relations and realities, has
directly influenced analytical proclivities and imaginative capacities.

* * *

Beyond and behind this state of affairs, capitalism typically faces crises not
due to limitations as to what it can produce but, rather, as a result of barriers in the realm of consumption. The micro-level activities of hundreds of
thousands of (usually competing) firms thrust investment and production
forward. Periodically, this leads to overproduction. Without consideration
for the tangible limits of the market or its long-term reproductive needs,
capitalists tend to generate too much productive capacity and too many commodities in relation to demand. The resulting economic crisis predictably
generates explicit inter- and intra-class conflicts. Consensual politics subsequently disintegrates and the hegemonic order is potentially challenged.

Such crises involve the imposition of coercive measures – state-led or -regulated methods of control applied as capitalism re-structures its accumulation dynamic. As in the past, these periods typically compel vested interests to 'write off' productive capacities and absorb excess capital through temporal and spatial displacement (as in long-term projects and overseas investments). But before such costly, destabilizing and potentially dangerous displacement strategies are employed, capitalists are compelled to get as much out of existing investments in established and emerging markets as possible. As such, a systemic dynamic is at work – the drive, accommodated by new and revised institutions, organizations and technologies, to penetrate and prospectively dominate daily life in different cultures through the institutionalization of capitalist consumption.[9]

The long-term result is the ascent of political cultures oriented towards the here-and-now of individual immediate gratification. This is not to say that cultural concerns for continuity, the future and community are entirely absent in contemporary political economies. Rather, these qualitative dimensions have been marginalized. But having said this, advertisers and marketers paradoxically reference these seemingly 'pre-modern' concerns, *as their primary means of promoting consumption itself.* As the most vociferous promoters of capitalist consumption seek to widen and deepen their reach, they find themselves referencing relationships and identities directly, as well as social-psychological desires such as love, happiness and autonomy to sell their products. By associating commodities with non-commodified relationships, and exchange values with intrinsic values, corporations themselves persistently (and remarkably) remind consumers of an essential truth – that the existential questions accompanying modernity *cannot* be answered satisfactorily through the world of things.

Marketing and advertising's expanding presence thus generally proceeds hand in hand with a growing admission that the products being sold can, at best, only represent or deliver the buyer to what's *really* important: non-commodified relationships.

* * *

The most important political point emerging from our research is that organized efforts facilitating sustained, creative thought are desperately needed. Again, those nation states able to carve out relatively autonomous development policies, particularly those on America's/capital's imperial margins, are best situated to pursue these. Indeed, the ongoing saliency of state sovereignty constitutes a structural paradox that progressives seeking respite from time-annihilating dynamics and mediators should exploit.

Out of our present circumstances, for those interested in a progressive non-reactionary future, nodal points of critical thought involving sustained reflection and activity must be defended and developed. We might refer to these as 'islands of resistance' – consciously structured mediators resisting, primarily, the annihilation of time. These constitute institutions, organizations and

technologies *relatively* protected from commercial forces and political pressures yet (at least occasionally) engaged in reflective, active critiques of modernity, consumer society and the public/private sector policies affecting them.[10]
This effort to forge alternative, historically aware ways of thinking and acting also entails various alliances. These are needed to access substantive resources and affect long-term change. Nation state, state/provincial/county/municipal governments, organized labour, environmental and human rights organizations, universities (and others), all can be mobilized with this agenda in mind. Rather than a post-modernist 'every viewpoint must be respected' orientation or a 'money talks, people mumble' marketplace approach, these alliances should be linked by a common need to redress market civilization's time–space imbalances generally and a mutual commitment to social justice and cultural-environmental (that is, ecological[11]) stewardship more specifically.

The policy reforms these 'islands' might facilitate include regulations limiting the further commercialization of television, the Internet and personal communication devices; efforts to rid cash-strapped schools and universities of advertising and promotions; the development of day care and public education facilities mandated to promote non-materialist values, creativity and a reflexive reading of history; and, perhaps most importantly, legislation – likely instigated by a difficult but increasingly crucial coalition of workers and environmentalists – crafted to promote practical alternatives to the commodification of both social relations and life itself.[12]

These, and many others, would constitute strategic nodes that, over time, could 'normalise' alternative ways of imagining the future. Barring a revolutionary turn in political economic trajectories, the primary goal of this strategy is the structuring of counter-balancing and prospectively counter-hegemonic realities. Rather than commercially mediated abstractions (characteristically acritical, ahistorical and relatively unimaginative) or similarly acritical (and sometimes reactionary) religious conceptualizations, reflexive and imaginative capacities should be prioritized.

The 'me' and 'now' that pervades much of today's anti-status quo activism, particularly in the West, constitutes the kind of thinking that enables rock star Bono to promote global change as an outgrowth of shopping. Marketing schemes such as his (or, more accurately, *American Express's, Giorgio Armani's, Converse's, Motorola's, Apple's* and the *Gap's*) 'Campaign Red', while funding humanitarian causes, reifies the marketplace amidst a fog of 'causumer' sincerity. The fact that this has taken form in a largely non-conscious culture reaffirms Innis's observation that time-annihilating conceptual systems are perniciously reproduced and elaborated through a spectrum of media.

One example of contemporary activists prioritizing reach and speed to the neglect of depth, reflection and time is the now defunct website *ifnotnow.com*. Established as an email-based pressure group targeting US Congressmen/women, the site provided visitors with a menu of issues from which selections could be made simply by clicking icons. This would automatically send a message to one's zip code-determined Representative or Senator (in 1999 this menu included 'Stop the bombing in Kosovo!' and a 'Safe roads campaign'). As Pietrzyk documents, such online anti-globalization activities tend to embrace a commercial news agenda *cause du jour*, occasionally culminating in some kind of 'day of action'. Once the act is performed, for most, it's time to move on to a new cause.[13] Illustrating this, an advertisement for the organization promised readers that activism now has become 'easy', taking just '5 minutes a week!' The irony of the ifnotnow.com's abbreviated existence speaks volumes (see Illustration 7.1).

If you care
you can
do something
...easy!

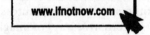
www.ifnotnow.com

BE A FULL-TIME CITIZEN ACTIVIST...
...for 5 minutes a week!
Over a dozen of the best social advocacy groups provide the information
—you read alerts, send letters, get responses, and monitor results—all at the click of a button.
It's a one-stop shop for staying involved.
We want to make it easy for you to make a difference!
MAKE YOUR VOICE HEARD!

www.ifnotnow.com
SIGN UP FOR A FREE TRIAL NOW!

"...www.ifnotnow.com tallies congressional votes on hot issues... so that visitors can easily see whether their official is getting the message."
The Washington Post, Oct. 12, 1998

"If Not Now keeps me informed and makes it easy for me to let my representatives hear how I think they should vote... And I'm using If Not Now to see who deserves my vote."
—Edward Asner, actor and political activist

"I'm clicking on If Not Now to help the officials I elected do something in office besides hold it. Use If Not Now to agitate, agitate, agitate!"
—Jim Hightower, syndicated radio talk show host

Agenda Information- Center for Science in the Public Interest • Children's Defense Fund • Common Cause • Environmental Defense Fund
Handgun Control • National Audubon Society • National Organization for Women (NOW) • Physicians for Social Responsibility
Public Citizen • Sierra Club • Union of Concerned Scientists • U.S. PIRG.

Source: *Mother Jones* (March/April 1999), p. 89, with permission from Phil and Paul Mitchell.

Illustration 7.1   ifnotnow.com advertisement

In anticipation of a globalization project in crisis, cultures that have escaped abject poverty but have not yet 'developed' into modern consumer societies are, at this juncture at least, relatively well positioned to take a *post*-globalization lead. Mixed but potentially important developments in parts of Latin America reveal this capacity.

In Venezuela, for example, the elected government of Hugo Chávez constitutes a problem for the United States and transnational capital, so much so that a (failed) US-backed coup was orchestrated in 2002. Beyond its strategic importance as a major oil-exporting country, the Chávez regime is a concern for official Washington because (like Cuba, especially during the Cold War) it *demonstrates* that an alternative, prospectively socialist future is possible. Among the country's notable reforms is a plan to implement worker-managed production centres.[14] Such a project, if successful, would constitute a bold step away from the seemingly unstoppable commodification of social relations.[15]

Through a political, economic and cultural rescinding of neoliberal processes, involving non modernist ways of thinking and nationalist/statist efforts to revise what is commonly thought feasible, a different future becomes imaginable. What Venezuela, as well as lingering aspects of China's and India's pre-globalization cultures suggest is that the time-annihilating dominance of a consumption-mediated empire of civil society, although probable, is not inevitable.[16]

* * *

At the beginning of this book, we cited Vergil Reed's 1949 report on India's prospects to become a modern consumer market. To 'move merchandise', Indian culture, he reported, would have to undergo a dramatic change:

> Indian genius runs more to introspection than to the practical. It has concerned itself mainly with abstract ideas and speculation on the nature of the soul rather than with physical laws, the properties of matter and the mastery of environment ... Did you ever try to shovel smoke or put a rubber band around a gaseous mass? It's easier than convincing Indians what they *must* do to become a modern nation ... Modernization will hurt quite a bit and will require action rather than philosophy.[17]

In his analysis of Indian advertising and consumption developments in the context of globalization, William Mazzarella perceptively demonstrates that Reed's metaphorical 'smoke' subsequently has been used to transform India into a marginally (but increasingly) commodified society. Marketers and advertisers took the traditional swadeshi and, even more remarkably, the Gandhian swaraj to make the consumption of commodities (including foreign-made goods) emblematic of India's maturity and independence. The fact that the abstract magic show of capitalist consumption can penetrate even the political, economic and cultural barriers of India says something quite profound as to the power of the institution and its capacity to adapt, develop and prospectively dominate.

The time-annihilating tendencies mediated through capitalist consumption now need to be redressed through, among other means, the critical recollection of pre- and non-capitalist norms in various cultures. In the case of India, the philosophical and political introspection of the past needs to be revisited and developed. Elsewhere, spatially biased, quantitatively oriented conceptual systems need to be critiqued. Barring the overnight resurrection of an organized and sustained working class politics – one focused on the decommodification of both work and leisure – we have suggested that through islands of resistance and the forging of creative alliances there exists at least some possibility of slowing down the forces and processes behind both the globalization project and commodification. Certainly the resurgence of domestic (as opposed to globalization-focused) politics involving mobilizations directed at government-mediated reforms constitutes a far more realistic and 'doable' course of action than now predominant strategies involving the networked 'multitude', discourse-focused identity politics, 'culture jamming', 'causumer' activities or, perhaps most delusional of all, the (largely voluntaristic) dawning of a progressive GCS.

What is needed is a re-assessment of what is 'normal', 'inevitable' and, indeed, what constitutes 'progress', involving an emphasis on the sustainable and culturally desirable. Following both Marcuse and Albert Schweitzer (the latter quoted at the outset of this chapter), humanity's survival may well depend on a shift away from immediate gratification towards delayed satisfaction, from pleasure to restraint – not through some kind of Maoist repression of one in favour of the other but, instead, a dialectical awareness of both.

While material goods provide people with the securities and comforts needed to live more liberated lives, as we have seen, there are limits to how much 'stuff' can make us happy.[18] Goods, in and of themselves, are neither liberating nor repressing; instead, once a culturally specific – but nevertheless generalizable – level of wealth is achieved, the liberation and happiness derived from the marketplace depends on how social relations and conceptual systems are organized through a range of time/space structuring institutions, organizations and technologies. The tangible elements of capitalist consumption – both its fleeting pleasures and the existential concerns linked to them – must, of course, be taken into account. Yet, clearly, in its current modern or neo-modern incarnations, the institution of capitalist consumption reflects a profound cultural imbalance of some characteristics and tendencies over others. Immediate gratification needs to be rebalanced with long-term needs – market expansion and control through sensations and imagery rebalanced with thought and discussion. Space needs to be rebalanced with time.

Associating *Coke* or *Tide* or *Cheerios* with identity, meaning, love and happiness implicitly re-affirms these existential needs and desires. However, the systemic commercial need to widen and deepen these abstractions, because they are experientially absurd, also cheapens and diminishes them. This quite possibly helps explain the cynicism and nihilism now so commonplace, especially among the West's traditionally most idealistic and radical – its youth. It is our collective capacity to perceive, reflect and act creatively and progressively that is at risk. Now perhaps more than ever it is time to mount an organized and lasting response.

Notes

Preface

1. In fact, as Marx demonstrated, capitalists are so productive that they are for-ever facing the prospect of not securing markets for their goods and services. At its worst, 'there breaks out an epidemic that, in all earlier epochs, would have seemed an absurdity – the epidemic of overproduction'. Karl Marx and Friedrich Engels, *The Communist Manifesto* (Harmondsworth: Penguin, 1979), p. 86.
2. Matthew Paterson, 'Shut Up and Shop!' (2002) http://www.theglobalsite.ac.uk/press/211paterson.htm.
3. Edward Comor, 'Introduction', in *The Global Political Economy of Communication*, Comor, ed. (London: Macmillan, 1994).
4. Other, relatively recent works taking substantive steps along these lines include Davies and Neimann's, *Rediscovering International Relations Theory* (London: Routledge, 2004); Stephen Gill, *Power and Resistance in the New World Order* (New York: Palgrave Macmillan, 2003); Ronnie Lipschutz's, *Global Environmental Politics* (Washington, DC: CQ Press, 2003); Kees Van Der Pijl, *Transnational Classes and International Relations* (London: Routledge, 1998); Princen, Maniates and Conca, eds, *Confronting Consumption* (Cambridge: MIT, 2002); and Leslie Sklair, *Globalization* (Oxford: Oxford University Press, 2002).
5. Samuel Huntington, 'The Clash of Civilizations?', *Foreign Affairs* Vol. 72 No. 3 (Summer 1993) http://www.foreignaffairs.org/19930601faessay5188/samuel-p-huntington/the-clash-of-civilizations.html.
6. Barber, 'Jihad vs. McWorld', *Atlantic Monthly* Vol. 269 No. 3 (March 1992) http://www.theatlantic.com/doc/199203/barber.
7. Ibid.
8. Justin Rosenberg, *Empire of Civil Society* (London: Verso, 1994).
9. Quoted in 'Woodward Shares War Secrets', *CBS News Online* (18 April 2004) http://www.cbsnews.com/stories/2004/04/15/60minutes/main612067.shtml.

1 Introduction

1. Quoted in William Mazzarella, *Shoveling Smoke* (Durham: Duke University Press, 2003), pp. 35–6.
2. Karl Marx, *Grundrisse* (Penguin: Harmondsworth, 1973), p. 164 (emphasis in original).
3. Robert Cox, 'Debt, Time, and Capitalism', *Studies in Political Economy* No. 48 (Autumn 1995), p. 168.
4. See, for example, Herbert Schiller, *Culture Inc.* (New York: Oxford University Press, 1989).
5. See, for example, Allan Pred and Michael Watts *Reworking Modernity* (1992) and Mike Featherstone, *Consumer Culture and Postmodernism* (London: Sage, 1991).
6. Neva R. Goodwin et al., eds, *The Consumer Society* (Washington, DC: Island Press, 1997), p. xxi.

7. Stephen Gill, 'Globalisation, Market Civilization, and Disciplinary Neoliberalism', *Millennium* Vol. 24 No. 3 (1995), p. 399.
8. Capitalist consumption is, after all, 'about continuous self-creation through ... things which are ... presented as new, modish, faddish or fashionable, always improved or improving'. Slater, *Consumer Culture and Modernity* (1997), p. 10.
9. Ibid., p. 3.
10. Ibid., p. 9.
11. Worldwatch Institute, *State of the World 2004* (8 January 2004) http://www.worldwatch.org/node/1783.
12. Ibid.
13. Mark Weisbrot et al., 'The Emperor Has No Growth', *Center for Economic and Policy Research* (26 September 2000) http://www.globalpolicy.org/globaliz/econ/growth.htm.
14. Worldwatch Institute (2004).
15. One recent threat stems from the 2007 crisis facing sub-prime mortgage lenders and its spillover effects on the availability of credit. According to the IMF, this constitutes one of the many threats to the ongoing buoyancy of consumer spending, particularly in the United States. Gary Duncan, 'US Recovery Under Threat from Sub-Prime Loan Crisis, IMF Says', *The Times* (2 August 2007) http://business.timesonline.co.uk/tol/business/economics/article2183297.ece.
16. *Economist.com*, 'Flying on One Engine' (18 September 2003) http://www.economist.com/surveys/showsurvey.cfm?issue=20030920.
17. Mark Weisbrot, 'Why Globalization Fails to Deliver', *The Observer* (28 July 2002) http://observer.guardian.co.uk/worldview/story/0,11581,764036,00.html.
18. Bob Coen, 'Bob Coen's Insiders Report 2003' (June 2003) http://www.mccann.com/insight/bobcoen.html.
19. The White House, *Helping Developing Nations* (21 June 2005) http://www.whitehouse.gov/infocus/developingnations/.
20. Marx, *Grundrisse* (1973),p. 251 (emphases in original).
21. John Agnew, *Hegemony, the Shape of Global Power* (Philadelphia: Temple University Press, 2005), pp. 179–81.
22. Ibid., pp. 179–80.
23. UNDP, *Human Development Report 1998* (New York: UNDP, 1998), p. 2.
24. Doug Saunders, 'The Fragile State of the Global Middle Class', *Globe and Mail* (21 July 2007) http://www.theglobeandmail.com/servlet/story/RTGAM.20070720.wmiddleclass0920/BNStory/International/home.
25. Mark Barnett, 'The Pentagon's New Map', *Esquire* (March 2003) http://www.thomaspmbarnett.com/published/pentagonsnewmap.htm.
26. Ibid., p. 6.
27. George W. Bush, 'Inaugural Speech' (21 January 2005) http://badinfluence.org/modules.php?name=News&file=article&sid=35.
28. Walter LaFeber, *The New Empire* (Ithaca, NY: Cornell University Press, 1963); William A. Williams, *The Tragedy of American Diplomacy* (New York: Delta, 1972).
29. The White House, *National Security Strategy of the United States of America* (Washington, 2002) in Introduction (n.p.).
30. Ibid., p. 18.
31. Rosenberg, *Empire of Civil Society* (1994); 'Globalization Theory: A Post Mortem', *International Politics* Vol. 42 No. 1 (March 2005), pp. 2–74.
32. David Harvey, *The Condition of Postmodernity.* (Cambridge: Basil Blackwell, 1989).
33. Rosenberg, 'Globalization Theory' (2005), p. 24.

34. Slater, *Consumer Culture and Modernity* (1997), p. 26.
35. Boal et al., *Afflicted Powers* (London: Verso, 2005), p. 76 (emphasis in original).
36. Karl Marx, *Capital, Vol. I* (Harmondsworth: Penguin, 1976), p. 875.
37. Paul Roberts, 'The New Food Anxiety', *Psychology Today* Vol. 31 No. 2 (March/April 1998) http://cms.psychologytoday.com/articles/pto-19980301-000028.html.
38. Thomas Freidman, 'A Manifesto for the Fast World', *New York Times Magazine* (28 March 1999) http://www.nytimes.com/books/99/04/25/reviews/friedman-mag.html.
39. Herbert Marcuse, *One Dimensional Man* (Boston: Beacon Press, 1964).
40. Barber, *Consumed* (New York: W.W. Norton, 2007), p. 248.
41. Boal et al., *Afflicted Powers* (2005), p. 173.
42. Beyond the now well-known environmental and health costs of capitalist consumption, the world's most active consumers are not even realizing the happiness promised by marketers and advertising executives. Several studies confirm that after a certain level of wealth is attained, people do not necessarily derive more joy or pleasure as a result of accumulating more things. One life-satisfaction survey conducted in 65 countries shows that rising incomes can be correlated with rising levels of reported happiness up to and until a certain annual income is reached ($13,000 per person in 1995 dollars). What this demonstrates is that money, in fact, *can* buy us happiness *but only to the extent that it is used to purchase basic* (and, to some degree, historically contingent) *levels of security and comfort*. Worldwatch Institute (2004).
43. According to a report commissioned by *MasterCard*, issued in 2006, in 'developing' countries such as India and China, when 'income exceeds the $5,000 threshold, marginal expenditures shift quickly to discretionary spending ... and these have a huge ... economic impact ...' Cited in Saunders, 'The Fragile State of the Global Middle Class' (2007).
44. Connor Dougherty, 'Exporting Christmas', *Wall Street Journal* (23 December 2006) http://online.wsj.com/article/SB116684145879058402.html?mod=googlewsj.
45. Barber, 'Jihad vs. McWorld' (1992).
46. Cox, 'Debt, Time, and Capitalism' (1995), p. 168.
47. Ibid., pp. 169–70.

2   Power, Hegemony and the Institution of Consumption

1. Steven Lukes, *Power, a Radical View* (London: Macmillan, 1974).
2. Ibid., p. 24.
3. See Robert Babe, *Cultural Ecology* (Toronto: University of Toronto Press, 2006) and his *Communication and the Transformation of Economics* (Boulder: Westview Press, 1995).
4. Goodwin, 'Volume Introduction' in Goodwin et al. (1997), p. xxxi.
5. Robert Cox, *Production, Power, and World Order* (New York: Columbia University Press, 1987), pp. 377–82.
6. Gaventa, *Power and Powerlessness* (Urbana: University of Illinois Press, 1982).
7. Ibid., p. 26 (emphases added).
8. Lukes, *Power, a Radical View* (1974), pp. 41–2.
9. Peter Berger and Thomas Luckmann, *The Social Construction of Reality* (Garden City, NY: Anchor Books, 1967), p. 54.
10. Ibid., p. 60.
11. The omnipresence of institutions, including consumption, also involves a functional necessity. By ordering thought and action, predictability in most interactions is facilitated. This relieves people (especially in relatively large scale, complex social formations) of having to spend considerable time and

effort in virtually every social encounter from having to repeatedly sort out the 'rules of engagement'.

12. Quoted in Russell Belk and Non Zhou, 'Learning to Want Things', *Advances in Consumer Research* Vol. 14 (Urbana: Association for Consumer Research, 1987), p. 478.

13. Ibid., p. 479.

14. Ibid.

15. As one analyst of contemporary Western anti-globalization activists argues, more than just reflecting the norms of consumer society, many appear to be influenced by the shallowness of their own consumerist-influenced identities. According to Ingolfur Blühdorn, 'the centre of social movement activity is, thus, no longer the political alternative, but *alterity*, the desire of individuals to be different from the system and experience themselves as autonomous subjects ... Social movements and other kinds of non-conventional political articulation can ... be interpreted as offering a supplementary form of identity construction which helps ... compensate for the shortcomings of consumption-oriented identity formation'. Blühdorn, 'Movements and Political Articulation in the Late-Modern Condition' *European Journal of Social Theory* Vol. 9 No. 1 (February 2006), p. 36.

16. James Watson, 'China's Big Mac Attack', *Foreign Affairs* Vol. 79 No. 30 (May/June 2000), pp. 120–34.

17. Fabrizio Perri and Dirk Krueger, 'Does Income Inequality Lead to Consumption Inequality?', *National Bureau of Economic Research* working paper 9202 (September 2002) http://papers.nber.org/papers/W9202.

18. Ibid.

19. Seth Sandronsky, 'A Rising Tide of Consumer Debt', *Common Dreams* (6 January 2001) http://www.commondreams.org/cgi-bin/print.cgi?file=/views01/0106-04.htm.

20. Helga Dittmar, 'Compulsive Buying – A Growing Concern?', *British Journal of Psychology*, Vol. 96 No. 4 (November 2005), pp. 467–91.

21. Cited in Barber, *Consumed* (2007), p. 239.

22. Steven Schlosser et al., 'Compulsive Buying' *General Hospital Psychiatry*, Vol. 15 No. 3 (May 1994), pp. 205–12.

23. Barber, *Consumed* (2007), p. 137.

24. While consumption ideals and practices at any given place and time play an important role in the complex structuring of human relationships, it is important to note that the institution is directly influenced by others. The law, for example, particularly property law, is influential. It provides individuals with state-sanctioned rights in relation to commodities while rules, regulations and social norms, to varying degrees, shape how consumption takes place. Without private property, there would be nothing to sell; in its absence, buyers would be unable to purchase something they then could not 'own'.

25. Among other theories, the globalization project's impelled application of neoliberal reforms has displaced or diminished many Third World bureaucrats and state industry officials who constituted, during the Cold War, a relatively small, 'elite' middle class. The result has been an existential vacuum, particularly among younger members or their children – a vacuum deepened by their eroding social status and waning economic ability to consume. Anti-Western, anti-modernist and anti-consumerist forms of religious fundamentalism subsequently have emerged, filling this vacuum for some. For a collection of papers addressing this and related issues, see The New America Foundation's *Global Middle Class Program* at http://www.newamerica.net/programs/global_middle_class#.

26. Rosenberg, 'Globalization Theory: A Post Mortem' (2005), pp. 2–74.

27. Pew Research Center for the People and the Press, *View of a Changing World 2003* (3 June 2003) http://people-press.org/reports/print.php3?PageID=712.
28. Quoted in David Harvey, *A Brief History of Neoliberalism* (New York: Oxford University Press, 2006), p. 176.
29. For a litany of covert activities orchestrated by the United States in the interest of capital, see Michael Parenti, *The Sword and the Dollar* (New York: St. Martin's Press, 1988).
30. Barber, *Consumed* (2007), p. 35.
31. Ibid., p. 36.
32. Ibid., pp. 296–303.
33. As is typically the case both with commercial and state-sponsored journalism, war coverage rarely focuses on arguably the worst affected victims – everyday people.
34. Denbighshire Record Office (report in file QSD/AG/1/79) cited in *Treadmill and Other Airing Ground Activities* www.ruthingaol.co.uk/English/Treadmill.htm.
35. C. Wright Mills, *The Power Elite* (Oxford: Oxford University Press, 1982), p. 162.
36. Sheldon Wolin, *Politics and Vision* (Boston: Little Brown, 1960), pp. 220–4.
37. Michael Mann, 'The Working Class', *New Society* (4 November 1976).
38. Paul Levinson, *Mind at Large* (Greenwich: JAI Press, 1988).
39. As noted previously and developed in Chapter 5, the recent 'opening up' of India to free trade and overseas commodities illustrates this point. In the late-1990s, despite the entry of transnational corporate brands, even the country's middle class remained remarkably utililtarian.
40. Berger and Luckmann, *The Social Construction of Reality* (1967).
41. Carey, 'Canadian Communication Theory', in *Studies in Canadian Communications*, G. Robinson and D. Theall, eds (Montreal: McGill University, 1975), p. 45.
42. The importance and implications of this point vis-à-vis the globalization project are discussed in Chapter 4.
43. This is not to say that hegemony, once established, is monolithic and irreversible. Instead, what we are arguing is that because institutional media, such as consumption, are *genuinely* participatory (within certain parameters, of course), the contemporary political economic (dis)order garners needed legitimacy.
44. Mann, 'The Working Class' (1976), p. 388.
45. Michael Mann, 'The Social Cohesion of Liberal Democracy', in *Classes, Power and Conflict*, D. Held and A. Giddens, eds (London: Macmillan 1982), pp. 373–95.
46. The corporate executive might have had different family, educational and social encounters than the environmentalist and, subsequently, these two people, despite living in the same political economic context, lead disparate lifestyles and thus may see themselves and the world differently. Indeed, it is likely that their respective backgrounds influenced the subsequent career choices of each and their experiences in these jobs further influenced their conceptual systems.

3   The Birth of Capitalist Consumption

1. Strauss, 'Things are in the Saddle', *The Atlantic Monthly*, Vol. 134 No. 5 (November 1924), pp. 577–88, esp. p. 579.
2. Quoted in Robert Cox, *Approaches to World Order* (Cambridge: Cambridge University Press, 1996), p. 80, n. 12 (emphases added).
3. The reason for this selection is as follows: the former was the birthplace of capitalist consumption while the latter emerged to become (and today remains) the institution's most important and dynamic centre.

4. Larry Patriquin, 'The Agrarian Origins of the Industrial Revolution in England', *Review of Radical Political Economics*, Vol. 36 No. 2 (Spring 2004), p. 204.
5. Robert Brenner, 'Agrarian Class Structure and Economic Development in Pre-Industrial Europe', *Past & Present*, No. 70 (February 1976), p. 52.
6. Ibid., pp. 56–8.
7. Ibid., p. 59.
8. Freeholders were the elite of peasants due largely to their undisputed Crown-recognized right to occupy and use a parcel of land. Patriquin, 'Agrarian Origins' (2004), p. 205.
9. D. J. Seipp, 'The Concept of Property in the Early Common Law', *Law and History Review*, Vol. 12 No. 1 (Spring 1994), p. 85.
10. Patriquin, 'Agrarian Origins' (2004), p. 206.
11. Ellen Wood, *The Origin of Capitalism* (New York: Monthly Review Press, 1999), p. 76.
12. By the early seventeenth century, one-quarter to one-third of the English peasantry no longer had customary access to land. See Patriquin, 'Agrarian Origins' (2004), p. 208 and William Lazonick, 'Karl Marx and Enclosures in England', *Review of Radical Political Economics*, Vol. 6 No. 2 (Summer 1974), p. 19.
13. C. E. Searle, 'Custom, Class Conflict and Agrarian Capitalism', *Past and Present*, No. 110 (1986), pp. 125–6.
14. Richard Lachmann, *From Manor to Market* (Madison: University of Wisconsin Press, 1987), p. 27.
15. Patriquin, 'Agrarian Origins' (2004), p. 211.
16. John Lie, 'Visualizing the Invisible Hand', *Politics & Society*, Vol. 21 No. 1 (September 1993), pp. 281–3.
17. Ibid., p. 301, fn. 49.
18. Ibid., p. 283.
19. Ibid., p. 286.
20. Christopher Chalkin, *The Rise of the English Town* (Cambridge: Cambridge University Press, 2001), pp. 1, 5.
21. Ibid., pp. 66–7. Among working class families, well into the nineteenth century, most spent at least half their incomes on food and beverage. It was not until the early twentieth century that England's proletariat earned the wages needed to purchase the kinds of goods and services bought by the middle-class bourgeoisie two centuries earlier. See Arthur J. Taylor, ed., 'Editor's Introduction', *The Standard of Living in Britain in the Industrial Revolution* (London: Metheun & Co., 1975), p. xxxiv.
22. Chalkin, *The Rise of the English Town* (2001), p. 10.
23. Lie, 'Visualizing the Invisible Hand' (1993), p. 288.
24. Ibid., pp. 288–90.
25. Ibid., p. 294.
26. Ibid., p. 296.
27. Grant McCracken, *Culture & Consumption* (Bloomington: Indiana University Press, 1990), pp. 11–16.
28. Neil McKendrick, 'The Consumer Revolution of Eighteenth-Century England', in *The Birth of Consumer Society*, McKendrick et al., eds (Bloomington: Indiana University Press, 1982), pp. 29–31. Commodities as varied and bizarre as Venice treacle, elephant's teeth, artificial eyes and even asses' milk were for sale in eighteenth-century London (McKendrick, p. 81). One advertisement, appearing in the *Salisbury Journal* in 1777, promoted 'night caps made of silver wire so strong that no mouse or … rat can gnaw through them'. Ibid., p. 64.
29. McCracken, *Culture and Consumption*, p. 19.

30. Ibid., pp. 16–22.
31. Slater, *Consumer, Culture and Modernity* (1997), p. 30.
32. According to a national Anglican census report published in 1851, the working class were 'thoroughly estranged from ... religious institutions'. Quoted in Hugh McLeod, *Religion and Irreligion* (Bangor: Headstart History, 1993), p. 13. Also see pp. 18–19.
33. Chalkin, *The Rise of the English Town* (2001), pp. 52, 68.
34. Ibid., p. 52 & pp. 68–70.
35. Ibid., p. 51.
36. Ibid., p. 55.
37. Benedict Anderson, *Imagined Communities* (London: Verso, 1983), pp. 29–39.
38. Ibid., pp. 39–40.
39. Chalkin, *The Rise of the English Town* (2001), p. 58.
40. The latter is a mechanized way of ordering time; the mechanical clock and its use in increasing efficiencies and disciplining labour constitute obvious examples. The former – cyclical time – relates more directly to the biological and ecological.
41. E. P. Thompson, 'Time, Work-Discipline, and Industrial Capitalism', *Past and Present*, No. 38 (December 1967), p. 61 (emphases in original [pp. 56–97]).
42. Quoted in Ibid., p. 80.
43. W. Cooke Taylor quoted in E. P. Thompson, 'Standards and Experiences', in *The Standard of Living in Britain in the Industrial Revolution*, Arthur J. Taylor, ed. (London: Metheun & Co., 1975), p. 126.
44. Thompson, Ibid., p. 130.
45. Huws, *The Making of a Cybertariat* (New York: Monthly Review Press, 2003), pp. 24–5.
46. Ibid., p. 25.
47. James Carrier, *Gifts and Commodities* (London: Routledge, 1995), pp. 75–9.
48. McKendrick, 'George Packwood and the Commercialization of Shaving', in *The Birth of Consumer Society*, McKendrick et al., eds (1982), p. 184.
49. Quoted in ibid., p. 183. Also on the subject of teeth (a growing concern among an ageing bourgeoisie exposed to a new staple – sugar) was a more truthful advertisement for *Mr. De Chamant's Improved Mineral Teeth* which substantiated its claim that it was superior to the false teeth taken from animals or the dead by underlining that the latter emanate a horrendous 'smell'. Ibid., p. 189.
50. Carrier, *Gifts and Commodities* (1995), pp. 82–3.
51. Harvey, *The Condition of Postmodernity* (Cambridge: Basil Blackwell, 1989), p. 101.
52. Thompson, 'Standards and Experiences', (1975), p. 139 & pp. 148–9.
53. Ibid., p. 141. Other researchers might speculate as to the extent to which this history is repeating itself in rapidly 'developing' political economies today, particularly in countries experiencing growing wage disparities.
54. Of course the pursuit of this particular freedom was not an autonomous enterprise. Social, political and economic change and, with them, existential uncertainty itself conditioned the quest for consumption. Furthermore, the parameters of what was consumable were delimited by what people could afford and, of course, by what was profitable for capitalists and retailers to provide.
55. William Leach, *Land of Desire* (New York: Pantheon Books, 1993), p. 9.
56. Frederick Taylor successfully promoted organizational principles aimed at increasing the efficiency of workers. These stressed the de-skilling of workers and the related management of factory activities. In effect, Taylorism reduced workers to unthinking extensions of assembly lines, minimizing creativity, increasing repetition and, more abstractly, further alienating people from their labour.

57. Electricity also led to the expansion of streetcar services, which, in effect, furthered suburbanization (itself a significant development, as discussed below).
58. Rosalynd Williams, 'Dream Worlds of Consumption', in *Communication in History*, D. Crowley and P. Heyer, eds (Pearson: Boston, 2007), p. 173.
59. Leach, *Land of Desire* (1993), p. 9 (emphasis in original).
60. Filene, *Successful Living in This Machine Age* (New York: Simon and Schuster, 1931), p. 157 (emphases added).
61. Paul David and Gavin Wright, 'Early Twentieth Century Growth Dynamics', *Oxford University Economic and Social Series*, Paper #033 (October 1999) http://ideas.repec.org/p/nuf/esohwp/_033.html.
62. Leach, *Land of Desire* (1993), p. 271.
63. Quoted in Ibid., p. 272.
64. Ibid., p. 266.
65. Quoted in Ibid., p. 268.
66. Stuart Ewen, *Captains of Consciousness* (New York: McGraw-Hill, 1976), p. 197.
67. William Leiss et al., *Social Communication in Advertising* (New York: Routledge, 1990), p. 102.
68. With advertising revenues exceeding monies generated directly from sales, many papers (and magazines) re-crafted their publications to deliver as many readers as they could to advertisers. Through this reorientation, 'balanced' reporting – now a principle of professional journalism – was born and the news was transformed from a forum dominated by facts (i.e. grain prices) and 'politically-biased' reports into a supposedly 'objective' portrayal of what is new, exciting and sensational. Dan Schiller, *Objectivity and the News* (Philadelphia: University of Pennsylvania Press, 1981).
69. Innis, *The Bias of Communication* (Toronto: University of Toronto Press, 1982), p. 78.
70. *Gillette*, for example, had its own show about beards and grooming.
71. Even before the First World War, signs of American labour's 'bourgeoisment' could be seen, particularly in the realm of consumption. In a speech given in 1913, William Haywood, who led the relatively radical Industrial Workers of the World, mapped out his vision of 'the ideal society': 'There will be a wonderful dining room where you will enjoy the best food that can be purchased,' he said. 'There will be a gymnasium and a great swimming pool and private bathrooms of marble ... Your work chairs will be morris chairs, so that when you become fatigued you may relax in comfort.' Quoted in Leach, *Land of Desire* (1993), p. 189.
72. Robert Lynd, 'The Consumer Becomes a "Problem"', in *The Ultimate Consumer*, J. Brainerd, ed. (Philadelphia: Annals of the American Academy of Political and Social Science, 1934), p. 6.
73. Lizabeth Cohen, *A Consumers' Republic* (New York: Vintage, 2004), pp. 21–2. Also see George Ross and Jane Jenson, 'Post-War Class Struggle and the Politics of Left Politics', in *Socialist Register 1985/86*, Ralph Miliband et al., eds (London: Merlin Press, 1986), pp. 25–6.
74. Quoted in Ewen, Captains of Consciousness (1976), p. 80.
75. Ibid., p. 58 (emphases added).
76. No other state-based consumer research department existed until Britain followed suit in the 1950s.
77. At the local level, in New York City, for example, business interests convinced city officials to enact zoning regulations that segregated 'factories from retail areas so that shoppers would not have to confront factory workers ...' Robbins, *Global Problems and the Culture of Capitalism* (Boston: Allyn & Bacon, 1999), pp. 18–19.

78. Ibid., pp. 19–20.
79. Leiss et al., *Social Communication in Advertising* (1990), p. 144.
80. Ross and Jenson, 'Post-War Class Struggle' (1986), p. 26.
81. Neil Postman, 'The Social Effects of Commercial Television', in *Critical Studies in Media Commercialism*, R. Anderson and L. Strate eds (Oxford: Oxford University Press, 2000), p. 62.
82. Ibid., p. 51 (emphases added).
83. Ibid.
84. Ibid., p. 64.
85. A relatively recent study confirming this trend is Robert Putnam's *Bowling Alone* (New York: Simon & Schuster, 2000).
86. Postman, p. 64.
87. Ibid., pp. 64–5.
88. Timothy Luke, 'The (Un)wise (Ab)use of Nature' (Unpublished paper prepared for the International Studies Association Annual Conference, Toronto, March 1997).

4   Global Civil Society or Global Consumer Society?

1. Barber, *Consumed* (2007), p. 163.
2. The concept of the multitude stems from the notion that a historical turning point has been ushered in alongside globalization – a political break away from class and nation state politics and towards the individual. Through ICTs and anti-globalization networking activities, the formation of an ever-changing transnational resistance is said to be underway. The definitive work on this perspective is Hardt and Negri's *Multitude* (London: Penguin, 2004).
3. For a Marxist-based critique of the multitude and Hardt and Negri's related concept of empire, see Amin, 'Empire and Multitude' (2005).
4. Mustapha Pasha and David Blaney, 'Elusive Paradise: The Promise and Peril of Global Civil Society', *Alternatives* Vol. 23 No. 4 (October–December 1998), p. 418.
5. James Rosenau, *Turbulence in World Politics* (Princeton, NJ: Princeton University Press, 1994).
6. Justin Rosenberg, *The Follies of Globalisation Theory* (London: Verso, 2000), p. 3.
7. Rosenberg, 'Globalization Theory: A Post Mortem' (2005), p. 13.
8. Ibid., p. 7.
9. Pasha and Blaney, 'Elusive Paradise' (1998), p. 419.
10. Martin Shaw, 'Global Society and Global Responsibility', in *International Society after the Cold War*, R. Fawn and J. Larkins, eds (London: Macmillan, 1996), p. 58.
11. Richard Falk, 'State of Siege', *International Affairs* Vol. 73 No. 1 (January 1997), p. 125.
12. See Gilles Deleuze and Felix Guattari, *A Thousand Plateaus* (Minneapolis: University of Minnesota Press, 1987).
13. Ironically, this heterogeneous and rhizomatic global justice movement has an Internet homepage. See http://www.globaljusticemovement.net/.
14. Huws, *The Making of a Cybertariat* (2003).
15. Susan Strange, *States and Markets*, (London: Pinter, 1988), p. 25.
16. Rosenberg, *Empire of Civil Society* (1994), p. 129.
17. Rosenberg, 'Globalization Theory' (2005), p. 18.
18. Marx regarded production as a process involving four inter-related 'moments': production, distribution, exchange and consumption. A breakdown in one

would undermine the perpetuation of the whole. Karl Marx, 'Introduction to a Critique of Political Economy', in *The German Ideology*, Marx and Engels, (New York: International Publishers, 1984), p. 129.

19. Rosenberg, 'Globalization Theory' (2005), p. 12.
20. Ibid.
21. As Milton Friedman summarized in what was a marginal perspective when he wrote it in 1962 (but had become mainstream by the 1980s), 'every act of government intervention limits ... individual freedom directly and threatens the preservation of freedom indirectly'. Friedman, *Capitalism and Freedom* (Chicago: University of Chicago Press, 1962), p. 33.
22. Rosenberg, 'Globalization Theory' (2005), pp. 43–8.
23. World Bank report cited in Leo Panitch, '"The State in a Changing World"', *Monthly Review* Vol. 50 No. 5 (October 1998), p. 20 (emphases added).
24. Francis Fukuyama, *The End of History and the Last Man* (New York: Avon Books, 1992).
25. On globalization's role as a means of managing uncertainty, see Ian Parker, 'Myth, Telecommunication and the Emerging Global Informational Order', in *The Global Political Economy of Communication*, Comor, ed. (1994), pp. 37–60.
26. Rosenberg, 'Globalization Theory' (2005), p. 52 (emphases added). Assessing the post-structuralist take on globalization, its assumptions regarding the decline of the nation state and the emergence of 'the multitude', Samir Amin, states that 'Our moment is one of defeat for the powerful social and political movements that shaped the twentieth century (workers', socialist, and national liberation movements). The loss of perspective that any defeat involves leads to ephemeral unrest and the profusion of para-theoretical propositions that both legitimate that unrest and give rise to the belief that it constitutes an "effective" means for "transforming the world" ...' Amin, 'Empire and Multitude' (2005).
27. For an overview of technology's role in facilitating capitalist consumption, see Edward Comor, 'New Technologies and Consumption', in *Information Technologies and Global Politics*, J. Rosenau and J. P. Singh, eds (Albany: SUNY Press, 2002), pp. 169–85.
28. *BlackBerry United States Homepage*, http://www.discoverblackberry.com/devices/.
29. See 'Web Ads Can Lure You In' (3 April 2006) www.ChronicleHerald.ca.
30. Thanks to James Bullbrook for informing us of this phenomenon.
31. Slater, *Consumer, Culture and Modernity* (1997), p. 126.
32. Ibid.
33. Richard Falk, 'The Making of Global Citizenship', in *Global Visions*, J. Brecher et al., eds (Boston: South End Press, 1993), p. 40.
34. Jeremy Brecher, et al., 'Introduction', in ibid., pp. xv–xvii.
35. Nancy Stefanik, 'Sustainable Dialogue/Sustainable Development', in ibid., p. 264.
36. Richard Falk, *Predatory Globalization, A Critique* (Cambridge: Polity Press, 1999), p. 6.
37. Reg Whitaker, *The End of Privacy* (New York: Kew Press, 1999), pp. 166–8.
38. Sean MacBride et al., *Many Voices, One World* (Paris: Kogan Page/UNESCO, 1984).
39. Herbert Schiller, *Mass Communications and American Empire* (Boulder, CO: Westview Press, 1992).
40. J. Becker et al., eds, *Communication and Domination* (Norwood: Ablex, 1986).
41. Vincent Mosco, *The Political Economy of Communication* (London: Sage, 1996).

42. Herbert Schiller, 'Transnational Media: Creating Consumers Worldwide', *Journal of International Affairs* Vol. 47 No. 1 (Summer 1993), pp. 47–58.
43. Rosenau, *Turbulence in World Politics* (1994).
44. Ronnie Lipschutz, 'Reconstructing World Politics', in *International Society after the Cold War*, R. Fawn and J. Larkins, eds (London: Macmillan, 1996), p. 114–15 (emphasis in the original).
45. By 'culture', we share with Lipschutz the general understanding that it involves historically constructed material and mental realities of day-to-day life and, as such, it is more complex than the sum of information flows or the meaningfulness of predominant discourse in any given place and time.
46. Lipschutz with J. Mayer, *Global Civil Society and Global Environmental Governance* (Albany: State University of New York Press, 1996), pp. 60–2.
47. Ibid., p. 63.
48. Quoted in Ibid., p. 65.
49. Ibid., p. 68.
50. Ibid., p. 72.
51. Lipschutz, 'Reconstructing World Politics' (1996), pp. 117–18.
52. Lipschutz with Mayer, *Global Civil Society* (1996), p. 74.
53. Martin Shaw, *Global Society and International Relations* (Cambridge: Polity, 1994), p. 4.
54. Ibid., p. 11.
55. Ibid., p. 13.
56. To understand the development and ongoing saliency of the nation as a comparatively powerful source of identity and meaning, particularly in relation to 'the global', see Anderson's definitive book, *Imagined Communities*, and John Tomlinson's *Globalization and Culture* (Cambridge: Polity Press, 1999). Generally, the pervasiveness of significant and meaningful institutions, organizations and technologies, mediating national and local relationships is far more extensive than those that are transnational or global. This pervasiveness, experienced through daily life, is particularly affecting in the context of socialization and the forging of conceptual systems. (Even the United Nations is an organization of nation states, not global citizens.)
57. Falk, *Predatory Globalization* (1999).
58. Ibid., pp. 140–1.
59. Ronald Deibert, 'International Plug 'n Play?', *International Studies Perspectives* Vol. 1 No. 3 (July 2000), pp. 255–72.
60. Richard Price, 'Reversing the Gun Sights', *International Organization* Vol. 52 No. 3 (July 1998), pp. 613–44.
61. Most particularly, see Giddens, *The Consequences of Modernity* (Stanford, CA: Stanford University Press, 1990). Rosenberg also makes this argument in his *The Follies of Globalisation Theory*.
62. Giddens, *The Consequences of Modernity* (1990).
63. Essential to this, of course, is the widening (i.e. the expansion) and deepening (i.e. the intensification) of various media in day-to-day life. In fact Giddens points to the importance of print and its rapid ascendancy over writing in the history of modernity. When books were produced by hand, they had to be passed along from one person to another. Spatial and temporal barriers were dramatically challenged when printing enabled many readers to share the same book over vast areas at the same time. Likewise, electronic media have facilitated the sharing of information on a global scale instantaneously. See Giddens, *Modernity and Self-Identity* (Stanford, CA: Stanford University Press, 1991).

64. John Tomlinson, 'Global Experience as a Consequence of Modernity', in *Globalization, Communication and Transnational Civil Society*, S. Braman et al., eds (Cresskill: Hampton Press, 1996), pp. 63–87.
65. Ibid., p. 75.
66. Lipschutz with Mayer, *Global Civil Society* (1996), p. 64.
67. In assessing time–space distanciation, an evaluation of assumptions related to the role of communication in shaping conceptual systems leads to an important corrective. For one thing, the extension to a global scale of shared information and experience is, in both quantitative and qualitative terms, varied and uneven. The experience of a long-distance telephone conversation is not very similar to the experience of watching television in that the levels of intimacy afforded by media shape what is communicated and, subsequently, its impact on the people involved. Again, there is a distinction between flesh-and-blood relationships (even when linked electronically) and others.
68. GCS progressives who recognize that the taking on of an activist lifestyle itself both reflects and can revise an individual's conceptual systems thus make a most salient point. As Paul Wapner argues in relation to the efforts of transnational environmental activist groups, their role in organizing participatory forms of local politics, 'can alter the way people interact with each other and their environment'. As such, and as with most forms of participatory democracy, some modification in how one thinks often is a consequence of one's actions. Wapner, 'Politics beyond the State', *World Politics* Vol. 47 No. 3 (Spring 1995), p. 336.
69. As we have detailed elsewhere, the American state, for example, has been a crucial and complex mediator of such domestic and transnational developments – 'complex' in the sense that the historical and power-laden structures of American domestic and foreign policy directly facilitate or retard different policy initiatives at different times. Thus, even the communications sector – itself often assumed to be an area that somehow transcends state authority – remains dependent on states and the state system. See Comor, *Communication, Commerce and Power* (London: Macmillan, 1998).
70. Supplementing this is the disintegration of class-based politics and organized labour, especially since the 1970s. Trentmann, 'Citizenship and Consumption', *Journal of Consumer Culture* Vol. 7 No. 2 (July 2007), p. 148.
71. Ibid., p. 151.
72. For an overview, see Mel Van Elteren, 'Rethinking Americanization Abroad', *The Journal of American Culture* Vol. 29 No. 3, pp. 345–67.
73. John Clarke, 'Mine Eyes Dazzle', in *New Times and Old Enemies*, J. Clarke, ed. (London: HarperCollins, 1991), p. 85.
74. Ibid.
75. Barber, *Consumed* (2007), p. 326.
76. Ibid., p. 120.
77. Even the nation state has become the object of this orientation, particularly through the popularity of branding as a marketing/public relations strategy. Recent examples include Tony Blair's 'Cool Brittania' and the second Bush administration's multi-billion-dollar push to promote 'Brand USA'. Ibid., pp. 206–9.
78. Peter Golding, 'Global Village or Global Pillage?', in *Capitalism and the Information Age*, R. McChesney et al., eds (New York: Monthly Review Press, 1998), pp. 69–86.
79. Robert Fortner, 'Excommunication in the Information Society', *Critical Studies in Mass Communication* Vol. 12 No. 2 (June 1995), p. 139.

80. Pasha and Blaney, 'Elusive Paradise' (1998), p. 423.
81. Luxembourg, *The Accumulation of Capital* (London: Routledge, 2003), p. 6.
82. Harvey, *The Condition of Postmodernity* (Cambridge: Basil Blackwell, 1989), pp. 180–1.
83. David Harvey, *A Brief History of Neoliberalism* (Oxford: Oxford University Press, 2005).
84. David Harvey, *The New Imperialism* (Oxford: Oxford University Press, 2003), p. 149.
85. Azizur Kahn, 'Growth and Distribution of Household Income in China between 1995 and 2002' (March 2004), p. 6 http://72.14.207.104/search?q=cache:9TllNwzFYW8J:www.economics.ucr.edu/seminars/spring04/05-28.
86. Ibid., p. 16 (emphases in original).
87. Ibid., pp. 28–32.
88. From 2003 to 2006, the number of *VISA* credit cards issued to Chinese residents increased from 1.7 to 11.7 million. Jacqueline Thorp, 'Chinese Becoming Avid Shoppers', *National Post* (24 July 2006), p. FP1.
89. OECD, *Trends and Recent Developments in Foreign Direct Investment* (June 2004), p. 5, http://www.oecd.org/dataoecd/37/39/32230032.pdf.
90. Harvey, *A Brief History of Neoliberalism* (2005), p. 161.
91. Slater, Consumer, Culture and Modernity (1997), p. 27.
92. Rosenberg, *Empire of Civil Society* (1994), p. 124.
93. Ibid., p. 125.
94. Exceptions or alternatives to this history – such as the communist revolutions in Russia, China and Cuba – took form in the midst of either primitive accumulation (to repeat, the initial period of capitalism's violent imposition) or in political economies whose development into 'developed' capitalist-consumerist societies was retarded by imperialism and/or authoritarian forces.
95. Margaret Keck and Kathryn Sikkink, *Activists beyond Borders* (Ithaca, NY: Cornell University Press, 1998).
96. Berger and Luckmann, *The Social Construction of Reality* (1967), pp. 174–83.
97. Deibert, *Parchment, Printing, and Hypermedia* (New York: Columbia University Press, 1997).
98. Scott Lash and John Urry, *Economies of Signs and Space* (London: Sage, 1994).
99. Arjun Appadurai, 'Disjuncture and Difference in the Global Cultural Economy', in *Global Culture: Nationalism, Globalization and Modernity*, M. Featherstone, ed. (London: Sage, 1990), p. 307.
100. Harvey (1990), p. 271.
101. Ibid., p. 303.
102. Innis, *The Bias of Communication* (1982), pp. 61–91.

5 'Developing' Political Economies and Global Consumer Society

1. Christian Frey and Jose Navarro de Pablo, *China and India, the Steady Progression towards Two Consumer Markets* (Zurich: UBS Wealth Management, 2004), p. 19.
2. Ibid., p. 20.
3. Ibid., p. 26.
4. Ibid., p. 27.
5. Quoted in 'Consumerism is King, Interview: Kishore Biyani', in *Financial Express* (29 April 2007), http://www.financialexpress.com/fe_full_story.php?content_id=162593# (emphasis added).

6. Frey and de Pablo, *China and India* (2004), pp. 36–7.
7. Mazzarella, *Shoveling Smoke* (2003), p. 272.
8. Margrit Van Wessel, 'Talking about Consumption', *Cultural Dynamics*, Vol. 16 No. 1 (July 2004), p. 94.
9. Mazzarella, *Shoveling Smoke* (2003), p. 5.
10. Quoted in Mazzarella, *Shoveling Smoke* (2003), p. 6.
11. Ibid., p. 8.
12. Quoted in Ibid.
13. Quoted in Ibid., p. 9.
14. Quoted in Ibid., pp. 10–11.
15. Quoted in Ibid., p. 11.
16. Ibid., p. 13.
17. Ibid., pp. 225–33.
18. Ibid., pp. 229–31.
19. Quoted in Ibid., p. 241.
20. Mazzarella, *Shoveling Smoke* (2003).
21. Mazzarella, *Shoveling Smoke* (2003), p. 225.
22. Ibid., p. 226.
23. Ibid., p. 244.
24. Van Wessel, 'Talking about Consumption' (2004), p. 95.
25. Ibid., p. 96.
26. Van Wessel, 'Talking about Consumption' (2004), p. 104.
27. Mazzarella, *Shoveling Smoke* (2003), esp. pp. 149–211.
28. Nandy et al., *Creating a Nationality* (Delhi: Oxford University Press, 1997).
29. Nandy, *The Intimate Enemy* (Delhi: Oxford University Press, 1983), p. 109 (emphases added).
30. Frey and de Pablo, *China and India* (2004), pp. 18 & 26.
31. Peter Ford, 'Consumer Tidal Wave on the Way', *The Christian Science Monitor* (2 January 2007) http://www.csmonitor.com/2007/0102/p01s02-woap.html.
32. Frey and de Pablo, *China and India* (2004), p. 42.
33. Jacqueline Thorpe, 'Chinese Becoming Avid Shoppers', *Financial Post* (24 July 2006), p. FP1, FP4.
34. Chen Juan quoted in Ford, 'Consumer Tidal Wave', (2007).
35. Karl Gerth, *China Made, Consumer Culture and the Creation of a Nation* (Cambridge: Harvard University Press, 2003).
36. Ibid., pp. 4–6.
37. Ibid., pp. 7–10.
38. Ibid., p. 10.
39. Ibid., p. 15.
40. For both China and India, capitalism initially was an exogenous force and, through imperialism, their political economies remained structurally 'underdeveloped'. In these circumstances, the institutional development of both the nation and consumption took place dialectically alongside one another. In China, says Gerth, 'The movement contributed to nation-making not only by spreading a new consumer culture of mass-produced consumer tastes and habits (that is, the basis of shared, nationwide consumption) but also by attempting to restrict consumption exclusively to national products, often through violence … The modern Chinese nation was not simply "imagined" – it was made in China.' Ibid., pp. 18–19.
41. Ibid., p. 16.
42. Ibid., p. 59.

43. Kerrie MacPherson, 'Introduction', in *Asian Department Stores*, MacPherson, ed. (Surrey: Curzon Press, 1998), pp. 5–6.
44. Yen Ching-hwang, 'Wing on and the Kwok Brothers', in ibid., pp. 58–9.
45. Ibid., pp. 7–16.
46. Guo Hongchi and Liu Fei, 'New China's Flagship Emporium', in ibid., p. 122.
47. Lonny Carlile, 'The Yaohan Group', in ibid., pp. 243–5. ExxonMobil is the largest.
48. Nick Knight, 'Reflecting on the Paradox of Globalization', *China: An International Journal* Vol. 4 No. 1 (March 2006), p. 8.
49. Ibid., p. 10.
50. Ibid.
51. Ibid., p. 12.
52. Ibid., p. 16.
53. Jiang Zemin quoted in Ibid., p. 21.
54. Ibid., p. 25.
55. See OpenNet Initiative, 'Internet Filtering in China in 2004–2005' (Toronto: Citizen Lab, 2005) http://www.opennetinitiative.net/studies/china/.
56. Ann Veeck and Alvin Burns, 'Changing Tastes', *Journal of Business Research* Vol. 58 No. 5 (May 2005), p. 646.
57. Ibid.
58. Ibid., pp. 647–48.
59. Veeck and Burns, 'Changing Tastes' (2005), p. 648.
60. Ibid., p. 649.
61. Ibid., pp. 649–50.
62. Quoted in Ibid., p. 650.
63. Mazzarella, Shoveling Smoke (2003), p. 12.
64. Ibid., p. 13.
65. Ibid., p. 19.
66. Ibid., p. 20.
67. Knight, 'Reflecting on the Paradox' (2006), p. 28.
68. Peter Jackson, 'Local Consumption Cultures in a Globalizing World', *Transactions of the Institute of British Geographers*, Vol. 29 No. 2 (June 2004), p. 167.
69. Ibid., pp. 170–1.
70. Quoted in Barber, *Consumed* (2007), p. 218.
71. Slater, *Consumer, Culture and Modernity* (1997), p. 114.
72. Martyn Lee, *Consumer Culture Reborn* (London: Routledge, 1993), p. 17 (emphases in original).
73. In relation to this point, the excuse commonly uttered by the defensive marketer that 'we're only giving the customer what she wants' is, in fact, a half-truth. What 'the customer' and, indeed, we all want (and need) is what the wealth and freedom of capitalism paradoxically has made increasingly difficult to secure – intimate relationships and a meaningful existence.
74. See Berger and Luckmann, *The Social Construction of Reality* (1967).
75. Barber, *Consumed* (2007), p. 270.
76. Williams, *Problems in Materialism and Culture* (London: New Left Books, 1980), p. 186.

6 Neo-Imperialism, Consumption and the Crisis of Time

1. Innis, *The Bias of Communication* (1982 [1950]), p. 169.
2. Walter LaFeber, *The New Empire* (Ithaca, NY: Cornell University Press, 1963); William A. Williams, *The Tragedy of American Diplomacy* (New York: Delta, 1972).

3. Richard Haas, *Imperial America* (Paper presented at the Atlanta Conference: Puerto Rico, 2000) http://www.brook.edu/views/articles/haass/2000imperial.htm.
4. Steven Peter Rosen, 'The Future of War and the American Military', *Harvard Review* Vol. 104 No. 5 (May–June 2002), p. 29.
5. Max Boot, 'The Case for American Empire', *The Weekly Standard* Vol. 7 No. 5 (15 October 2001) http://www.weeklystandard.com/Content/Public/Articles/000/000/000/318qpvmc.asp.
6. The timing and political implications of Hardt and Negri's *Empire* (2000) surely has played some part in this.
7. William Arkin, 'Military Bases Boost Capability but Fuel Anger', *Los Angeles Times*, (6 January 2002), p. A-1.
8. Rosen, 'The Future of War' (2002), p. 29.
9. White House, *The National Security Strategy of the United States of America* (NSS), (Washington, 2002) http://www.whitehouse.gov/nsc/nssall.html.
10. White House, *The National Security Strategy of the United States of America* (NSS), (Washington, 2006), p. 25. http://www.whitehouse.gov/nsc/nss/2006/nss2006.pdf.
11. Ibid., pp. 25–6.
12. Ibid., p. 30.
13. Panitch, 'The State in a Changing World' (1998).
14. *NSS* (2006), p. 47.
15. For an example of this perspective, see Michael Ignatieff, 'Nation-Building Lite', *New York Times Magazine* (28 July 2002), http://www.globalpolicy.org/security/issues/afghan/2002/0728buildinglite.htm.
16. William Finnegan, 'The Economics of Empire', *Harper's* Vol. 306 No. 1836 (May 2003), p. 42 (pp. 41–52).
17. For examples of the American state rewarding its foreign policy allies and punishing dissenters, see Paul Blustein, 'Trade Accords Become a US Foreign Policy Tool', *The Washington Post* (29 April 2003), p. E1; and Lewis Lapham, 'The Demonstration Effect', *Harper's* Vol. 306 No. 1837 (September 2003), pp. 9–11.
18. Quoted in Michael Parenti, *Against Empire* (New York: City Lights Books, 1995), p. 135.
19. Marx quoted in Rosenberg, *Empire of Civil Society* (1994), p. 124 (emphases added).
20. Ibid., p. 131.
21. Quoted in Ibid., p. 143.
22. Ibid., p. 149.
23. Parker in Comor, *The Global Political Economy of Communication* (1994).
24. Mythologies also serve to de-politicize such developments. As Roland Barthes writes, through myth 'history evaporates ... Nothing is produced, nothing chosen ... This miraculous evaporation of history is another form of concept common to most bourgeois myths: *the irresponsibility of man*'. Quoted in Babe, *Communication and the Transformation of Economics* (1995), p. 182 (emphases added).
25. Stiglitz, *Globalization and Its Discontents* (New York: W.W. Norton, 2002). See also George Soros, *George Soros on Globalization* (New York: Public Affairs, 2002).
26. Project for the New American Century, *Statement of Principles* (3 June 1997) http://www.newamericancentury.org/statementofprinciples.htm.
27. Brzezinski, *The Grand Chessboard: American Primacy and Its Geostrategic Imperatives* (New York: Basic Books, 1997), p. 40.
28. Kiesling, 'Letter of resignation to Secretary of State Colin L. Powell', *New York Times* (27 February 2003), http://truthout.org/docs_03/030103A.shtml.
29. Brzezinski, *Second Chance* (New York: Basic Books, 2007), p. 216.
30. Innis, *Bias of Communication* (1982), p. 141.

31. We might note here a parallel between Islamic suicide bombings and the seemingly unrelated public shootings that now take place almost routinely in the United States. Rather than targeting a culture in the context of a *collective* struggle (in the case of the former), the latter almost always constitutes an attack on other *individuals* in response to *personally perceived* indignities or injustices. 'Unabomber' Ted Kasinski arguably was something of a hybrid; opposed as he was to the individual agents of capitalist modernity, thus targeting corporate executives and other elites.

32. TV also facilitates the separation of people sharing the same residence. Moreover, the popularity of the Internet, gaming and personal computing likely is deepening the search for human connection and community – a search now paradoxically pursued through the use of telecommunications and consumer electronics.

33. Todd Gitlin, *Media Unlimited* (New York: Metropolitan Books, 2001), p. 72.

34. Edward Comor, 'Household Consumption on the Internet', *Journal of Economic Issues* Vol. 34 No. 1 (March 2000), pp. 105–16.

35. Gitlin, *Media Unlimited* (2001), p. 165.

36. Pentagon Defense Policy Board member Ken Adelman hopes that the conquest of Baghdad 'emboldens leaders [in the United Sates] to take drastic, not measured approaches'. Quoted in Lapham, 'Demonstration Effect' (2003), p. 11.

37. Quoted in Comor, *Communication, Commerce and Power* (1998), p. 150.

38. Perle et al., *A Clean Break* (Washington, DC: Institute for Advanced Strategic and Political Studies, 1996) http://www.israeleconomy.org/strat1.htm.

39. According to one business reporter, 'Flows of Iraqi oil to the world market unconstrained by OPEC quotas could further erode the cartel's already limited ability to set prices and might even trigger a price war … Such an outcome would surely delight the Bush administration as well as buyers of gasoline in the United States … With this in mind, commentators … have contended that the real purpose of Bush's war in Iraq was to put in place a government that would break OPEC. Such an outcome would dismay the world's largest oil producer, Saudi Arabia …' Peter Goodman, 'US Advisor Says Iraq May Break with OPEC', *The Washington Post* (17 May 2003), pp. E1–E2.

40. *NSS* (2002), Section IX.

41. Quoted in Lapham, 'Demonstration Effect' (2003), p. 11.

42. Williams, *The Tragedy of American Diplomacy* (1972), p. 303. Just before declaring war on Iraq in March 2003, President Bush tried to explain his pending decision. More insightful than his reasons for overthrowing the Hussein regime was what the event revealed in regard to *how* the President was thinking. As columnist David Broder observed, what it made clear 'was his [Bush's] extraordinary capacity to reject any efforts to put this matter in any broader context – his ability to simplify what otherwise would be a wrenching decision'. Broder, 'Bush's Minimalist Mantra', *The Washington Post* (11 March 2003), p. A23 (emphases added).

43. Rosenberg, *Empire of Civil Society* (1994), p. 169.

44. Quoted in Rosenberg, 'Globalization Theory: A Post Mortem' (2005), p. 25.

45. Quoted in Ibid.

46. Marilyn Deegan and Simon Tanner, 'The Digital Dark Ages', *Library & Information Update* Vol. 1 No. 2 (May 2002), pp. 42–3.

47. Kamilla Pietrzyk, 'Exit from the Myopic Impasse', MA Dissertation. University of Western Ontario (Unpublished, 2007), Ch. 2.

48. Rosa, 'The Speed of Global Flows and the Pace of Democratic Politics', *New Political Science* Vol. 27 No. 4 (December 2005), pp. 453–4.
49. Gorz, *Farewell to the Working Class* (London: Pluto Press, 1982), pp. 39–40.
50. Ibid., p. 41.
51. Ibid., p. 40, fn. 3 (emphases in original).
52. Innis, *Bias of Communication* (1982), p. 205.
53. Georges Gurvitch, *The Spectrum of Social Time* (Dordrecht: D. Reidel, 1964).
54. Innis, *Bias of Communication* (1982), pp. 69–91.
55. Mike Davis, 'Planet of Slums', *New Left Review* No. 26 (March–April 2004), p. 13.
56. Brzezinski, *Second Chance* (2007), p. 206.
57. Davis, 'Planet of Slums' (2004), p. 29.
58. Ibid., p. 30.
59. Ibid., p. 33.
60. Brzezinski, *Second Chance* (2007), p. 215.
61. Gurvitch, *The Spectrum of Social Time* (1964).
62. Parker in Comor, *Global Political Economy* (1994).
63. David Harvey, *Spaces of Hope* (Berkeley: University of California Press, 2000).

7 Conclusion

1. Harvey, *The Condition of Postmodernity* (Cambridge: Basil Blackwell, 1989), pp. 106–07.
2. John Kenneth Galbraith, *The Affluent Society* (Boston: Houghton Mifflin, 1958). For a more contemporary analysis, see Vincent Manzerolle, 'The Consumer Database, Consumer Sovereignty, and the Commercial Mediation of Identity in the United States', MA Dissertation. University of Western Ontario (Unpublished, 2006).
3. Building on Marcuse, Benjamin Barber argues that contemporary consumer identities 'are less one-dimensional than no-dimensional, because such [an] identity … is entirely heteronomous. A product of what is bought, eaten, worn, and imbibed. This is not really identity at all, but merely a coat worn to cover nakedness'. Barber, *Consumed*, p. 250–1.
4. Lewis, *Time and Western Man* (New York: Chatto and Windus, 1927).
5. See Scott Lucas and Liam Kennedy, 'Enduring Freedom: Public Diplomacy and US Foreign Policy', *American Quarterly* Vol. 57 No. 2 (June 2005), pp. 309–33 and Barber (2007), pp. 205–9.
6. For a jarring overview of the rise of anti-Americanism overseas, dating from the US invasion of Iraq, see Pew Global Attitudes Project, *America's Image Slips* (13 June 2006), http://pewglobal.org/reports/display.php?ReportID=252.
7. Alexander Watson, *Marginal Man* (Toronto: University of Toronto Press, 2006), p. 328.
8. Debates concerning the Pentagon's aspirations to develop a new class of nuclear weapons designed to penetrate bunkers further illustrate this reactionary cycle. Beyond ending the taboo against using such weapons for anything other than deterrence, their development likely will accelerate the efforts of 'rogue states' – fearing American 'intervention' – to develop chemical, biological and even nuclear arsenals.
9. Indeed, life itself constitutes the 'last frontier' of this commodification process. Beyond the ownership of land and the use of animals for food and entertainment, oceans, the sky, human organs, body parts and, more abstractly, the human genome have become the subjects of private ownership and exchange.

Life itself and its intrinsic values thus are being eclipsed by exchange value and, as Marx put it, 'the icy water of egotistical calculation'. Marx and Engels, *The Communist Manifesto* (1979), p. 82.

10. Existing media – from working class community associations in the West to extended families found in some 'developing' cultures, from a selection of content-rich websites to environmental groups, from progressive religious organizations to critically minded university departments – today constitute such 'islands'; collectivities structured in ways that facilitate the maintenance or development of reflexive, historically aware, non-commodified values and practices.

11. We direct the reader to the general approach laid out in Babe, *Culture of Ecology* (Toronto: University of Toronto Press, 2006).

12. Innumerable examples come to mind: non-commercial educational services explicitly organized to stimulate critical, long-term thinking; universal day care programmes implemented to promote creative, ecologically aware children; local governments instituting environmentally minded reforms citing the long-term needs of their communities; national-level carbon tax programmes that hold corporate polluters accountable for emissions, diverting monies towards the development and implementation of 'green' technologies, and many others.

13. Pietrzyk, 'Exiting the Myopic Impasse' (2007).

14. Brian Ellsworth, 'Venezuela Tries the Worker-Managed Route', *International Herald Tribune* (3 August 2005) http://www.iht.com/articles/2005/08/02/business/worker.php.

15. The proposed policy involves an adaptation of similar efforts in Tito's Yugoslavia.

16. In 2007, São Paulo became the first city in the non-communist world to ban all outdoor advertising. David Harris, 'São Paulo: A City Without Ads', *Adbusters* #73 (August–September 2007) http://adbusters.org/the_magazine/73/So_Paulo_A_City_Without_Ads.html. Examples, however, also abound in which identity, meaning and, through these, happiness itself are being explicitly related to consumption by regimes embracing modernist ambitions. In Thailand, for example, in 2007, its government introduced what it called its *yoo dee mee suk* or 'happy living' policy – an effort to stoke domestic consumption through various state programmes or, to be even more explicit, a plan, similar to China's, to wean the countries economic fortunes away from exports and towards domestic consumption. Pattnapong Chantranontwong, 'Kosit Says Domestic Consumption Overlooked', *BangkokPost.com* (30 April 2007) http://www.bangkokpost.com/News/30Apr2007_news25.php.

17. Quoted in Mazzarella, *Shoveling Smoke* (2003), pp. 35–6 (emphasis in original).

18. Stanley Lebergott, *Pursuing Happiness* (New Jersey: Princeton University Press, 1993), pp. 13–14.

Bibliography

Agnew, John. *Hegemony, the Shape of Global Power*. Philadelphia: Temple University Press, 2005.

Altvater, Elmar. 'The Growth Obsession'. In *A World of Contradictions: Socialist Register 2002*, ed. Leo Panitch & Colin Leys. New York, NY: Monthly Review Press, December 2001.

Amin, Samir. 'Empire and Multitude'. *Monthly Review*, vol. 57 no. 6 (November 2005), http://www.monthlyreview.org/1105amin.htm.

Anderson, Benedict. *Imagined Communities*. London: Verso, 1983.

Appadurai, Arjun. 'Disjuncture and Difference in the Global Cultural Economy'. In *Global Culture*. ed. Mike Featherstone. London: Sage Publications, 1990.

Arkin, William M. 'Military Bases Boost Capability but Fuel Anger'. *Los Angeles Times*, 6 January 2002, A-1.

Babe, Robert E. *Communication and the Transformation of Economics*. Boulder: Westview Press, 1995.

Babe, Robert E. *Cultural Ecology, Reconciling Economics and Environment*. Toronto: University of Toronto Press, 2006.

Barber, Benjamin. *Consumed*. New York: W.W. Norton, 2007.

Barber, Benjamin. 'Jihad vs. McWorld'. *Atlantic Monthly* vol. 269 no. 3 (March 1992).

Barnett, Mark P.M. 'The Pentagon's New Map'. *Esquire* (March 2003), http://www.thomaspmbarnett.com/published/pentagonsnewmap.htm.

Becker, J., G. Hedebroan and D L. Paldan, eds. *Communication and Domination*. Norwood: Ablex, 1986.

Belk, Russell and Non Zhou. 'Learning to Want Things'. In *Advances in Consumer Research* vol. 14, ed. Melanie Wallendorf & Paul Anderson. Urbana: Association for Consumer Research, 1987.

Beninger, James, *The Control Revolution*. Cambridge: Harvard University Press, 1989.

Berger, Peter L. and Thomas Luckmann. *The Social Construction of Reality*. Garden City, NY: Anchor Books, 1967.

Blustein, Paul. 'Trade Accords become a U.S. Foreign Policy Tool'. *The Washington Post*, 29 April 2003, E1.

Boal, Iain, T. J. Clark, Joseph Matthews and Michael Watts. *Afflicted Powers*. London: Verso, 2005.

Boot, Max, 'The Case for American Empire'. *The Weekly Standard*, vol. 7 no. 5 (2001), http://www.weeklystandard.com/Content/Public/Articles/000/000/000/318qpvmc.asp.

Brecher, J. et al., eds. *Introduction to Global Visions*. Boston: South End Press, 1993.

Brenner, Robert. 'Agrarian Class Structure and Economic Development in Pre-Industrial Europe'. *Past & Present*, no. 70 (February 1976).

Breslin, Shaun and Timothy M. Shaw. *China and the Global Political Economy*. New York: Palgrave Macmillan, 2007.

Broder, David. 'Bush's Minimalist Mantra'. *The Washington Post*, 11 March 2003, A23.

Brzezinski, Zbigniew. *The Grand Chessboard*. New York: Basic Books, 1997.

Brzezinski, Zbigniew. *Second Chance*. New York: Basic Books, 2007.

Bush, George W. 'Inaugural Speech' (21 January 2005), http://badinfluence.org/modules.php?name=News&file=article&sid=35.

Carey, James. 'Canadian Communication Theory'. In *Studies in Canadian Communications*. ed. G. Robinson and D. Theall. Montreal: McGill University, 1975.

Carrier, James. *Gifts and Commodities*. New York : Routledge, 1995.

Chalkin, Christopher. *The Rise of the English Town*. Cambridge: Cambridge University Press, 2001.

Chantranontwong, Pattnapong. 'Kosit Says Domestic Consumption Overlooked'. *BangkokPost.com* (30 April 2007), http://www.bangkokpost.com/News/30Apr2007_news25.php.

Cheng, Hong and John C. Schweitzer. 'Cultural Values Reflected in Chinese and U.S. Television Commercials'. *Journal of Advertising Research*, vol. 36 no. 3 (May 1996).

Ching-hwang, Yen. 'Wing On and the Kwok Brothers'. In *Asian Department Stores*. ed. Kerrie MacPherson. Surrey: Curzon Press, 1998.

Clarke, John. 'Mine Eyes Dazzle'. In *New Times and Old* Enemies. ed. J. Clarke. London: HarperCollins, 1991.

Coen, Bob. 'Bob Coen's Insiders Report 2003'. *Universal McCann* (Universal McCann: June 2003), http://universalmccann.com/downloads/reports/June2003.pdf.

Cohen, Lizabeth. *A Consumers' Republic*. New York: Vintage, 2004.

Comor, Edward, *Communication, Commerce and Power*. London: Macmillan, 1998.

Comor, Edward, ed. *The Global Political Economy of Communication*. London: Macmillan, 1994.

Comor, Edward. 'Household Consumption on the Internet'. *Journal of Economic Issues*, vol. 34 no. 1 (March 2000).

Comor, Edward. 'New Technologies and Consumption'. In *Information Technologies and Global Politics*. ed. James Rosenau and J. P. Singh. Albany: SUNY Press, 2002.

'Consumerism is King, Interview: Kishore Biyani'. *Financial Express* (29 April 2007), http://www.financialexpress.com/fe_full_story.php?content_id=162593#.

Cox, Robert W. *Approaches to World Order*. Cambridge: Cambridge University Press, 1996.

Cox, Robert W. 'Debt, Time, and Capitalism'. *Studies in Political Economy*, no. 48 (Autumn 1995).

David, Paul A. and Gavin Wright. 'Early Twentieth Century Growth Dynamics'. *Oxford University Economic and Social Series*, Paper #033 (October 1999), http://ideas.repec.org/p/nuf/esohwp/_033.html.

Davies, Matthew and Michael Neimann, *Rediscovering International Relations Theory*. London: Routledge, 2004.

Davis, Mike. 'Planet of Slums'. *New Left Review*, no. 26 (March–April 2004).

Deegan, Marilyn and Simon Tanner. 'The Digital Dark Ages'. *Library & Information Update*, vol. 1 no. 2 (May 2002).

Deibert, Ronald J. 'International Plug 'n Play?'. *International Studies Perspectives*, vol. 1 no. 3 (July 2000).

Deibert, Ronald J. *Parchment, Printing, and Hypermedia*. New York: Columbia University Press, 1997.

Deleuze, Gilles and Felix Guattari. *A Thousand Plateaus*. Minneapolis: University of Minnesota Press, 1987.

Dittmar, Helga. 'Compulsive Buying – A Growing Concern?'. *British Journal of Psychology*, vol. 96 no. 4 (November 2005).

Dougherty, Connor. 'Exporting Christmas'. *Wall Street Journal* (23 December 232006), http://online.wsj.com/article/SB116684145879058402.html?mod=googlewsj.

Economist.com, 'Flying on One Engine' (18 September 2003), http://www.economist.com/surveys/showsurvey.cfm?issue=20030920.

Ellsworth, Brian. 'Venezuela Tries the Worker-Managed Route'. *International Herald Tribune* (3 August 2005), http://www.iht.com/articles/2005/08/02/business/worker.php.

Elteren, Mel Van. 'Rethinking Americanization Abroad'. *The Journal of American Cuture*, vol. 29 no. 3.

Ewen, Stuart. *Captains of Consciousness*. New York: McGraw-Hill, 1976.

Falk, Richard. 'The Making of Global Citizenship'. In *Global Visions*. ed. J. Brecher et al. Boston: South End Press, 1993.

Falk, Richard. 'State under Siege'. *International Affairs*, 73 (1997).

Falk, Richard. *Predatory Globalization, a Critique*. Cambridge: Polity Press, 1999.

Featherstone, M. *Consumer Culture and Postmodernism*. London: Sage, 1991.

Filene, Edward A. *Successful Living in the Machine Age*. New York: Simon and Schuster, 1932.

Finnegan, William. 'The Economics of Empire'. *Harper's* (May 2003), 41–54.

Ford, Peter. 'Consumer Tidal Wave on the Way'. *The Christian Science Monitor* (2 January 2007), http://www.csmonitor.com/2007/0102/p01s02-woap.html.

Fortner, R. S. 'Excommunication in the Information Society'. *Critical Studies in Mass Communication*, vol. 12 no. 2 (June 1995).

Friedman, Milton. *Capitalism and Freedom*. Chicago: University of Chicago Press, 1962.

Friedman, Thomas. 'A Manifesto for the Fast World'. *New York Times Magazine* (28 March 1999), http://www.nytimes.com/books/99/04/25/reviews/friedman-mag.html.

Frey, Christian and Jose Navarro de Pablo. *China and India*. UBS Wealth Management: Zurich, 2004.

Fukuyama, Francis. *The End of History and the Last Man*. New York: Avon Books, 1992.

Galbraith, John Kenneth. *The Affluent Society*. Boston: Houghton Mifflin, 1958.

Gaventa, John. *Power and Powerlessness*. Urbana: University of Illinois Press, 1982.

Gerth, Karl. *China Made*. Cambridge: Harvard University Press, 2003.

Giddens, Anthony. *Modernity and Self-Identity*. Stanford, CA: Stanford University Press, 1991.

Giddens, Anthony. *The Consequences of Modernity*. Stanford, CA: Stanford University Press, 1990.

Gill, Stephen. 'Globalisation, Market Civilisation, and Disciplinary Neoliberalism'. *Millennium*, vol. 24 no. 3 (December 1995).

Gill, Stephen. *Power and Resistance in the New World Order*. New York: Palgrave Macmillan, 2003.

Gitlin, Todd. *Media Unlimited*. New York: Metropolitan Books, 2001.

Golding, Peter. 'Global Village or Global Pillage?'. In *Capitalism and the Information Age*. ed. Robert W. McChesney et al. New York: Monthly Review Press, 1998.

Goldstein, Andrea, *Multinational Companies from Emerging Economies*. New York: Palgrave Macmillan, 2007.

Golub, Philip S. 'The Dynamics of World Disorder'. *Le Monde Diplomatique* (September, 2002), http://www.arena.org.nz/westemp.htm.

Goodman, Peter S. 'U.S. Advisor Says Iraq May Break with OPEC'. *The Washington Post*, 17 May 2003, E1–E2.

Goodwin, Neva R., Frank Ackerman and David Kiron. eds. *The Consumer Society*. Washington, DC: Island Press, 1997.

Gorz, André. *Farewell to the Working Class*. London: Pluto Press, 1982.

Gramsci, Antonio. *Prison Notebooks*. New York: International Publishers, 1971.

Gurvitch, Georges. *The Spectrum of Social Time*. Dordrecht: D. Reidel, 1964.

Haas, Richard. 'Imperial America' (Paper presented at the Atlanta Conference: Puerto Rico, 2000), http://www.brook.edu/views/articles/haass/2000imperial.htm.

Hardt, Michael and Antonio Negri. *Empire*. Cambridge, MA: Harvard University Press, 2000.

Hardt, Michael and Antonio Negri. *Multitude*. London: Penguin, 2004.

Harris, David. 'São Paulo: A City Without Ads.' *Adbusters* #73, August–September 2007, http://adbusters.org/the_magazine/73/So_Paulo_A_City_Without_Ads.html.

Harvey, David. *A Brief History of Neoliberlism*. Oxford: Oxford University Press, 2005.

Harvey, David. *Spaces of Hope*. Berkeley: University of California Press, 2000.

Harvey, David. *The Condition of Postmodernity*. Cambridge: Basil Blackwell, 1989.

Harvey, David. *The New Imperialism*. New York: Oxford University Press, 2003.

Heath, Joseph and Andrew Potter. *The Rebel Sell*. Toronto: Harper Collins, 2004.

Huntington, Samuel. 'The Clash of Civilizations?'. *Foreign Affairs* vol. 72 no. 3 (Summer 1993).

Huws, Ursula. *The Making of a Cybertariat*. New York: Monthly Review Press, 2003.

Ignatieff, Michael. 'Nation-Building Lite'. *New York Times Magazine*, 28 July 2002, http://www.globalpolicy.org/security/issues/afghan/2002/0728buildinglite.htm.

Innis, Harold A. *The Bias of Communication*. Toronto: University of Toronto Press, 1982.

Jackson, Peter. 'Local Consumption Cultures in a Globalizing World'. *Transactions of the Institute of British Geographers*, 29 (2004).

Kahn, Azizur Rahman. 'Growth and Distribution of Household Income in China between 1995 and 2002' (March 2004), http://www.economics.ucr.edu/seminars/spring04/05-28-04AzizurKhan.pdf.

Keck, Margaret E. and Kathryn Sikkink. *Activists beyond Borders*. Ithaca, NY: Cornell University Press, 1998.

Kiesling, John Brady. 'Letter of resignation to Secretary of State Colin L. Powell'. *New York Times*, 27 February 2003, http://truthout.org/docs_03/030103A.shtml.

Kingston, Anne. 'The Trouble with Buying for a Cause'. *Maclean's*, 26 March 2007, 40–1.

Knight, Nick. 'Reflecting on the Paradox of Globalization'. *China*, vol. 4 no. 1 (March 2006).

Lachmann, Richard. *From Manor to Market*. Madison: University of Wisconsin Press, 1987.

LaFeber, Walter. *The New Empire*. Ithaca, NY: Cornell University Press, 1963.

Lapham, Lewis. 'The Demonstration Effect'. *Harper's* (June 2003), 9–11.

Lash, Scott and John Urry. *Economies of Signs and Space*. London: Sage, 1994.

Lazonick, William. 'Karl Marx and Enclosures in England'. *Review of Radical Political Economics*, vol. 6 no. 2 (Summer 1974).

Leach, William. *Land of Desire*. New York: Pantheon, 1993.

Lebergott, Stanley. *Pursuing Happiness*. New Jersey: Princeton University Press, 1993.

Lee, Martyn J. *Consumer Culture Reborn*. London: Routledge, 1993.

Leiss, William, S. Klein and S. Jhally. *Social Communication in Advertising*. Scarborough: Nelson Canada, 1990.

Levinson, Paul. *Mind at Large*. Greenwich, CT: JAI Press, 1988.

Lewis, Wyndham. *Time and Western Man*. New York: Chatto and Windus, 1927.

Lie, John. 'Visualizing the Invisible Hand'. *Politics & Society*, vol. 21 no. 1 (September 1993).

Lipschutz, Ronnie. 'Reconstructing World Politics'. In *International Society after the Cold War*. ed. R. Fawn and J. Larkins. London: Macmillan, 1996.

Lipschutz, Ronnie. *Global Environmental* Politics. Washington, DC: CQ Press, 2003.

Lipschutz, Ronnie and J. Mayer. *Global Civil Society and Global Environmental Governance*. Albany: State University of New York Press, 1996.

Lucas, Scott and Liam Kennedy. 'Enduring Freedom'. *American Quarterly*, vol. 57 no. 2 (Summer 2005).

Luke, Timothy. 'The (Un)wise (Ab)use of Nature'. Unpublished paper prepared for the International Studies Association Annual Conference, Toronto, March 1997.

Lukes, Steven. *Power: A Radical View*. London: Macmillan, 1974.

Luxembourg, Rosa. *The Accumulation of Capital*. London: Routledge, 2003.

Lynd, Robert S. 'The Consumer becomes a "Problem"'. In *The Ultimate Consumer*. ed. J. G. Brainerd. Philadelphia: American Academy of Political and Social Science, 1934.

MacBride, Sean, et al. *Many Voices, One World*. Paris: Kogan Page/UNESCO, 1984.

Macleod, Lijia. 'Pressures of Capitalism Put Chinese in Therapy'. *The Independent*, 13 May 2001.

Mann, Michael. 'The Social Cohesion of Liberal Democracy'. In *Classes, Power and Conflict*, ed. D. Held and A. Giddens. London: Macmillan, 1982.

Mann, Michael. 'The Working Class'. *New Society* (4 November 1976).

Manzerolle, Vincent. 'The Consumer Database, Consumer Sovereignty, and the Commercial Mediation of Identity in the United States'. Unpublished MA Dissertation: University of Western Ontario, 2006.

Marcuse, Herbert. *One Dimensional Man*. Boston: Beacon Press, 1964.

Marx, Karl. *Grundrisse*. Harmondsworth: Penguin, 1973.

Marx, Karl and Friedrick Engels. *The Communist Manifesto*. Harmondsworth: Penguin, 1979.

Marx, Karl and Frederick Engels. *The German Ideology*. New York: International Publishers, 1970.

Mazzarella, William. *Shoveling Smoke*. Durham: Duke University Press, 2003.

McCracken, Gant. *Culture & Consumption*. Bloomington: Indiana University Press, 1990.

McKendrick, Neil. 'The Consumer Revolution of Eighteenth-Century England'. In *The Birth of Consumer Society*. ed. N. McKendrick et al. Bloomington: Indiana University Press, 1982.

McLeod, Hugh. *Religion and Irreligion*. Bangor: Headstart History, 1993.

Mills, C. Wright. *The Power Elite*. Oxford: Oxford University Press, 1982.

Mosco, Vincent. *The Political Economy of Communication*. London: Sage, 1996.

Mukherjee-Reed, Ananya. *Corporate Capitalism in Contemporary South Asia*. New York: Palgrave Macmillan, 2007.

Nandy, Ashis et al. *Creating a Nationality*. Delhi: Oxford University Press, 1997.

Nandy, Ashis. *The Intimate Enemy*. Delhi: Oxford University Press, 1983.

OpenNet Initiative. 'Internet Filtering in China in 2004–2005' (Toronto: Citizen Lab, 2005), http://www.opennetinitiative.net/studies/china/.

OECD. *Trends and Recent Developments in Foreign Direct Investment* (June 2004), http://www.oecd.org/dataoecd/37/39/32230032.pdf.

'Our Devices'. *Blackberry.com*. http://www.discoverblackberry.com/devices/.

Panitch, Leo. '"The State in a Changing World"'. *Monthly Review*, vol. 50 no. 5 (October 1998).

Parenti, Michael. *Against Empire*. City Lights Books, May 1995.

Parenti, Michael. *The Sword and the Dollar*. New York: St. Martin's Press, 1988.

Parker, Ian. 'Myth, Telecommunication and the Emerging Global Informational Order'. In *The Global Political Economy of Communication*. ed. Edward A. Comor. New York: St. Martin's Press.

Pasha, Mustapha Kamal and David L. Blaney. 'Elusive Paradise'. *Alternatives*, vol. 23 no. 4 (October–December 1998).

Patriquin, Larry, 'The Agrarian Origins of the Industrial Revolution in England'. *Review of Radical Political Economics*, vol. 36 no. 2 (Spring 2004).

Perle, Richard et al. *A Clean Break*. Washington, DC: Institute for Advanced Strategic and Political Studies, 1996. http:// www.israeleconomy.org/strat1.htm.

Perri, Fabrizio and Dirk Krueger. 'Does Income Inequality Lead to Consumption Inequality?'. *National Bureau of Economic Research* (August 2003), http://www.iue.it/ FinConsEU/ResearchActivities/krueger2005.pdf.

Pew Global Attitudes Project. *America's Image Slips* (13 June 2006), http://pewglobal. org/reports/display.php?ReportID=252.

Pietrzyk, Kamilla. 'Exiting the Myopic Impasse'. Unpublished MA Dissertation: University of Western Ontario, 2007.

Pijl, Kees Van Der. *Transnational Classes and International Relations*. London: Routledge, 1998.

Polanyi, Karl, *The Great Transformation*. Boston: Beacon Press, 1957.

Postman, Neil. 'The Social Effects of Commercial Television'. In *Critical Studies in Media Commercialism*. ed. R. Anderson and L. Strate. Oxford: Oxford University Press, 2000.

Power, Samantha. 2002. Interview by Bill Moyers. 8 November 2002 NOW, PBS television.

Pred, Allan and Michael Watts. *Reworking Modernity*. New Brunswick, NJ: Rutgers University Press, 1992.

Price, Richard. 'Reversing the Gun Sights: Transnational Civil Society Targets Land Mines'. *International Organization*, vol. 52 no. 3 (July 1998).

Princen, Thomas, Michael Maniates and Ken Conca. eds., *Confronting Consumption*. Cambridge: MIT, 2002.

Project for the New American Century. *Statement of Principles*. (1997), http://www. newamericancentury.org/statementofprinciples.htm.

Putnam, Robert. *Bowling Alone*. New York: Simon & Schuster, 2000.

Robbins, Richard H. *Global Problems and the Culture of Capitalism*. Boston, MA: Allyn and Bacon, 1999.

Roberts, Paul. 'The New Food Anxiety'. *Psychology Today* (March/April 1998), http://cms.psychologytoday.com/articles/pto-19980301-000028.html.

Rosa, Hartmut. 'The Speed of Global Flows and the Pace of Democratic Politics'. *New Political Science*, vol. 27 no. 4 (December 2005).

Rosen, Steven Peter. 'The Future of War and the American Military'. *Harvard Review*, vol. 104 no. 5 (May–June 2002).

Rosenau, James N. *Turbulence in World Politics*. Princeton, NJ: Princeton University Press, 1994.

Rosenberg, Justin. *Empire of Civil Society*. New York: Verso, 1994.

Rosenberg, Justin. *The Follies of Globalization Theory*. London: Verso, 2000.

Rosenberg, Justin. 'Globalization Theory: A Post Mortem'. *International Politics*, vol. 42 no. 1 (March 2005).

Ross, George and Jane Jenson. 'Post-War Class Struggle and the Politics of Left Politics'. In *Socialist Register 1985/86*. ed. Ralph Miliband et al. London: Merlin Press, 1986.

Sandronsky, Seth. 'A Rising Tide of Consumer Debt'. *Common Dreams* (6 January 2001), http://www.commondreams.org/cgi-bin/print.cgi?file=/views01/0106-04. htm.

Saunders, Doug. 'The Fragile State of the Global Middle Class'. *Globe and Mail* (21 July 2007), http://www.theglobeandmail.com/servlet/story/RTGAM.20070720. wmiddleclass0920/BNStory/International/home.

Schiller, Dan. *Objectivity and the News*. Philadelphia: University of Pennsylvania Press, 1981.

Schiller, Herbert I. *Culture, Inc*. New York: Oxford University Press, 1991.

Schiller, Herbert I. *Mass Communications and American Empire*. Boulder, CO: Westview Press, 1992.

Schiller, Herbert I. 'Transnational Media: Creating Consumers Worldwide'. *Journal of International Affairs*, 47 (1993).

Schlosser, Steven, D. W. Black, S. Repertinger and D. Freet. 'Compulsive Buying'. *General Hospital Psychiatry*, vol. 15 no. 3 (May 1994).

Searle, C. E. 'Custom, Class Conflict and Agrarian Capitalism'. *Past and Present*, 110 (1986).

Seipp, D. J. 'The Concept of Property in the Early Common Law'. *Law and History Review*, 12 (1994).

Shaw, Martin. 'Global Society and Global Responsibility'. In *International Society after the Cold War*. ed. R. Fawn and J. Larkins. London: Macmillan, 1996.

Shaw, Martin. *Global Society and International Relations*. Cambridge: Polity, 1994.

Sklair, Leslie. *Globalization*. Oxford: Oxford University Press, 2002.

Slater, Don. *Consumer Culture and Modernity*. Cambridge: Polity Press, 1997.

Soros, George. *George Soros on Globalization*. New York: Public Affairs, 2002.

Stefanik, Nancy. 'Sustainable Dialogue/Sustainable Development'. In *Global Visions*. ed. J. Brecher et al. Boston: South End Press, 1993.

Stiglitz, Joseph E. *Globalization and Its Discontents*. New York: W.W. Norton, 2002.

Strange, Susan. *States and Markets*. London: Pinter, 1988.

Thompson, E.P. *The Making of the English Working Class*. New York: Vintage Books, 1966.

Thompson, E. P. 'Standards and Experiences'. In *The Standard of Living in Britain in the Industrial Revolution*. ed. Arthur J. Taylor. London: Metheun & Co., 1975.

Thorpe, Jacqueline. 'Chinese Becoming Avid Shoppers'. *National Post*, 24 July 2006, FP1 & FP4.

Tomlinson, John. 'Global Experience as a Consequence of Modernity'. In *Globalization, Communication and Transnational Civil Society*. ed. Sandra Braman & Annabelle Sreberny-Mohammadi. Cresskill, NJ: Hampton Press, 1996.

Tomlinson, John. *Globalization and Culture*. Cambridge: Polity Press, 1999.

Trentmann, Frank. 'Citizenship and Consumption'. *Journal of Consumer Culture*, vol. 7 no. 2 (July 2007).

UNDP. *Human Development Report 1998*. New York: Oxford University Press, 1998.

Veblen, Thorstein. *The Theory of the Leisure Class*. Mentor: New York, 1953.

Veeck, Ann and Alvin Burns. 'Changing Tastes'. *Journal of Business Research*, vol. 58 no. 5 (May 2005).

Wapner, Paul. 'Politics beyond the State'. *World Politics*, vol. 47 no. 3 (Spring 1995).

Watson, J. 'China's Big Mac Attack'. *Foreign Affairs*, vol. 79 no. 30 (May/June 2000).

Watson, A. John. *Marginal Man*. Toronto: University of Toronto Press, 2006.

'Web Ads Can Lure You In'. (April 3, 2006), http://thechronicleherald.ca/Business/494339.html.

Weisbrot, Mark. 'Why Globalization Fails to Deliver'. *The Observer* (28 July 2002), http://observer.guardian.co.uk/worldview/story/0,11581,764036,00.html.

Wessel, Margrit Van. 'Talking about Consumption'. *Cultural Dynamics*, vol. 16 no. 1 (July 2004).

White House. 'Helping Developing Nations' (21 June 2005), http://www.whitehouse. gov/infocus/developingnations/.

White House. *The National Security Strategy of the United States of America*, (Washington, 2002), http://www.whitehouse.gov/nsc/nssall.html.

White House. *The National Security Strategy of the United States of America*, (Washington, 2006), http://www.whitehouse.gov/nsc/nss/2006/nss2006.pdf.

Weisbrot, Mark, Robert Naiman & Joyce Kim. 'The Emperor Has No Growth'. Center for Economic and Policy Research (26 September 2000), http://www.globalpolicy. org/globaliz/econ/growth.htm.

Whitaker, Reg. *The End of Privacy*. New York: Kew Press, 1999.

Williams, Raymond. 'Advertising: The Magic System'. In *Problems in Materialism and Culture*. ed. Raymond Williams. London: New Left Books, 1980.

Williams, Rosalynd. 'Dream Worlds of Consumption'. In *Communication in History*. ed. D. Crowley and P. Heyer. Pearson: Boston, 2007.

Williams, William A. *The Tragedy of American Diplomacy*. New York: Delta, 1972.

Wolin, Sheldon S. *Politics and Vision*. Boston: Little Brown, 1960.

Wood, Ellen. *The Origin of Capitalism*. New York: Monthly Review Press, 1999.

'Woodward Shares War Secrets'. *CBS News Online* (18 April 2004), http://www.cbsnews. com/stories/2004/04/15/60minutes/main612067.shtml.

Worldwatch Institute, *The State of the World, 2004: Worldwatch Institute Report on Progress Toward a Sustainable Society*. New York: W.W. Norton & Co., 2004.

Index

Mexico, 77, 89, 100, 111
  also see Zapatistas
Microsoft, 164
Middle East, 7, 77, 135, 147–8, 164
Midle East Free Trade Area, 138
  also see Iraq
Mills, C. Wright, 38, 43
modernity/modernization, xi, 2, 23,
  65, 75–9, 94, 107, 112, 114,
  116, 122–4, 127–32, 134, 154–6,
  161, 166–7, 169–70, 182n, 188n,
  190n
  and cultural biases, 136, 161–2
  pre-modern use of commodities,
  127–8, 130, 161, 166
Motorola, 167
Mutilateral Agreement on Investments,
  93
mythology, 23, 36, 83, 92, 97, 114, 121,
  142, 153, 158, 187n

Nader, Ralph, 142
Nandy, Ashis, 116
Nandy, Pritish, 109
the nation
  nation states and progressive politics,
    18, 97, 107, 122–4, 134, 158, 160,
    166–7, 169–70
  national identity, xi, 83, 94, 113,
    118–19, 127, 129, 182n, 185n
  nationalism, xi, 9, 83, 97, 104–5, 108,
    114, 118–20, 150, 164
  radio marketing, 69
  and state sovereignty, 17, 83, 108,
    142, 149, 158
Negri, Antonio, 82, 83, 187n
neoclassical/'mainstream' economics,
  22, 31, 71, 85, 109
  as an institution, 22–3
  maximisation of utility, 22–3, 25
  also see exchange, neoliberalism
neoliberalism, xi, 5, 8–9, 17, 20, 22, 23,
  31, 34, 56, 86, 90, 97, 100–1, 107,
  126, 135, 141–2, 148, 158, 160,
  169, 175n
  and global civil society, 81, 82
  and 'market fundamentalism', 8
  and neo-imperialism, 8, 141
  opposition to, 18, 169
  privatization, 10, 56, 101, 160

and United States foreign policy, xi,
  7, 14–15, 100, 142, 165
  also see 'developing' countries,
    neoclassical economics
neorealism, 14–15, 20, 86, 149, 151,
  165
news media, 35, 73, 147, 168, 176n,
  179n
Nicaragua
  Sandinistas, 35
'9/11', x, xii, 5, 7, 8, 17, 35, 135–7, 141,
  142, 147, 149, 164–5
Nixon, Richard, 35
non-governmental organizations, 31,
  90, 96
North America, 13, 111, 114, 120, 123
North Korea, 104

Olin Institute for Strategic Studies, 137
Organization of Petroleum Exporting
  Countries, 100, 148
  'petrodollars', 100, 188n

Palestine, 46
Palmerston, Lord, 150
Panitch, Leo, 85–6
Parker, Ian, 158
Pasha, Mustapha Kamal, 82, 99
Pepsi, 34, 111
Perle, Richard, 148
Perri, Fabrizio, 27, 29
Pew Research Center, 32
Pickford, Mary, 68
Pietrzyk, Kamilla, 152, 168
pluralists, 20
pornography, 77, 103
post-Fordism, 44
post-structuralism, 80, 82, 97, 136, 152,
  156–7, 170, 181n
  analytical biases, 136, 151
  and capitalism, 127, 164
  'the multitude', 80, 82–3, 97, 170,
    180n, 181n
post-modernism, 107, 167
Postman, Neil, 73–4
poverty, 17, 20, 23, 79, 98, 142, 156,
  169
  in China, 101
  and consumption, 13, 21, 27–8, 36–7,
    134